W9-DCX-468

zen pencils

INSPIRATIONAL QUOTES FOR KIDS

zen pencils

INSPIRATIONAL QUOTES FOR KIDS

GAVIN AUNG THAN

Andrews McMeel
PUBLISHING®

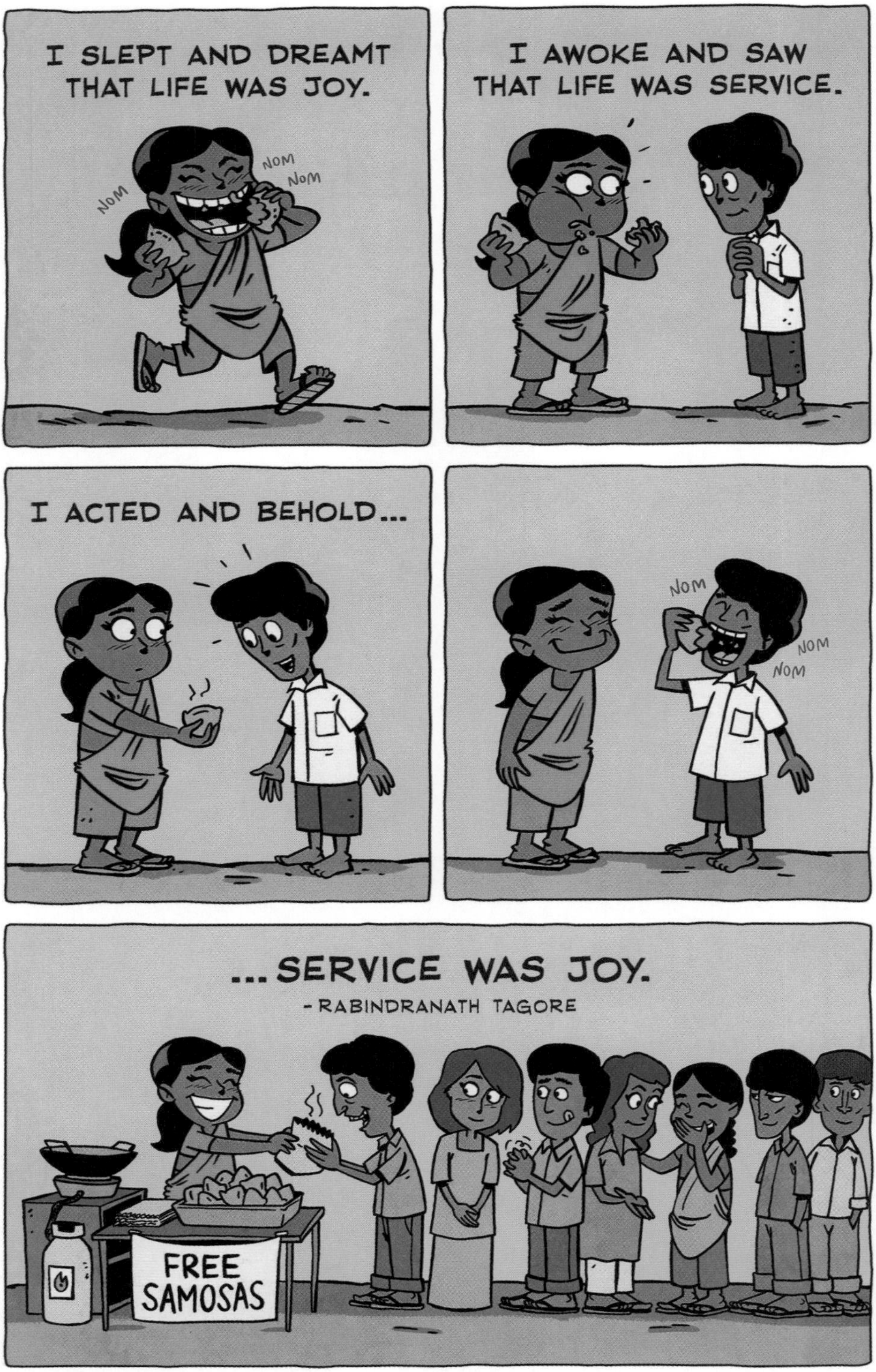
I SLEPT AND DREAMT THAT LIFE WAS JOY.
NOM
NOM
NOM
I AWOKE AND SAW THAT LIFE WAS SERVICE.
I ACTED AND BEHOLD...
NOM
NOM
NOM
...SERVICE WAS JOY.
- RABINDRANATH TAGORE
FREE SAMOSAS

CONTENTS

CHOOSE A JOB YOU LOVE Confucius

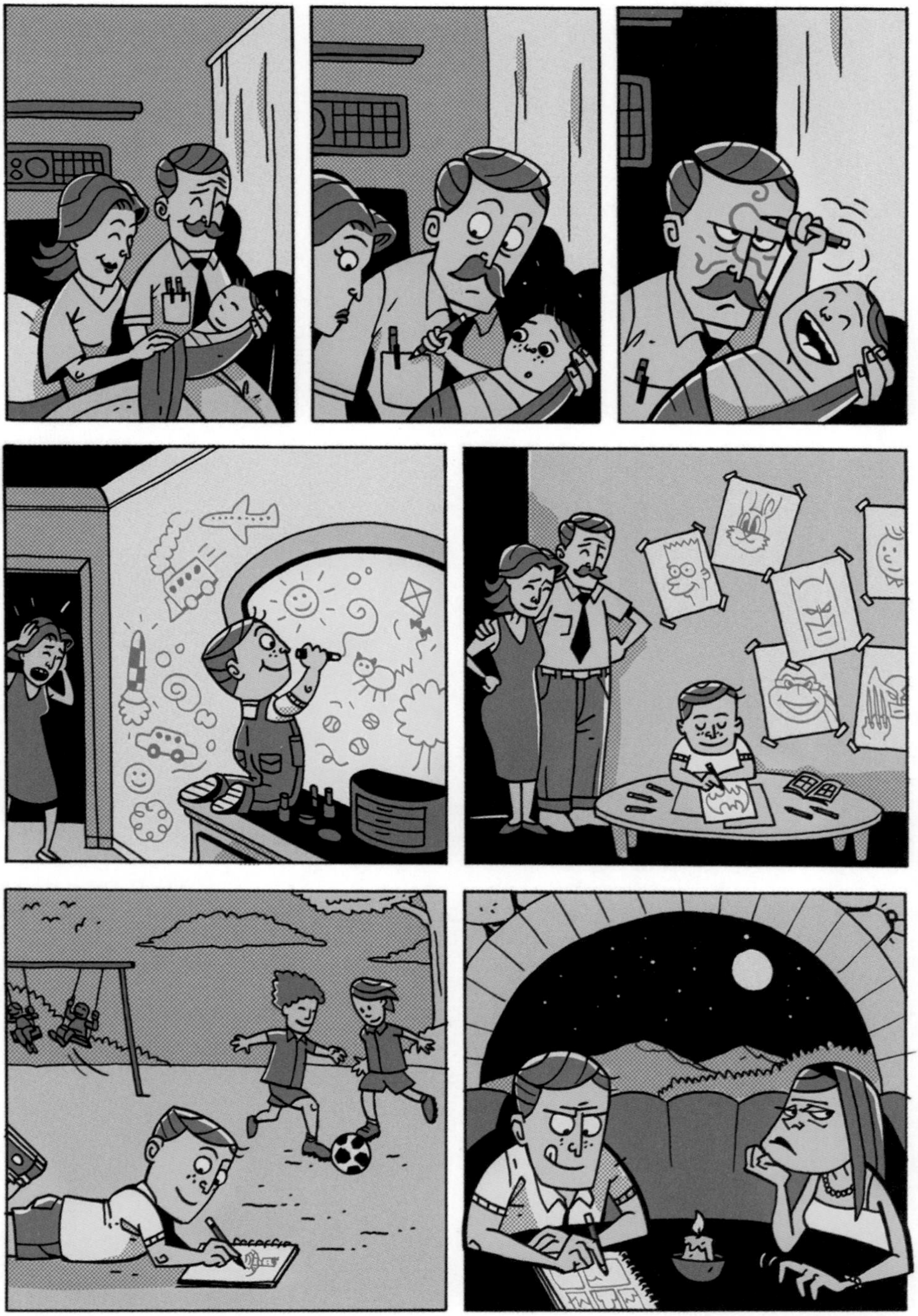

CHOOSE A JOB YOU LOVE,
AND YOU WILL NEVER HAVE
TO WORK A DAY IN YOUR LIFE.

–CONFUCIUS

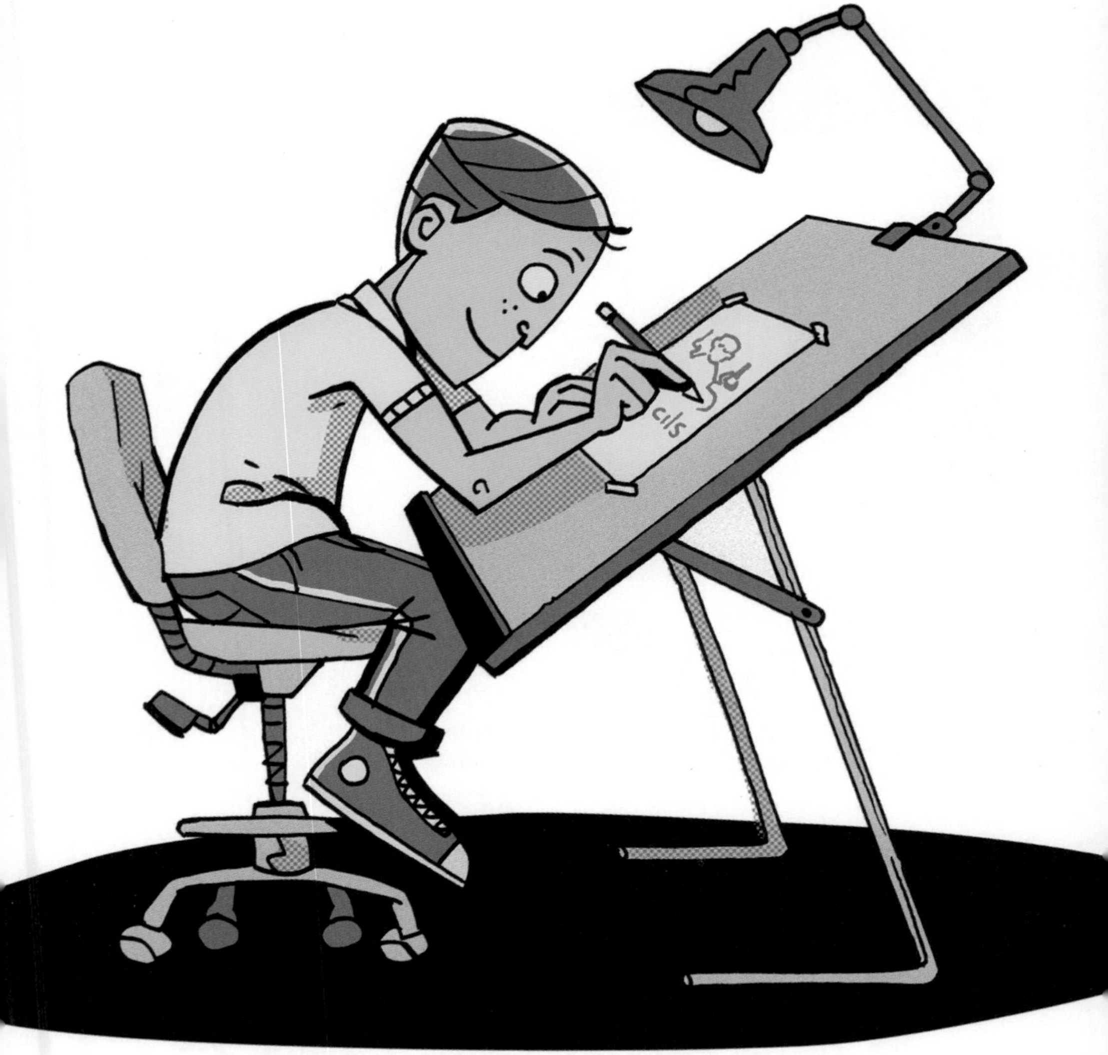
cils

ALWAYS BE PREPARED

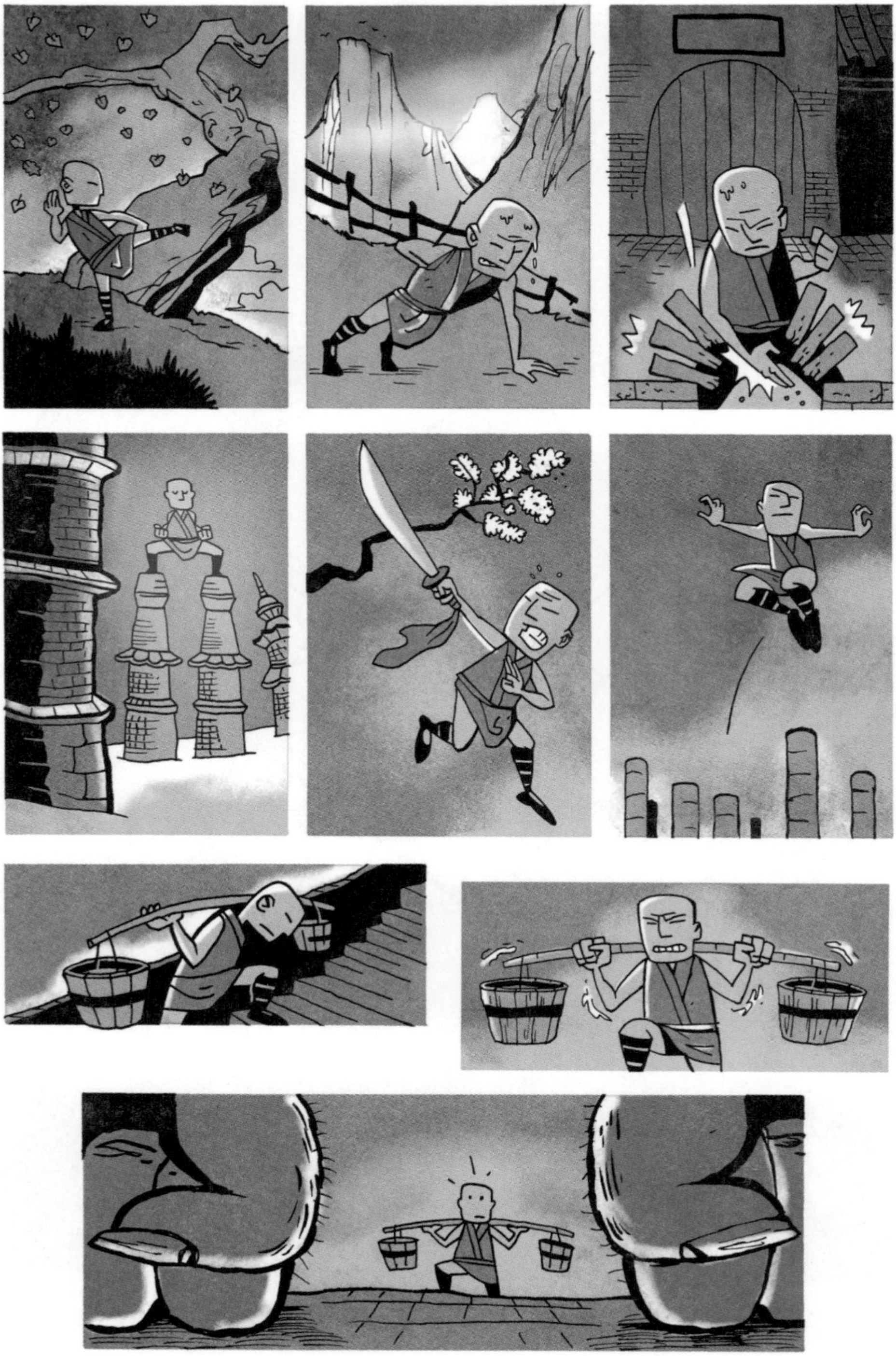

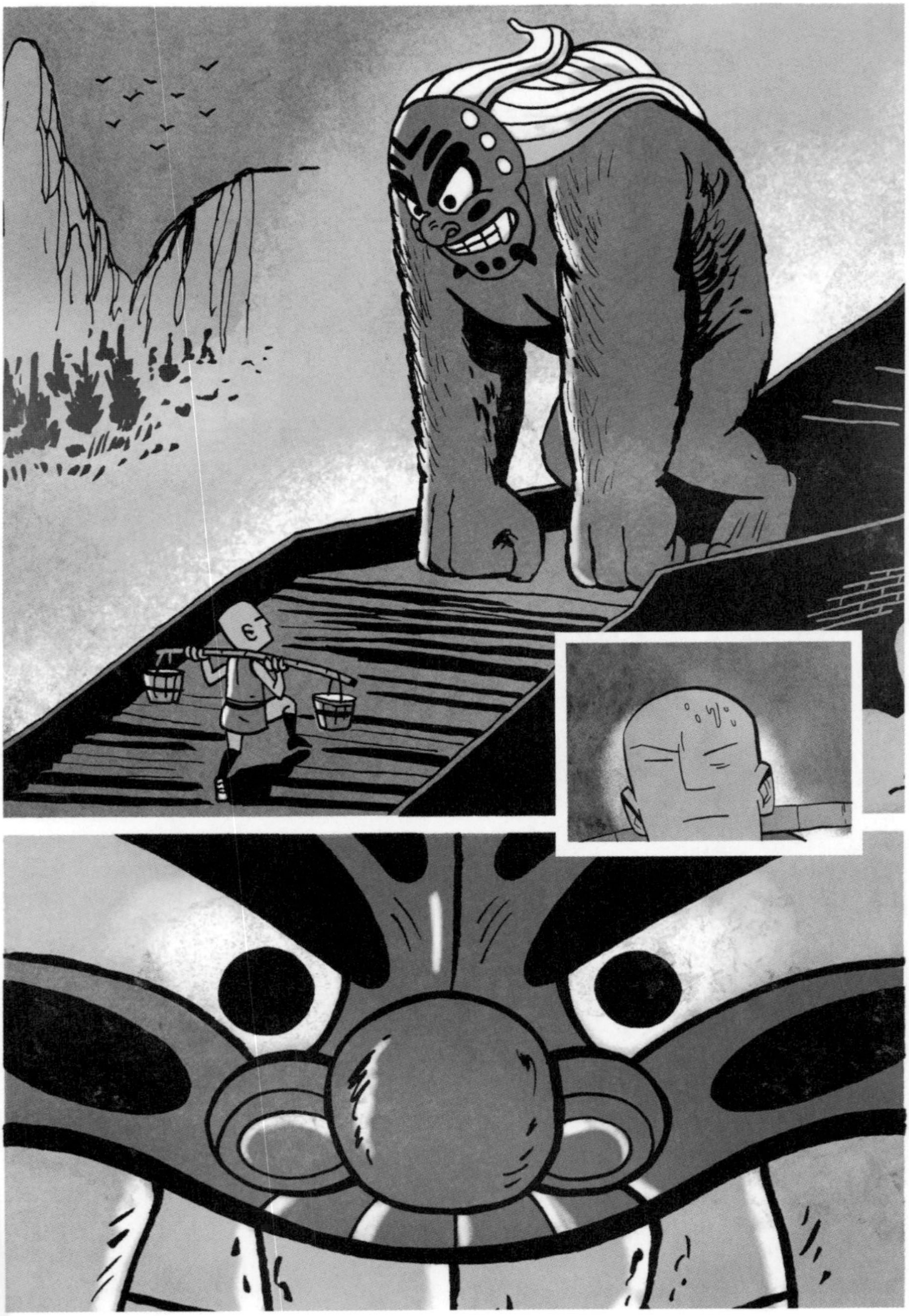

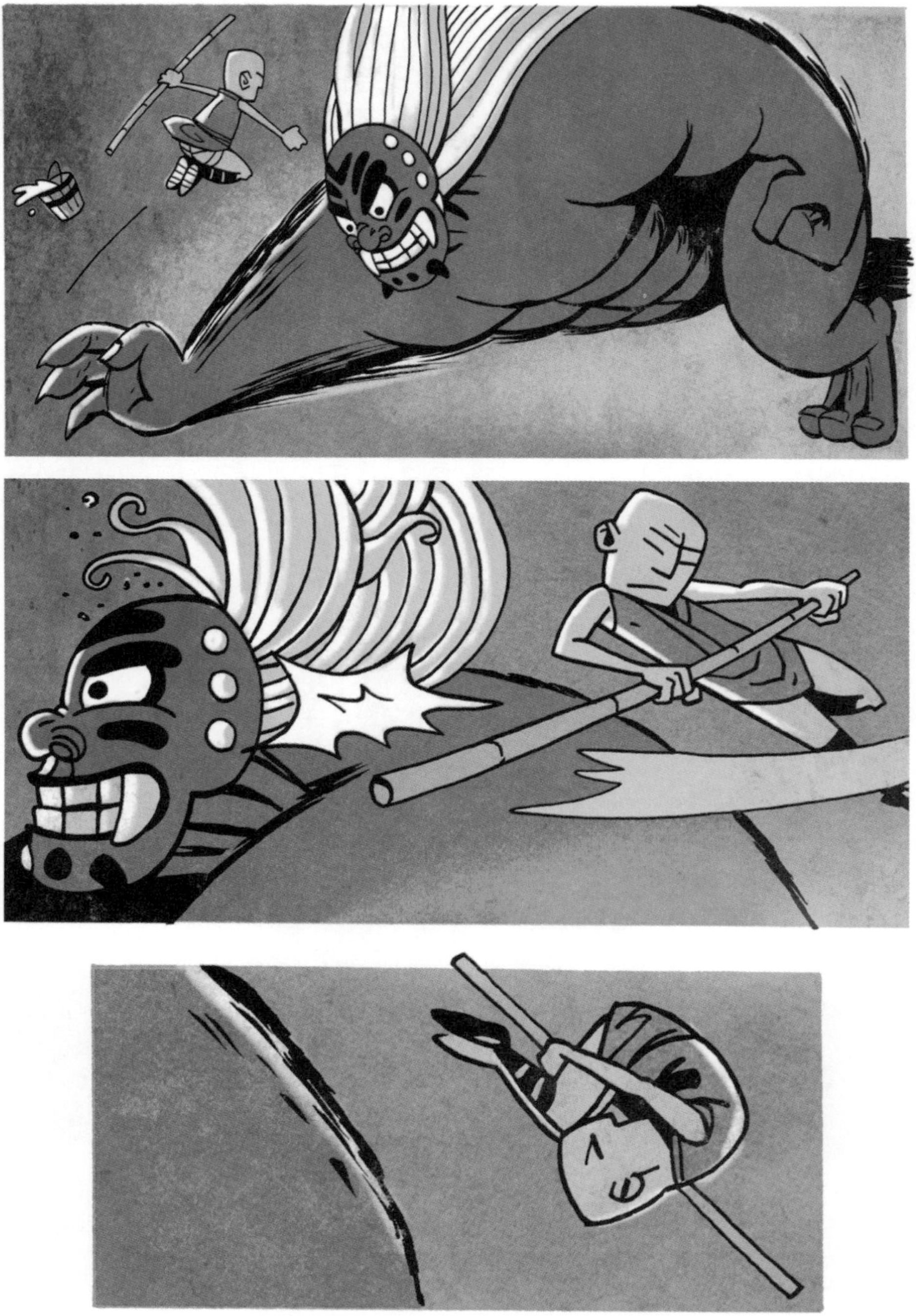

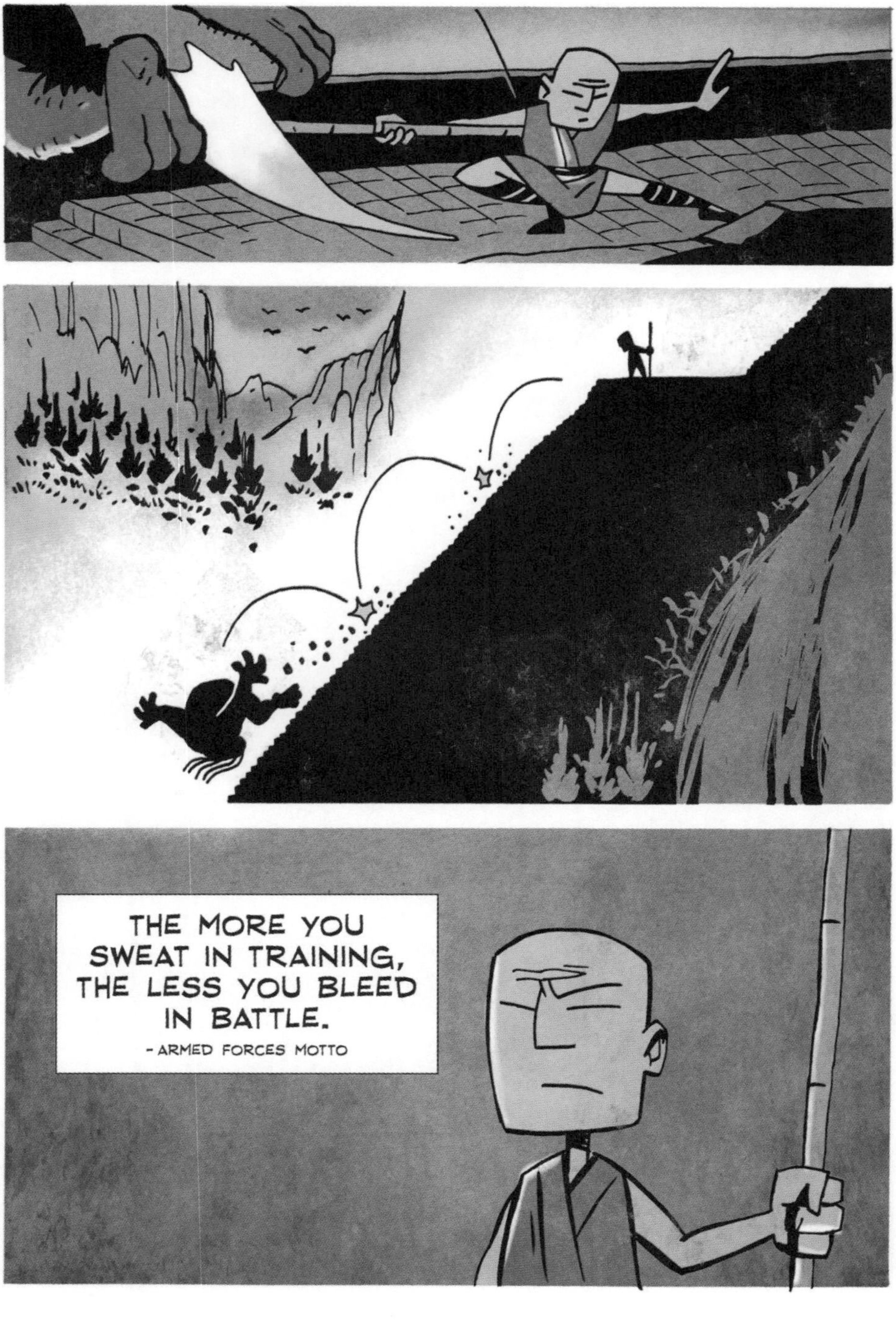
THE MORE YOU SWEAT IN TRAINING, THE LESS YOU BLEED IN BATTLE.
- ARMED FORCES MOTTO

THE MAN IN THE ARENA Theodore Roosevelt

IT IS NOT THE CRITIC WHO COUNTS.

HAPPY BIRTHDAY JAMES

OUR LITTLE ASTRONAUT!

NASA

NOT THE MAN WHO POINTS OUT HOW THE STRONG MAN STUMBLED.

TAX ACCOUNTS

JAMES FOX

CONGRATULAT

SENIOR ACCOUNT

OR WHERE THE DOER OF DEEDS COULD HAVE DONE BETTER.

Everest expedition

Everest expedition

THE CREDIT BELONGS TO THE MAN IN THE ARENA.

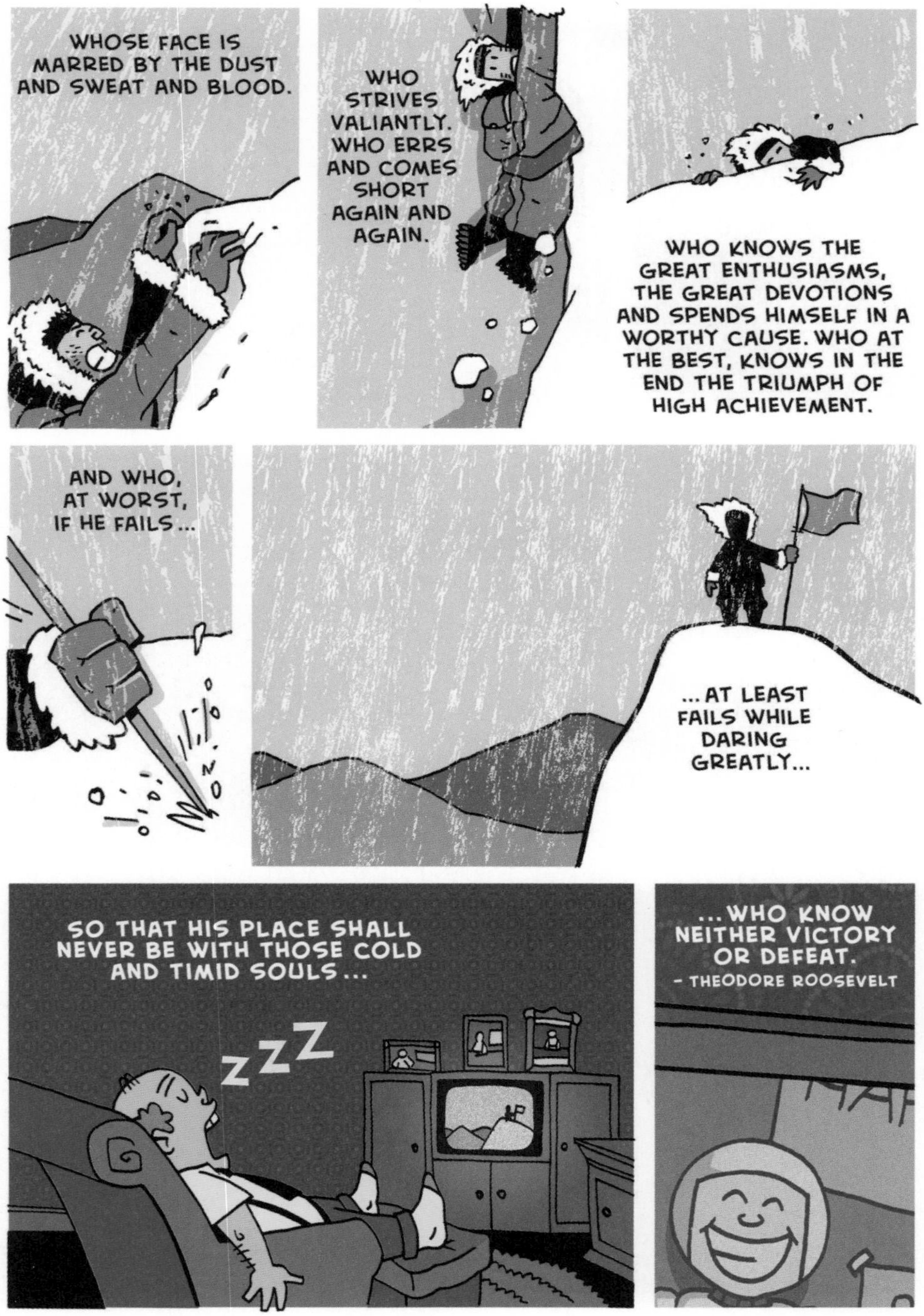
WHOSE FACE IS MARRED BY THE DUST AND SWEAT AND BLOOD.
WHO STRIVES VALIANTLY. WHO ERRS AND COMES SHORT AGAIN AND AGAIN.
WHO KNOWS THE GREAT ENTHUSIASMS, THE GREAT DEVOTIONS AND SPENDS HIMSELF IN A WORTHY CAUSE. WHO AT THE BEST, KNOWS IN THE END THE TRIUMPH OF HIGH ACHIEVEMENT.
AND WHO, AT WORST, IF HE FAILS...
...AT LEAST FAILS WHILE DARING GREATLY...
SO THAT HIS PLACE SHALL NEVER BE WITH THOSE COLD AND TIMID SOULS...
ZZZ
...WHO KNOW NEITHER VICTORY OR DEFEAT.
- THEODORE ROOSEVELT

STRANGE LIKE ME Rebecca Martín

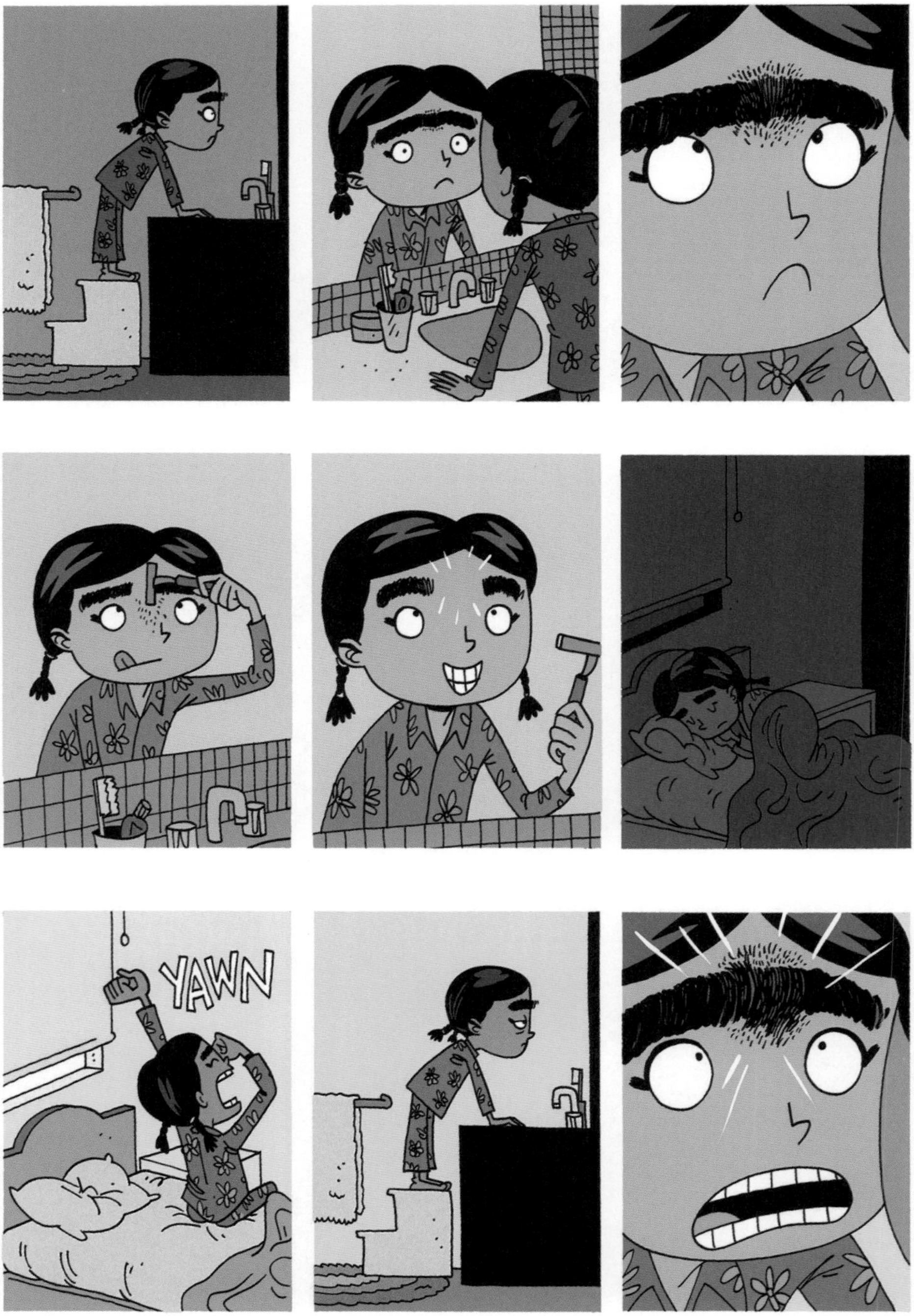
YAWN

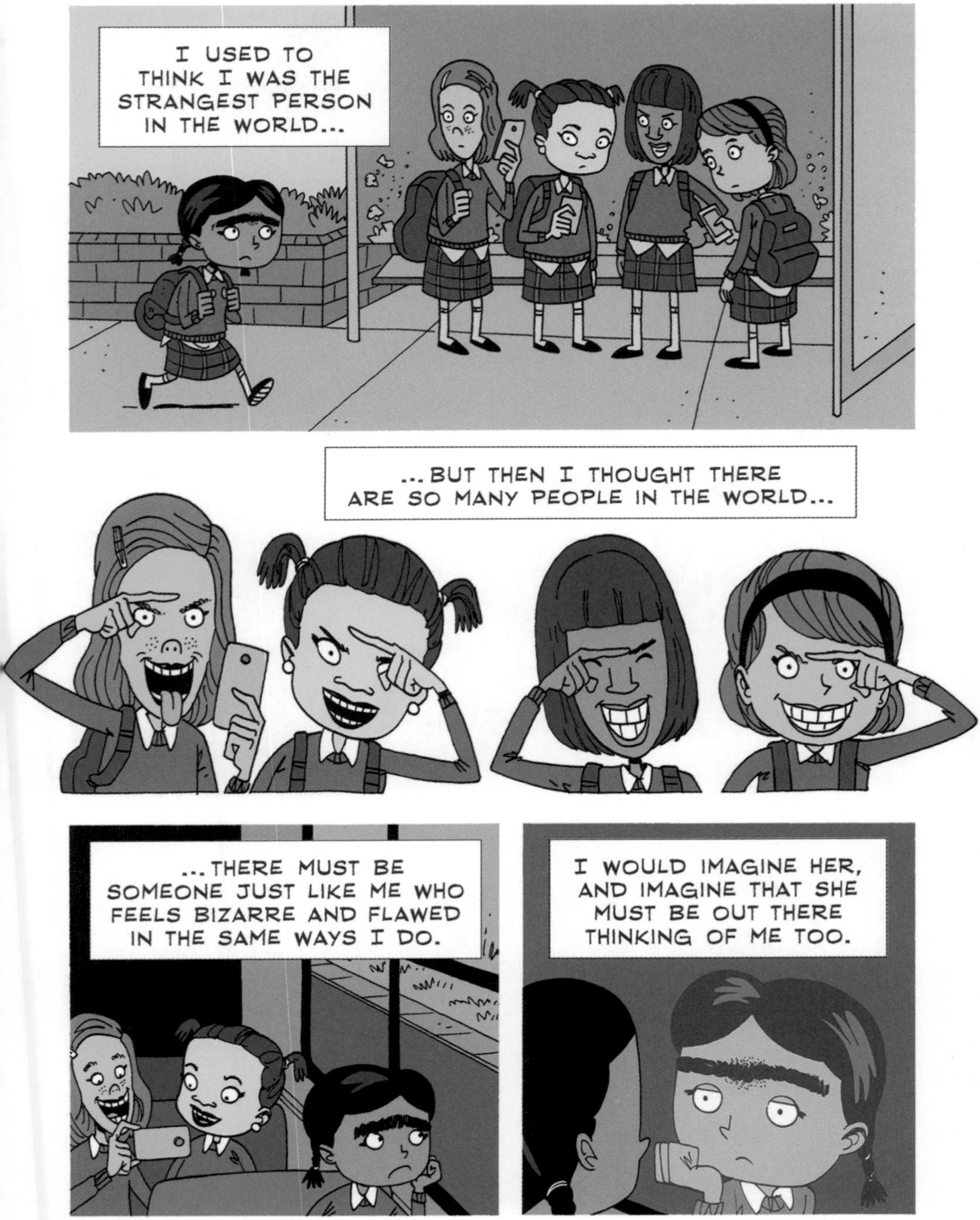
I USED TO THINK I WAS THE STRANGEST PERSON IN THE WORLD...
...BUT THEN I THOUGHT THERE ARE SO MANY PEOPLE IN THE WORLD...
...THERE MUST BE SOMEONE JUST LIKE ME WHO FEELS BIZARRE AND FLAWED IN THE SAME WAYS I DO.
I WOULD IMAGINE HER, AND IMAGINE THAT SHE MUST BE OUT THERE THINKING OF ME TOO.

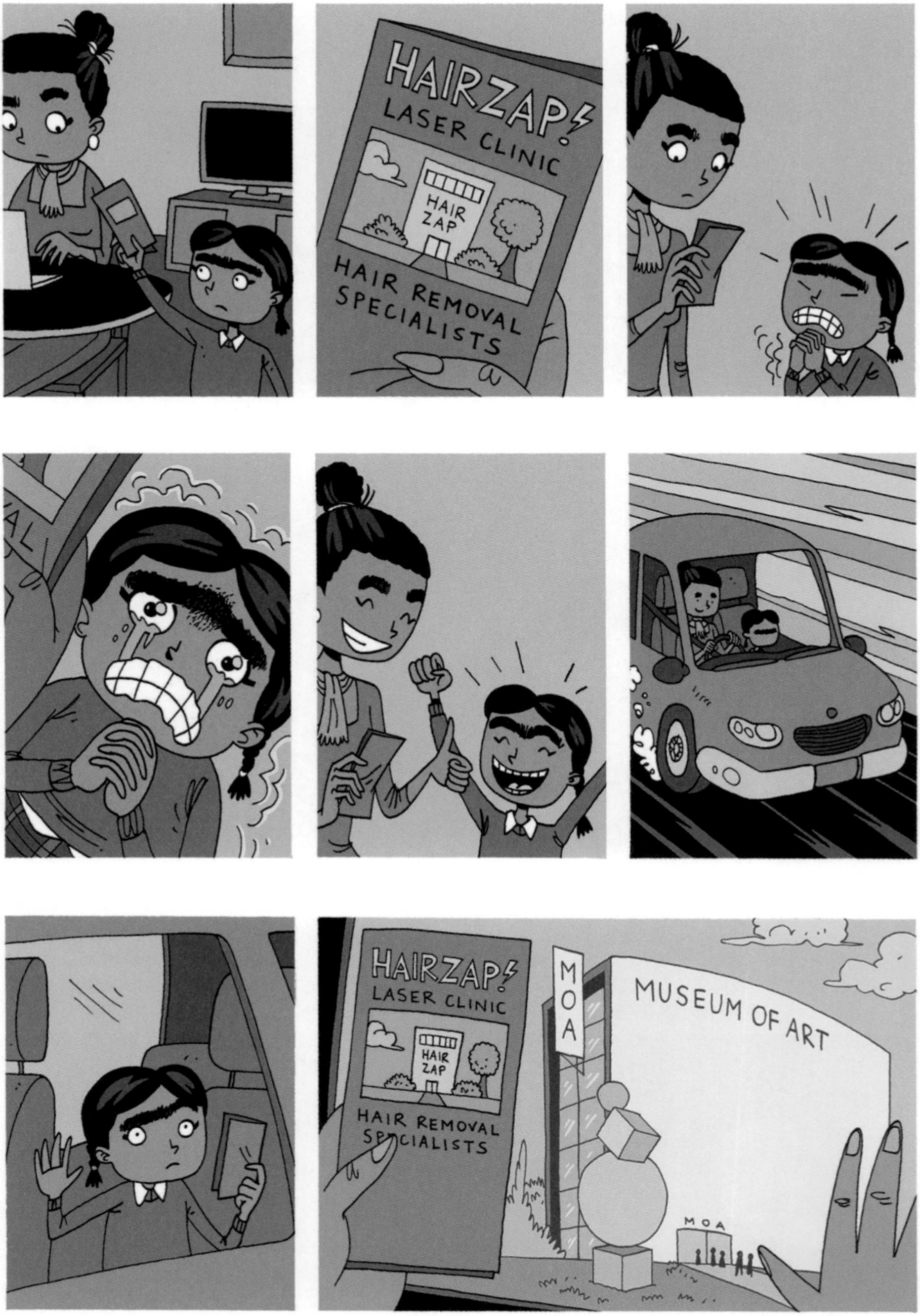

HAIRZAP!
LASER CLINIC
HAIR ZAP
HAIR REMOVAL SPECIALISTS
HAIRZAP!
LASER CLINIC
HAIR ZAP
HAIR REMOVAL SPECIALISTS
MOA
MUSEUM OF ART
MOA

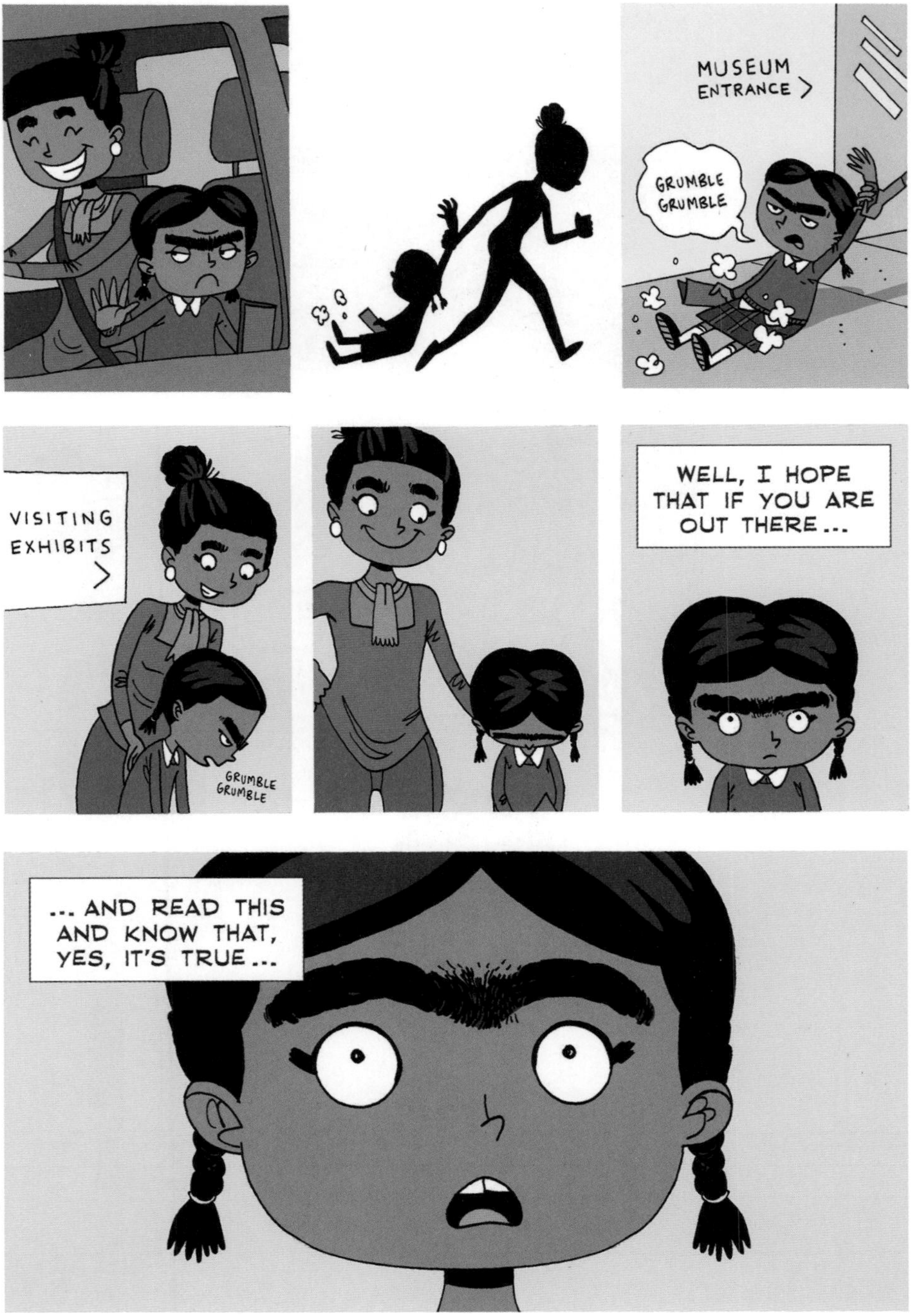
MUSEUM
ENTRANCE >
GRUMBLE
GRUMBLE
VISITING
EXHIBITS
>
GRUMBLE
GRUMBLE
WELL, I HOPE THAT IF YOU ARE OUT THERE...
... AND READ THIS AND KNOW THAT, YES, IT'S TRUE...

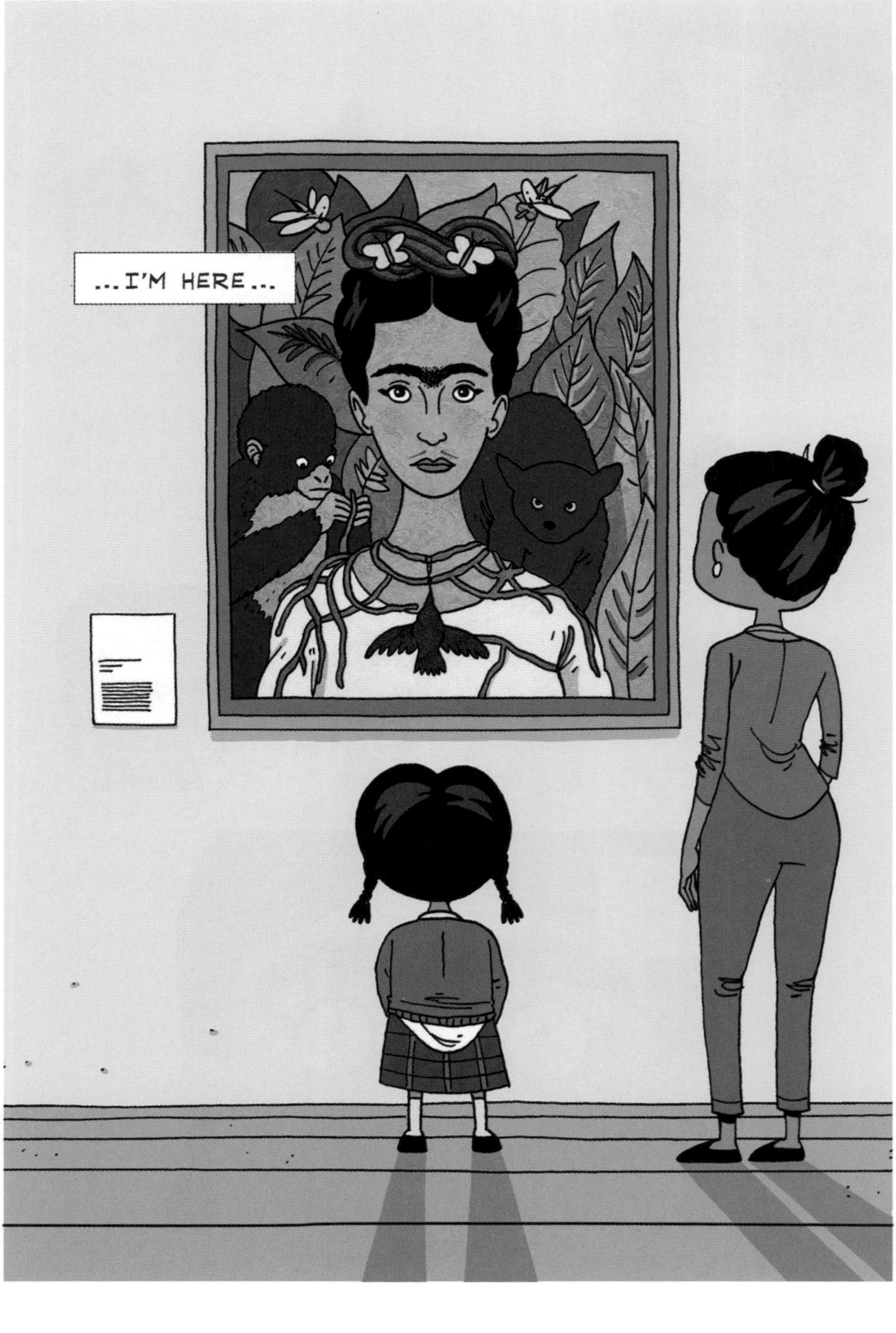
...I'M HERE...

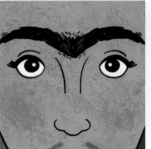

Frida
Her life & work

...AND I'M JUST
AS STRANGE AS YOU.
— REBECCA MARTIN

TRASH

ASK YOURSELF Howard Thurman

ANDRE THE GIANT
HULK POWER
HULKAMANIA
JUNIOR STATE WRESTLING CHAMPI
ULTIMATE WARRIOR
OH YEEAH!
MACHO MAN
HOMEWORK
HOMEWORK
HOMEWORK
HOMEWORK
HOMEWORK
HOMEWORK
STAGE NAME: RISING PHOENIX!
ELBOW GUARD
SIGNATURE MOVE: FLYING ELBOW DROP
REPORT CARD
A+ MATH
A+ BIOLOGY
A+ PHYSICS
HISTORY
NGLISH
HARVARD LAW SCH
DON'T ASK YOURSELF WHAT THE WORLD NEEDS.

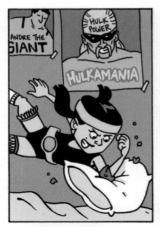

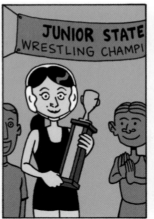

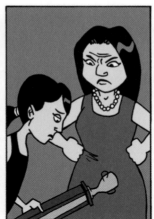

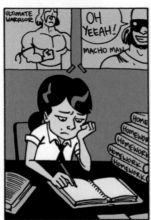

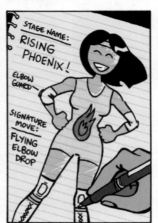

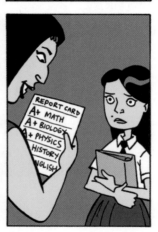

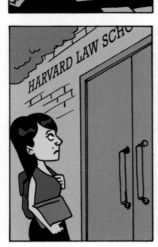

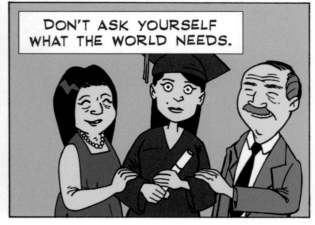

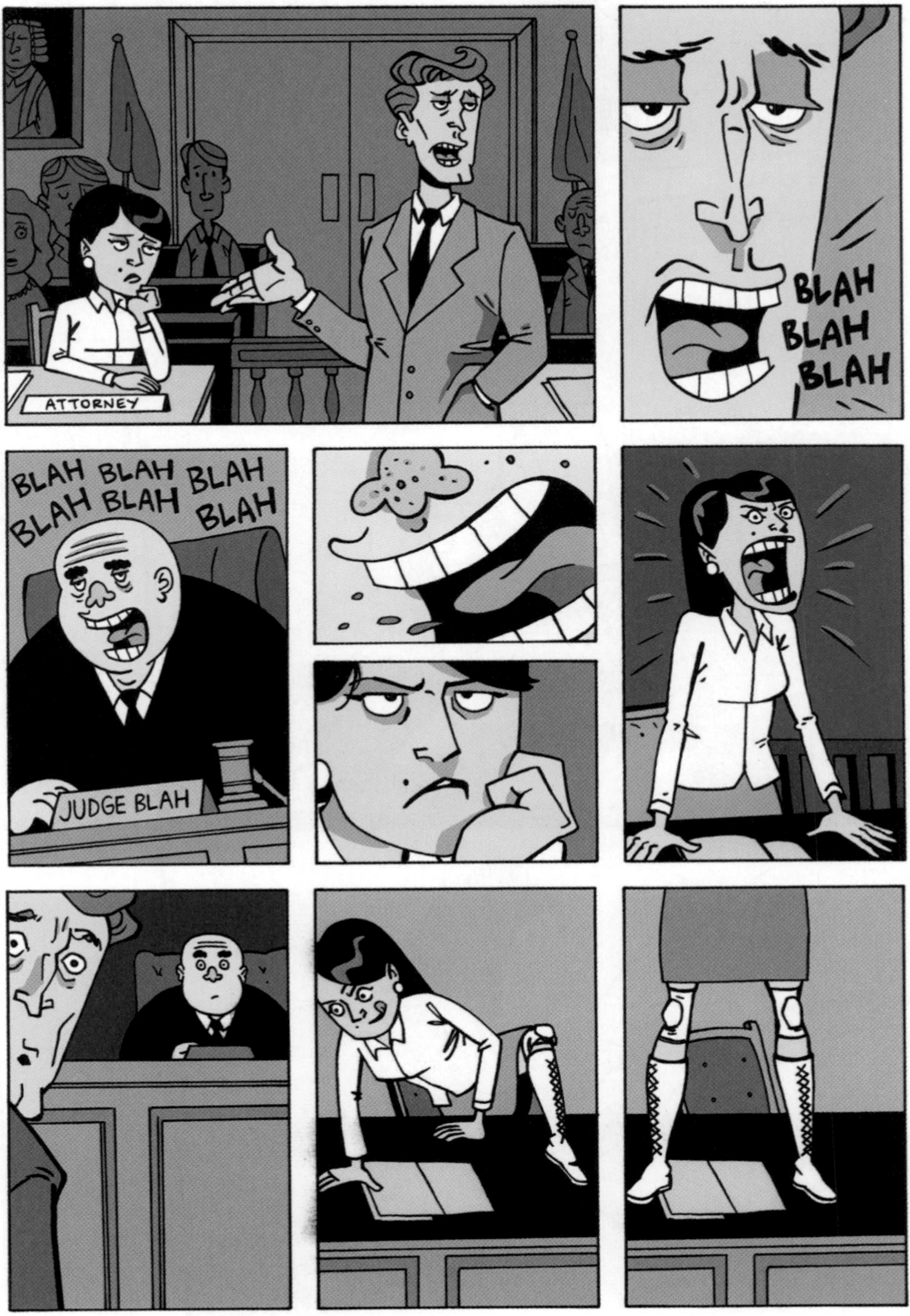
ATTORNEY
BLAH
BLAH
BLAH
BLAH BLAH BLAH
BLAH BLAH BLAH
JUDGE BLAH

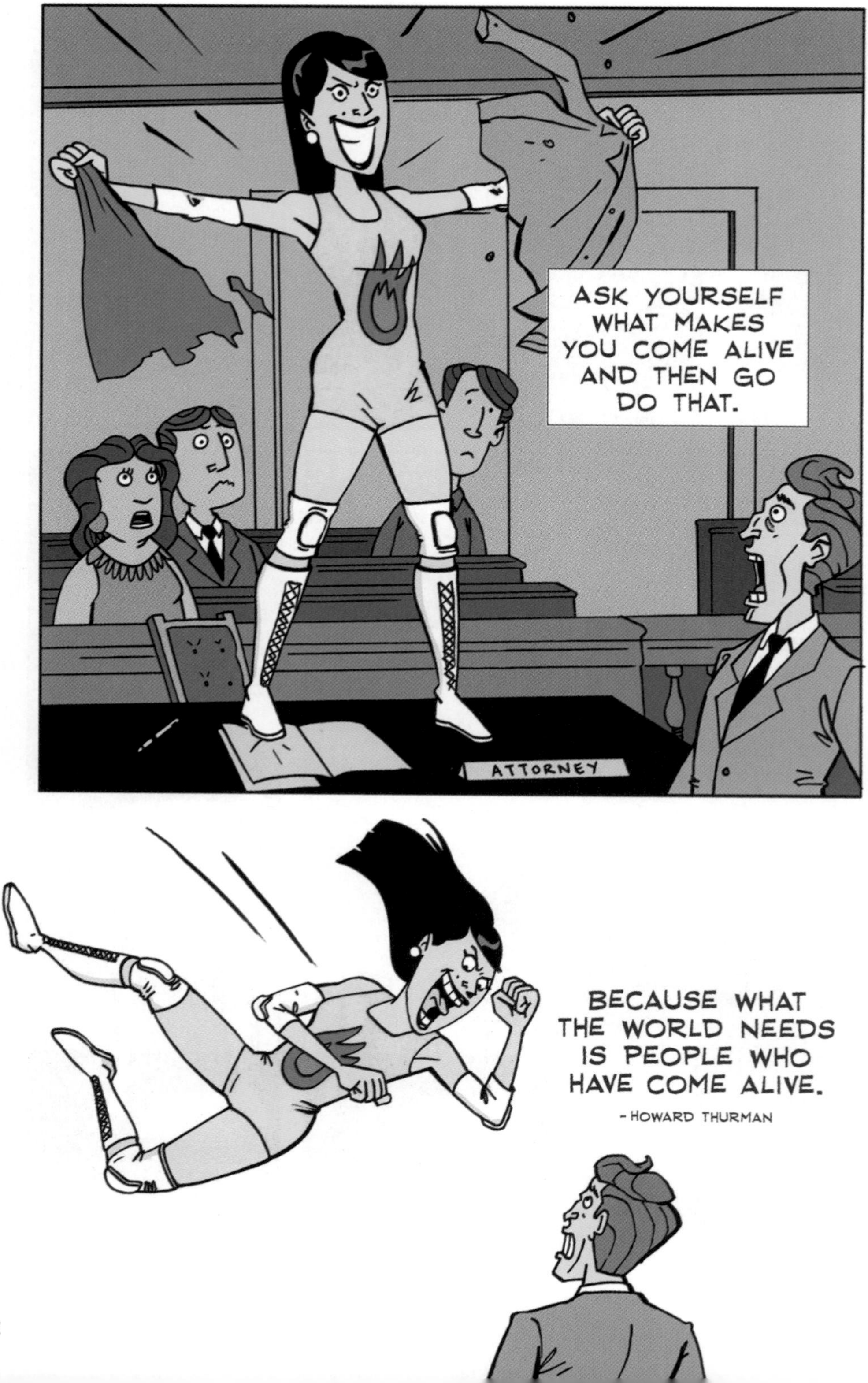
ASK YOURSELF WHAT MAKES YOU COME ALIVE AND THEN GO DO THAT.
ATTORNEY
BECAUSE WHAT THE WORLD NEEDS IS PEOPLE WHO HAVE COME ALIVE.
- HOWARD THURMAN

THE TWO WOLVES

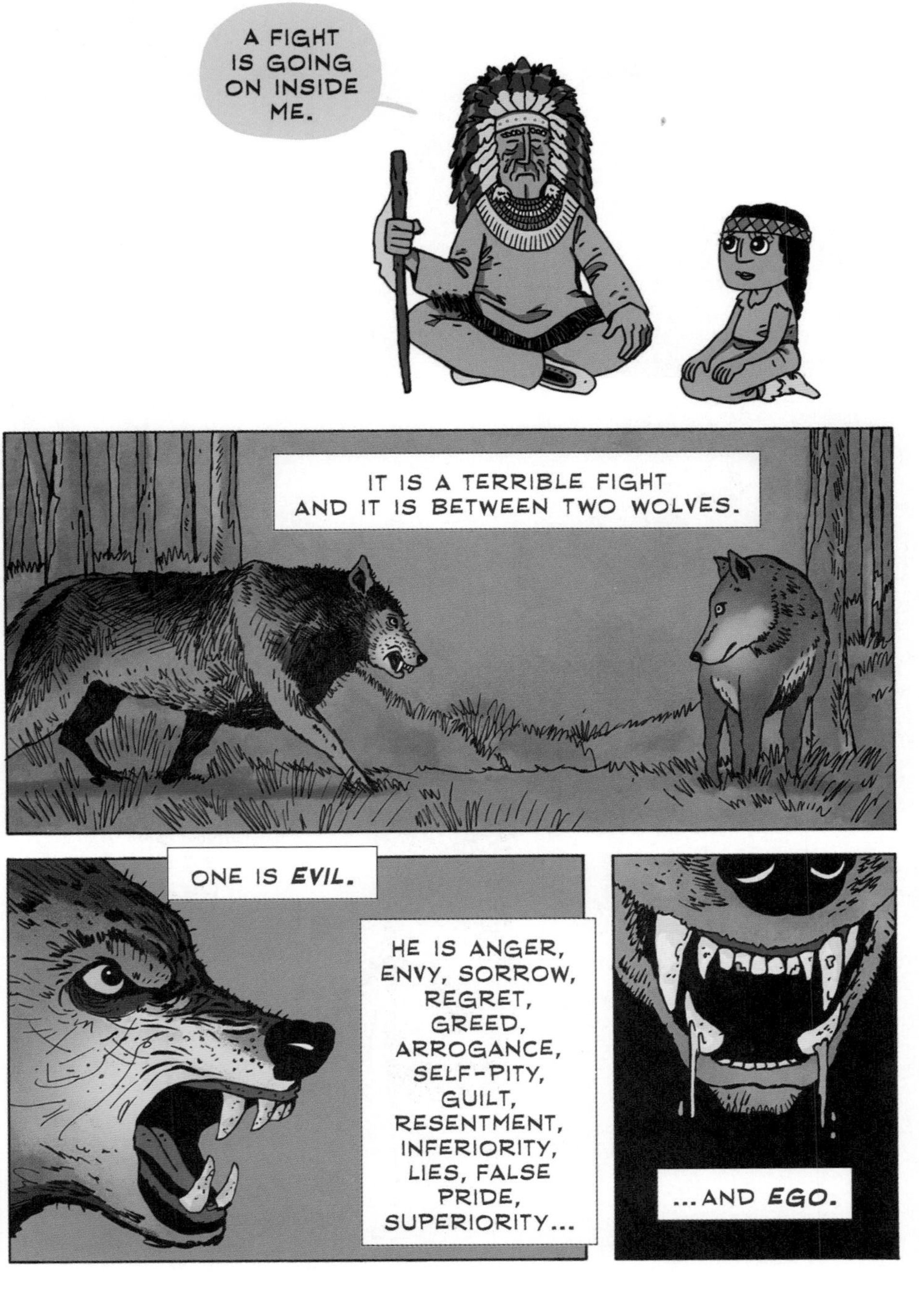
A FIGHT IS GOING ON INSIDE ME.
IT IS A TERRIBLE FIGHT AND IT IS BETWEEN TWO WOLVES.
ONE IS *EVIL.*
HE IS ANGER, ENVY, SORROW, REGRET, GREED, ARROGANCE, SELF-PITY, GUILT, RESENTMENT, INFERIORITY, LIES, FALSE PRIDE, SUPERIORITY...
...AND *EGO.*

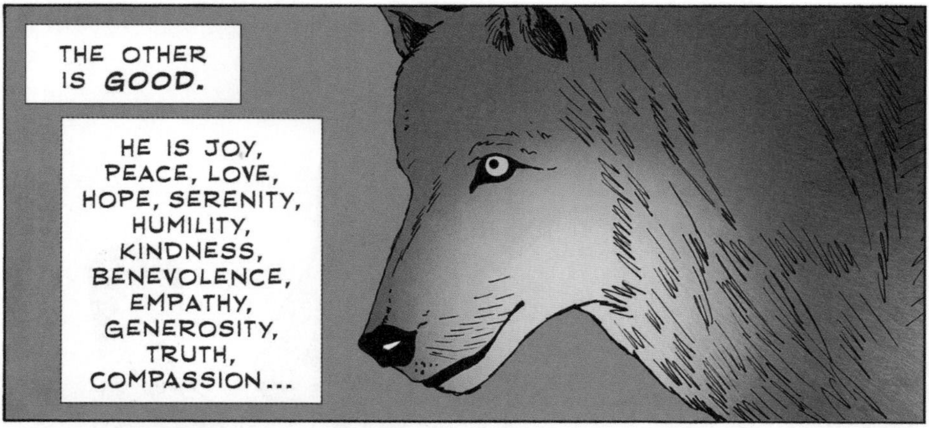
THE OTHER IS *GOOD*.
HE IS JOY, PEACE, LOVE, HOPE, SERENITY, HUMILITY, KINDNESS, BENEVOLENCE, EMPATHY, GENEROSITY, TRUTH, COMPASSION...

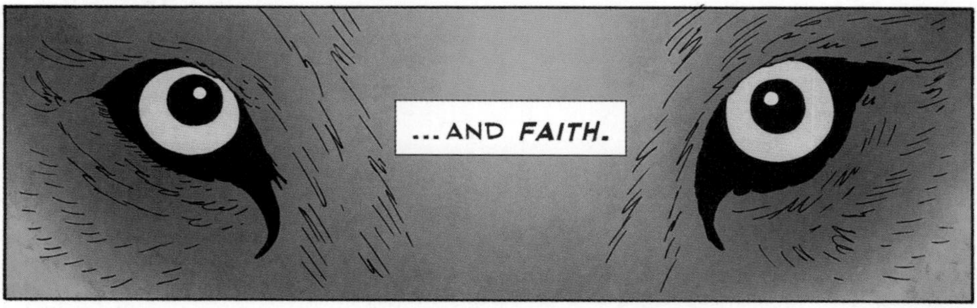
...AND *FAITH*.

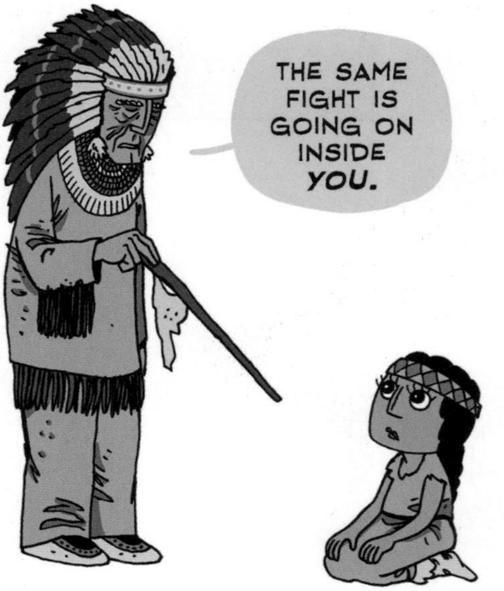
THE SAME FIGHT IS GOING ON INSIDE *YOU*.

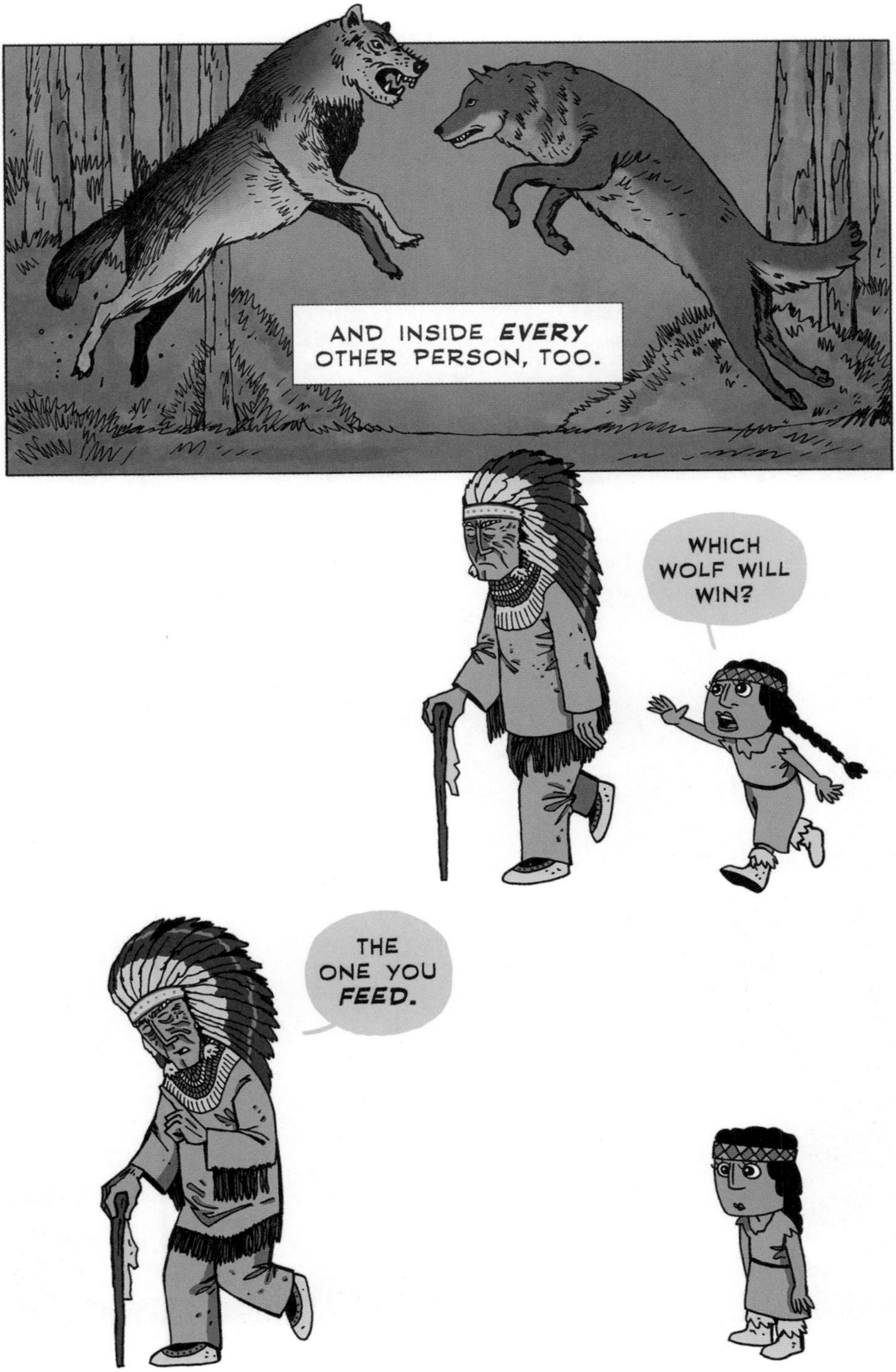
AND INSIDE EVERY OTHER PERSON, TOO.
WHICH WOLF WILL WIN?
THE ONE YOU FEED.

ASHES OR DUST Jack London

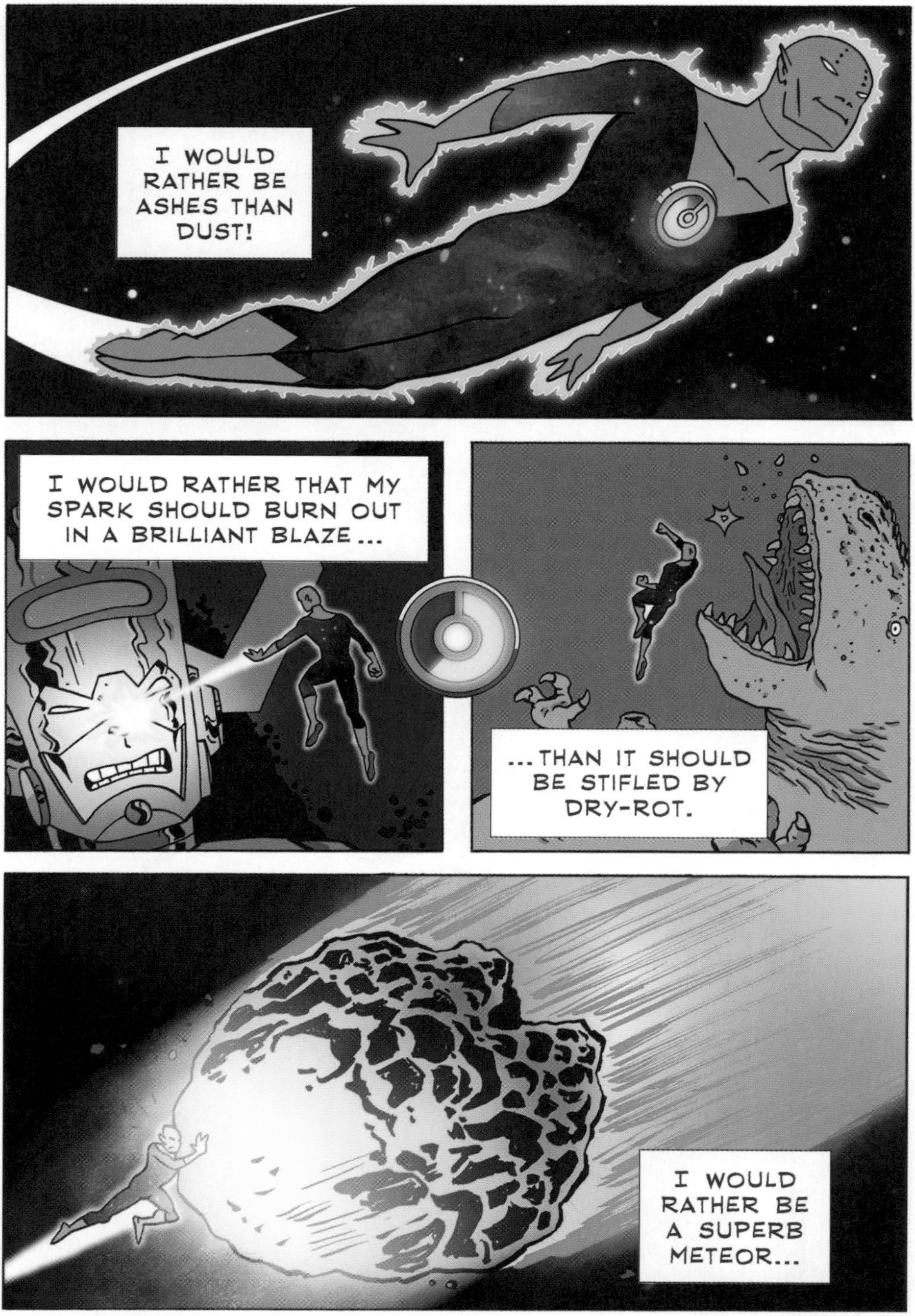
I WOULD RATHER BE ASHES THAN DUST!
I WOULD RATHER THAT MY SPARK SHOULD BURN OUT IN A BRILLIANT BLAZE...
...THAN IT SHOULD BE STIFLED BY DRY-ROT.
I WOULD RATHER BE A SUPERB METEOR...

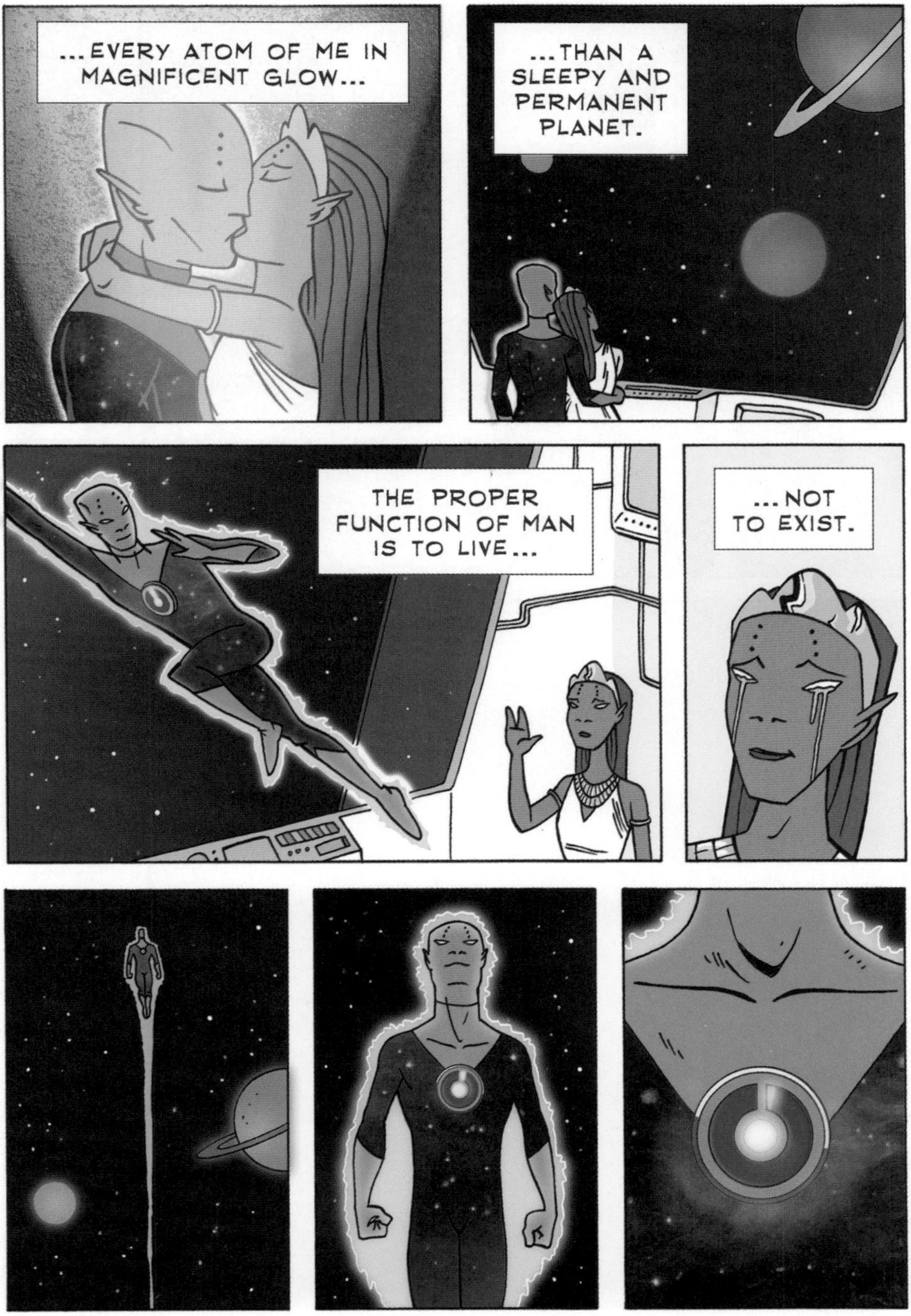

...EVERY ATOM OF ME IN MAGNIFICENT GLOW...
...THAN A SLEEPY AND PERMANENT PLANET.
THE PROPER FUNCTION OF MAN IS TO LIVE...
...NOT TO EXIST.

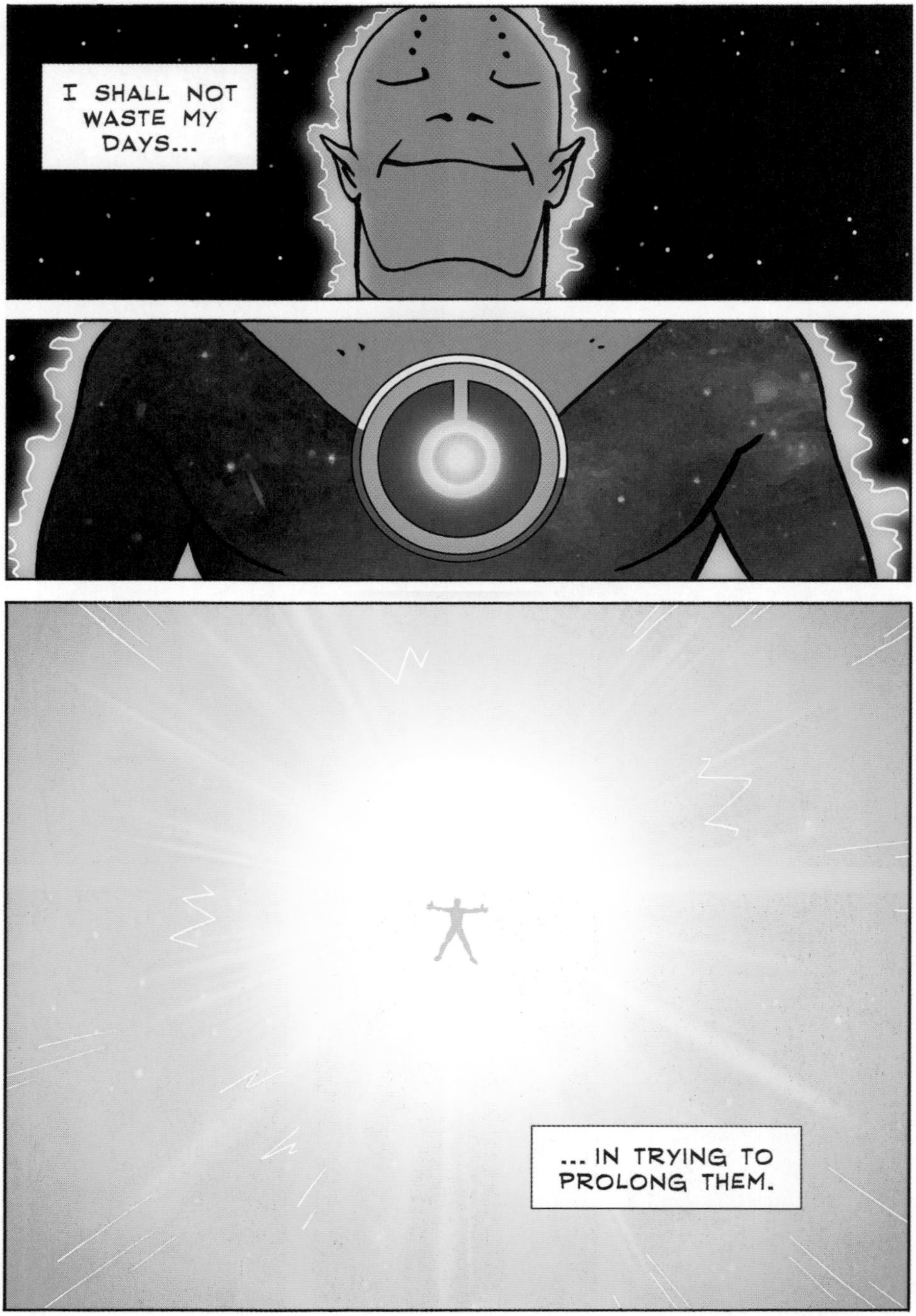
I SHALL NOT WASTE MY DAYS...
...IN TRYING TO PROLONG THEM.

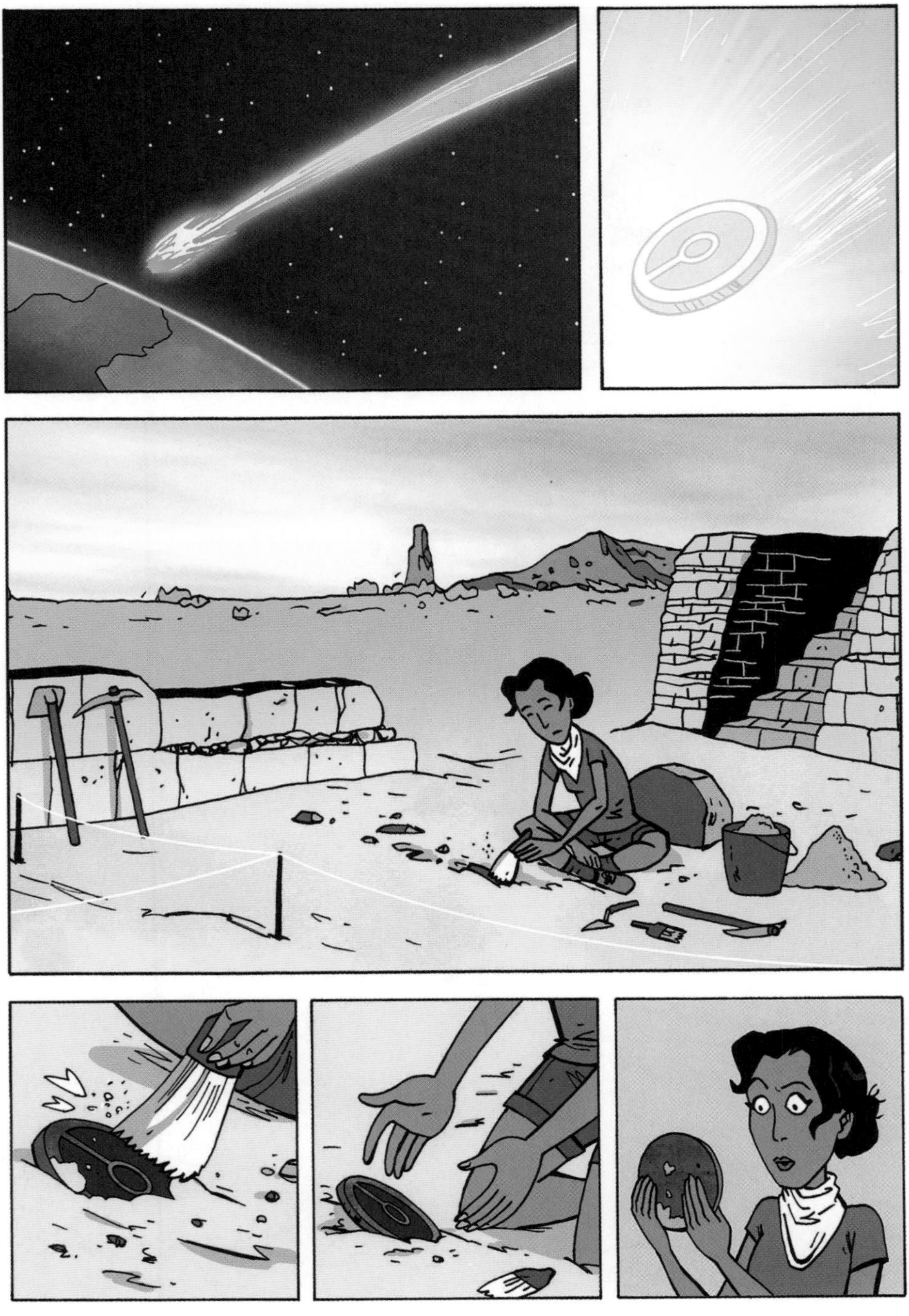

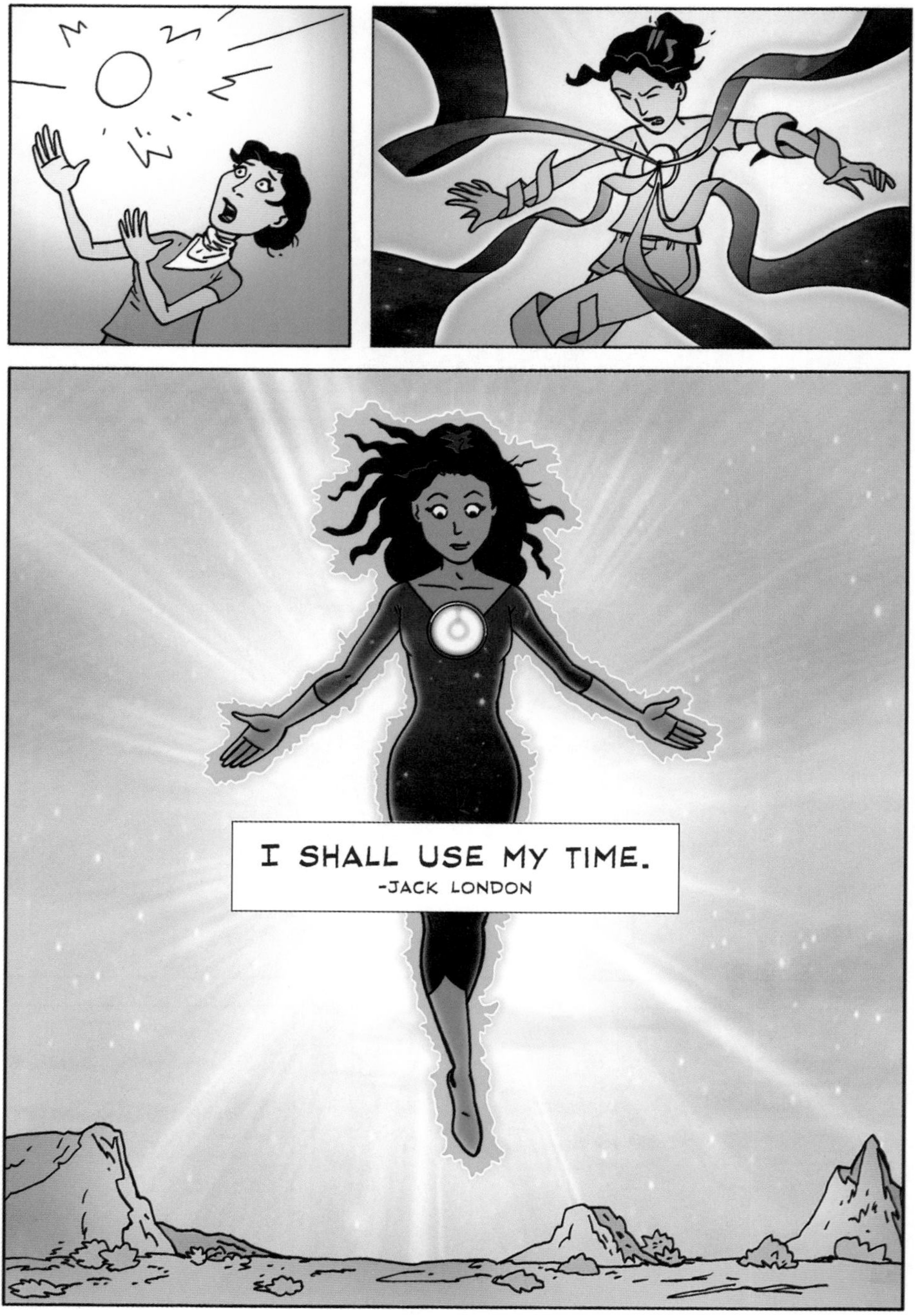
I SHALL USE MY TIME.
-JACK LONDON

NEVER GIVE UP Calvin Coolidge

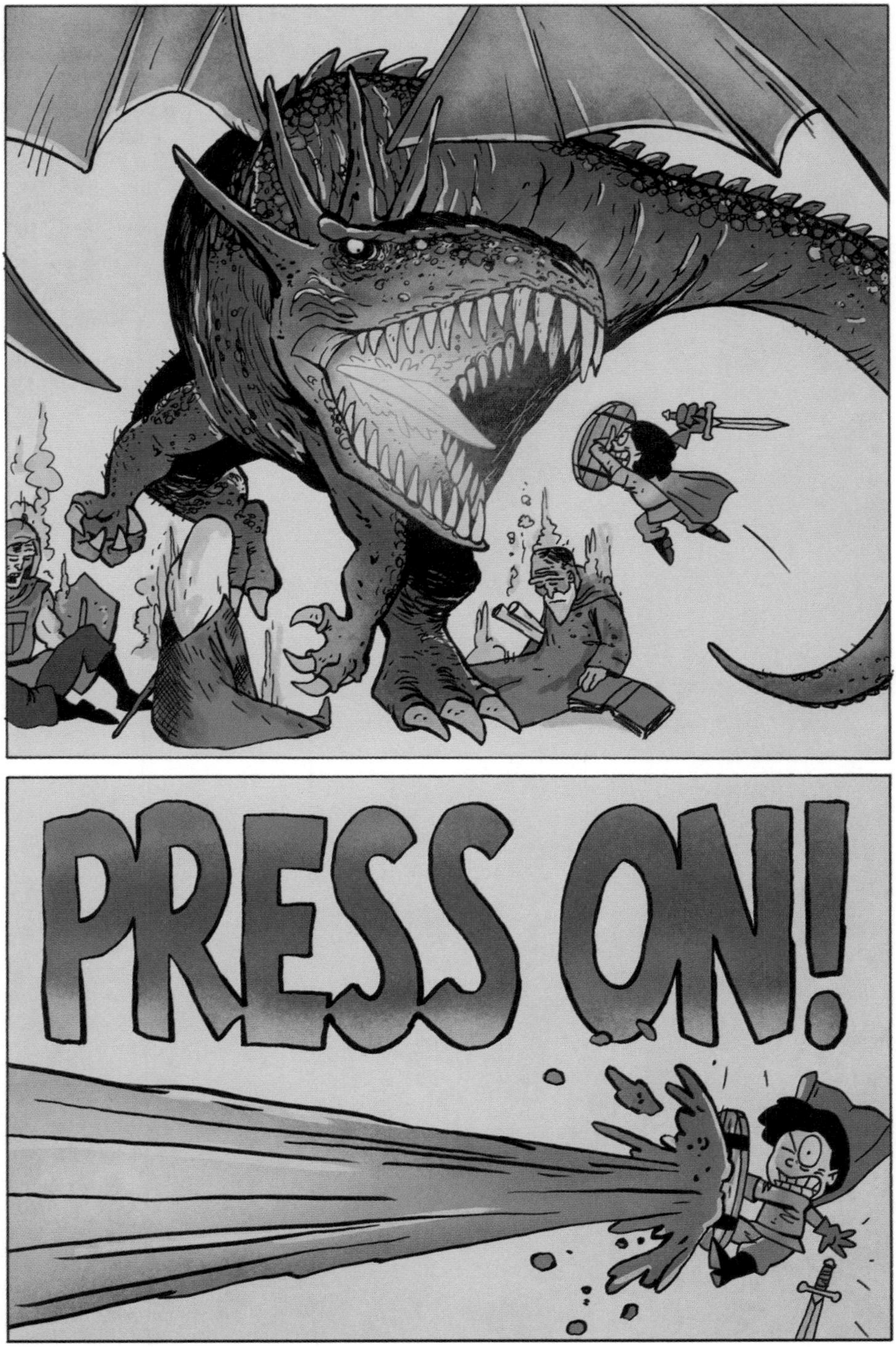
PRESS ON!

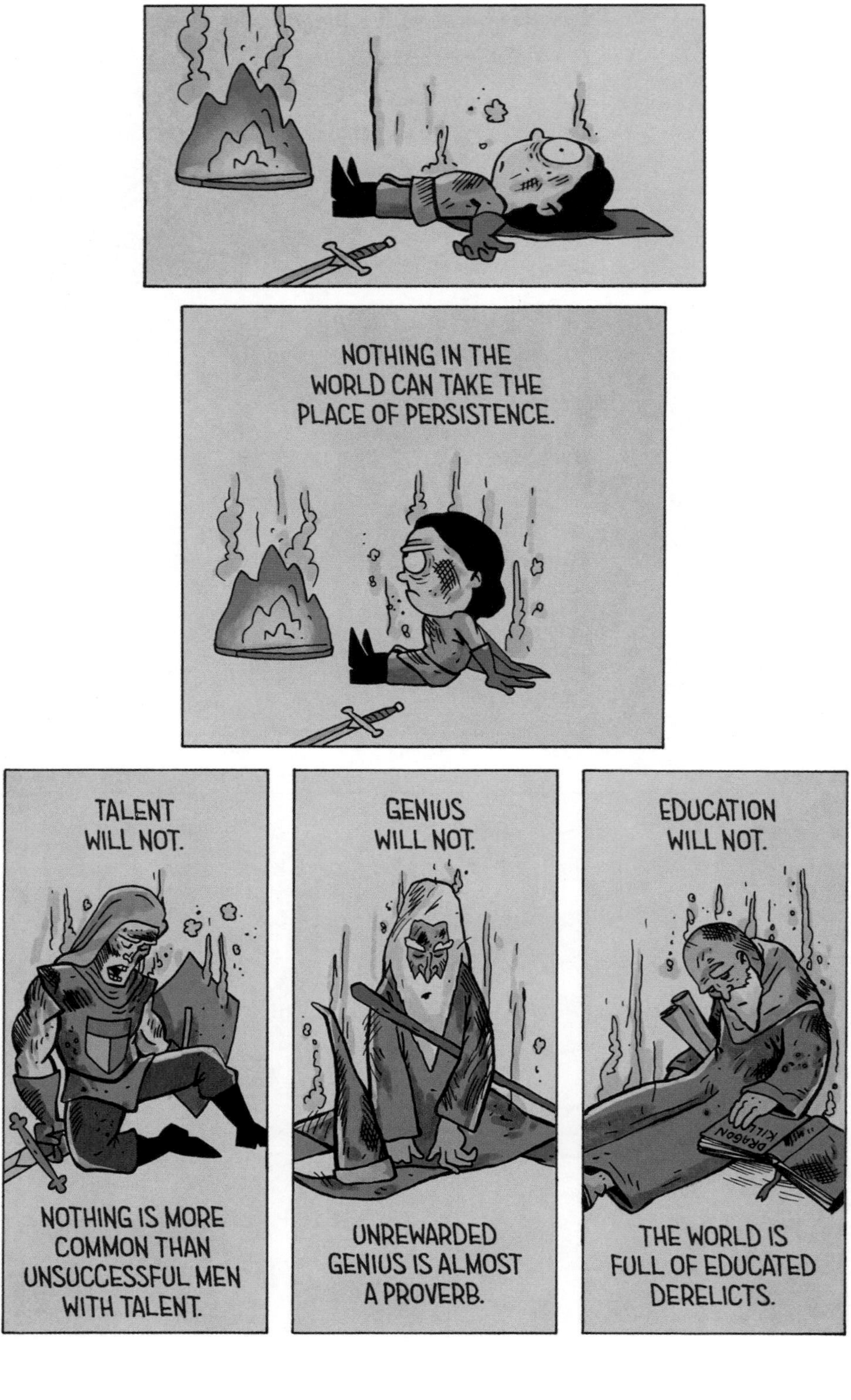
NOTHING IN THE WORLD CAN TAKE THE PLACE OF PERSISTENCE.
TALENT WILL NOT.
NOTHING IS MORE COMMON THAN UNSUCCESSFUL MEN WITH TALENT.
GENIUS WILL NOT.
UNREWARDED GENIUS IS ALMOST A PROVERB.
EDUCATION WILL NOT.
THE WORLD IS FULL OF EDUCATED DERELICTS.

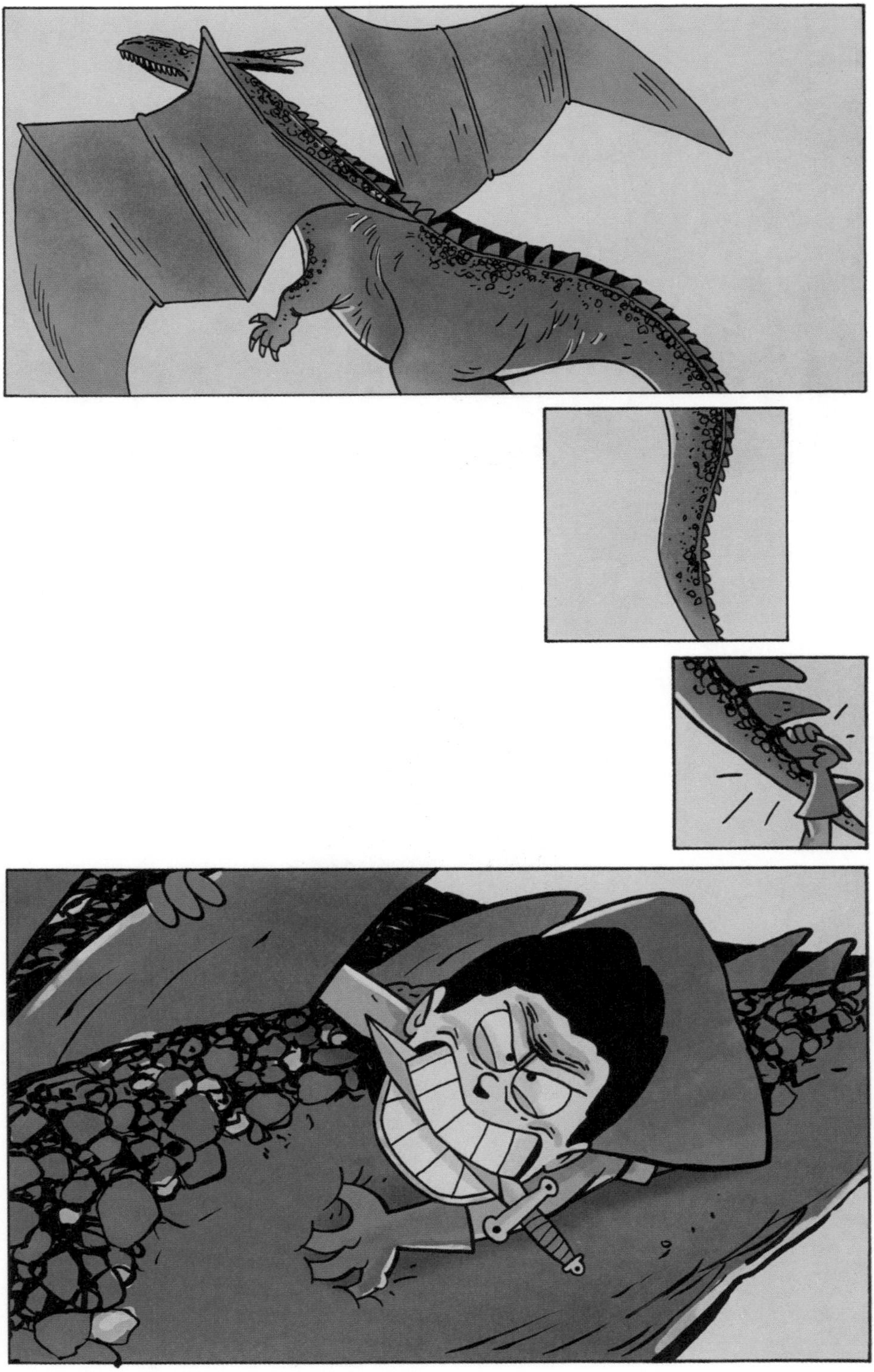

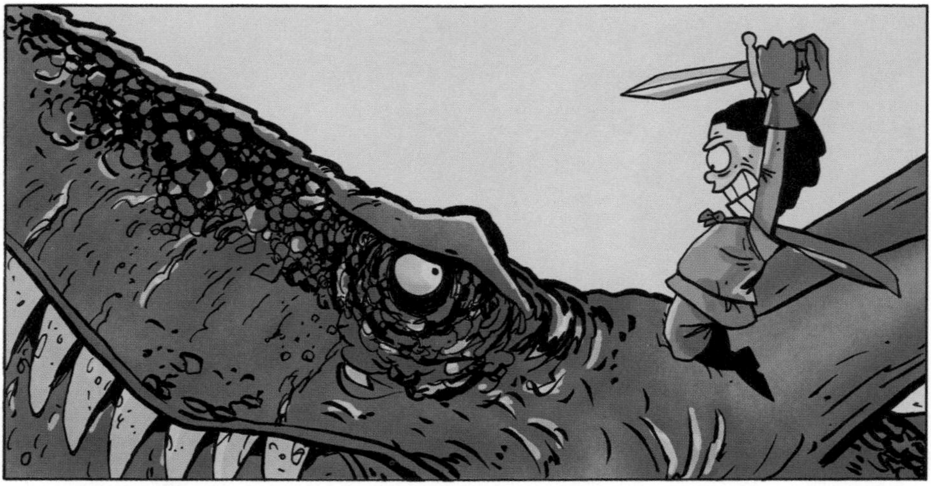

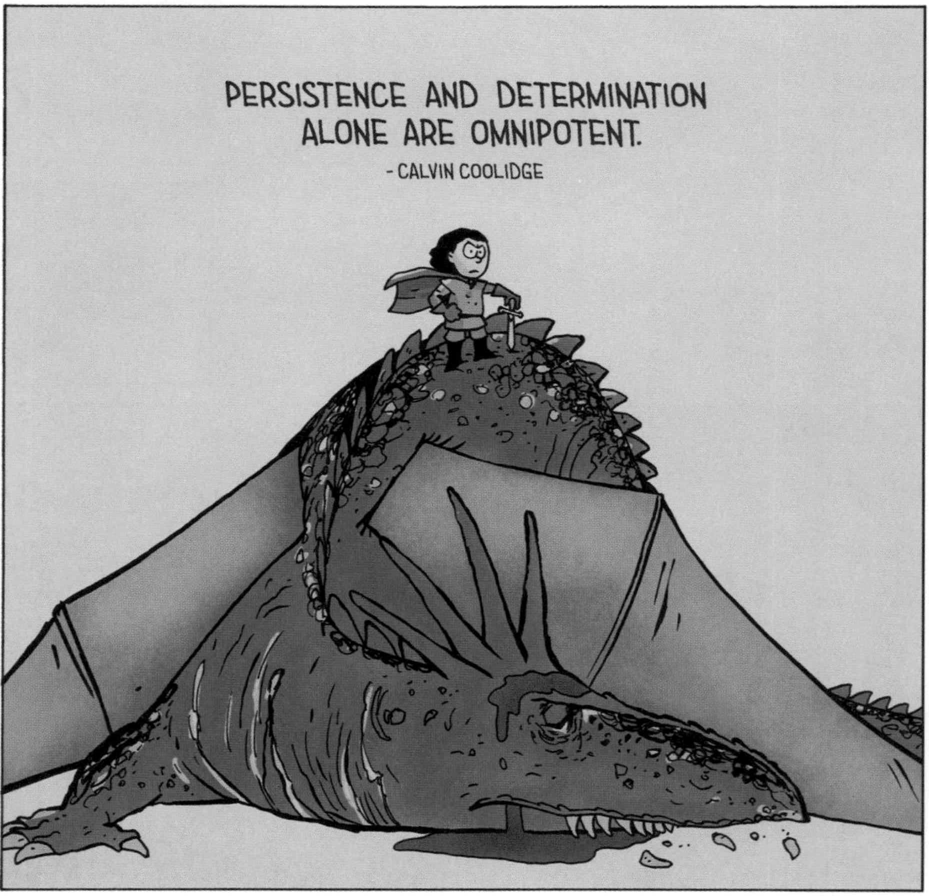
PERSISTENCE AND DETERMINATION ALONE ARE OMNIPOTENT.
- CALVIN COOLIDGE

FEARS ARE PAPER TIGERS Amelia Earhart

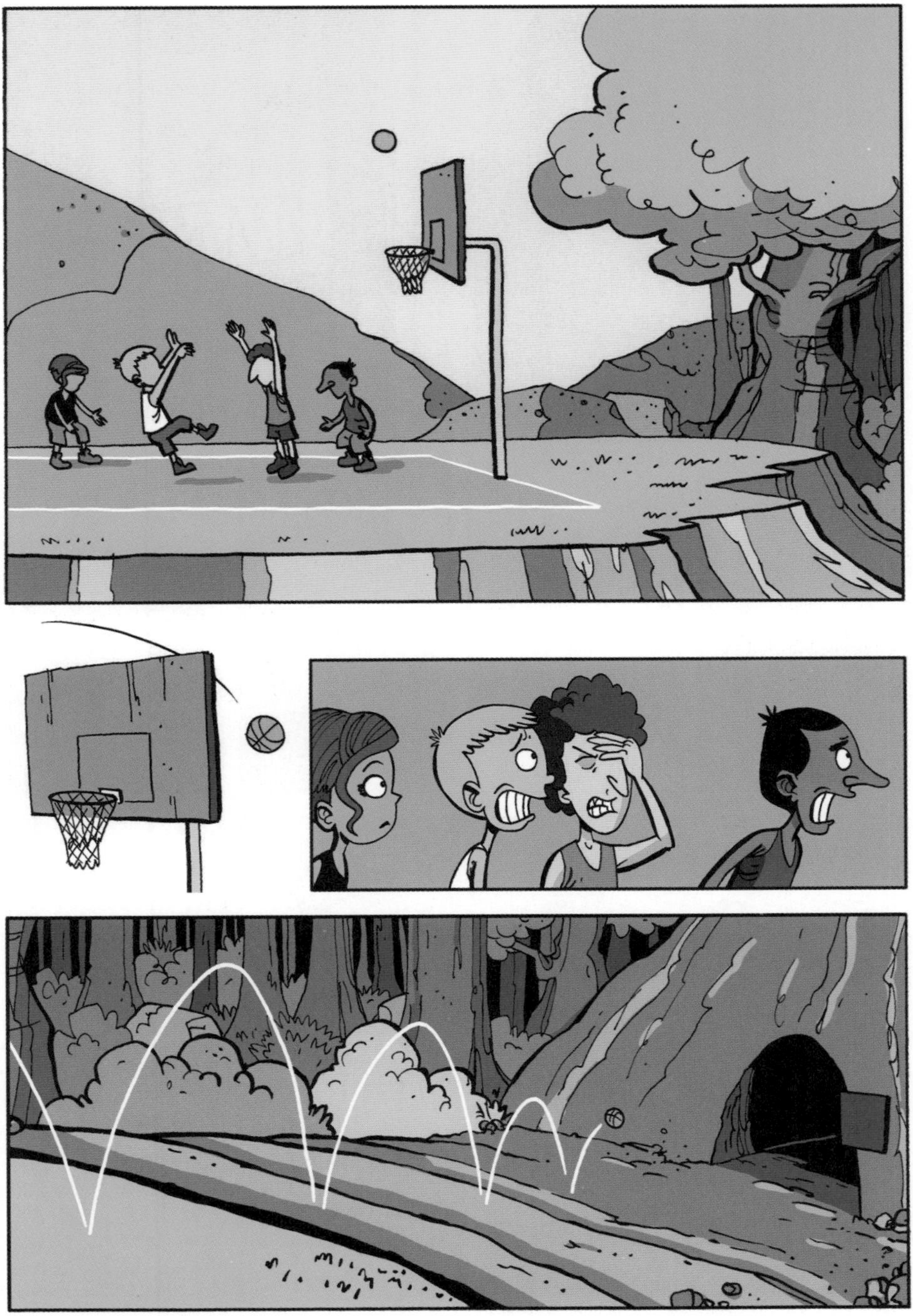

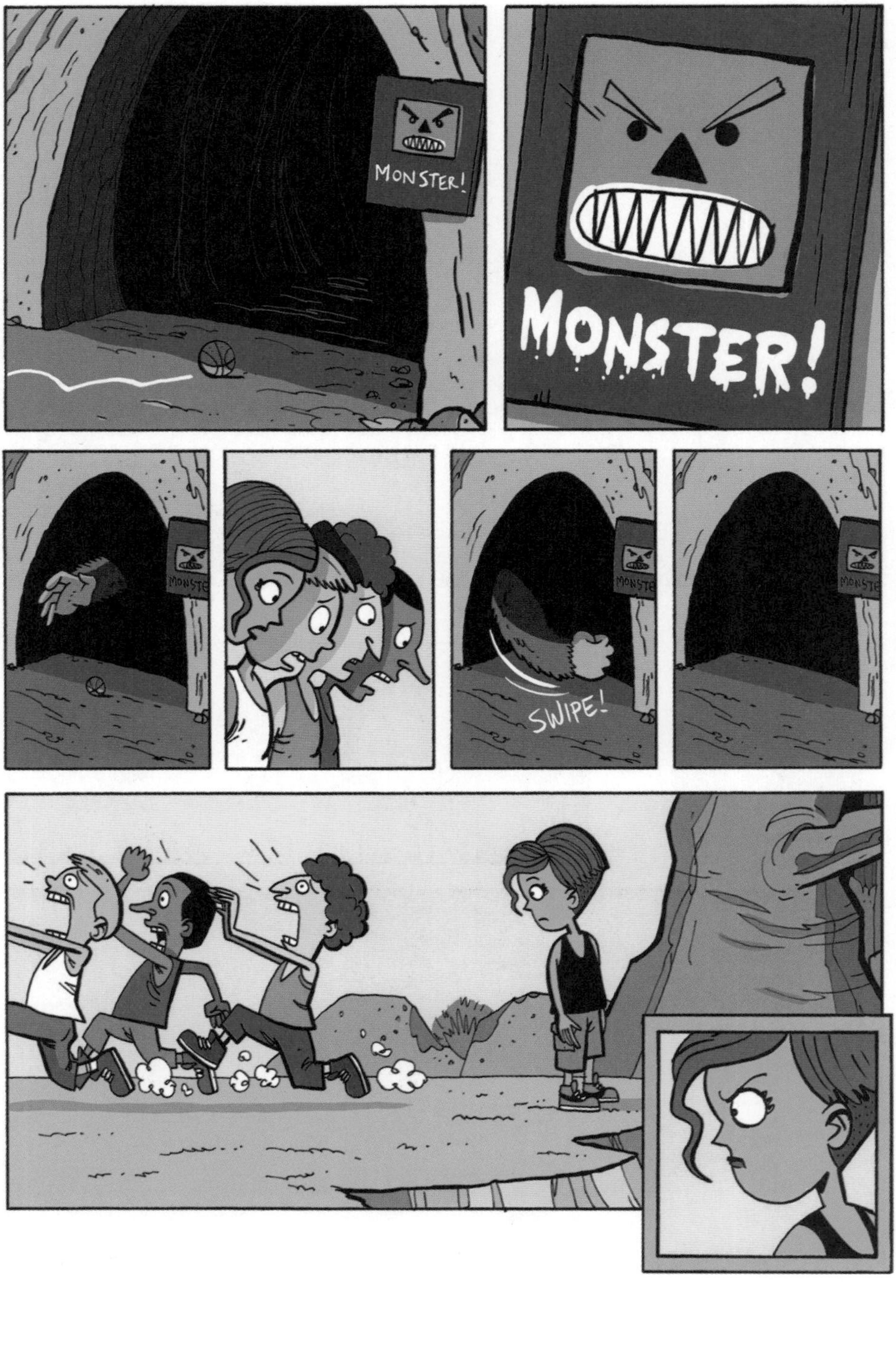
MONSTER!
MONSTER!
MONSTE
SWIPE!
MONSTE
MONSTE

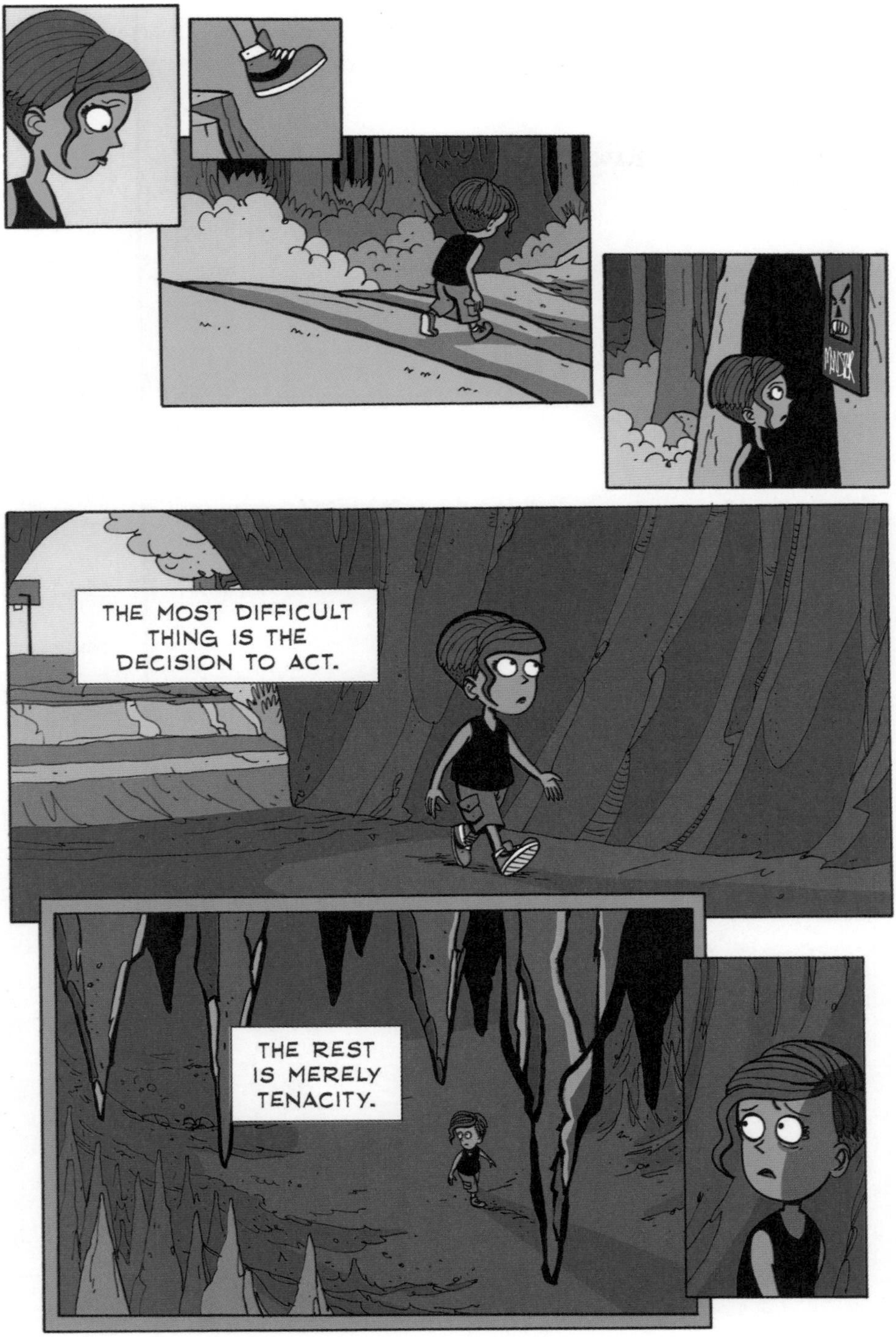
THE MOST DIFFICULT THING IS THE DECISION TO ACT.
THE REST IS MERELY TENACITY.

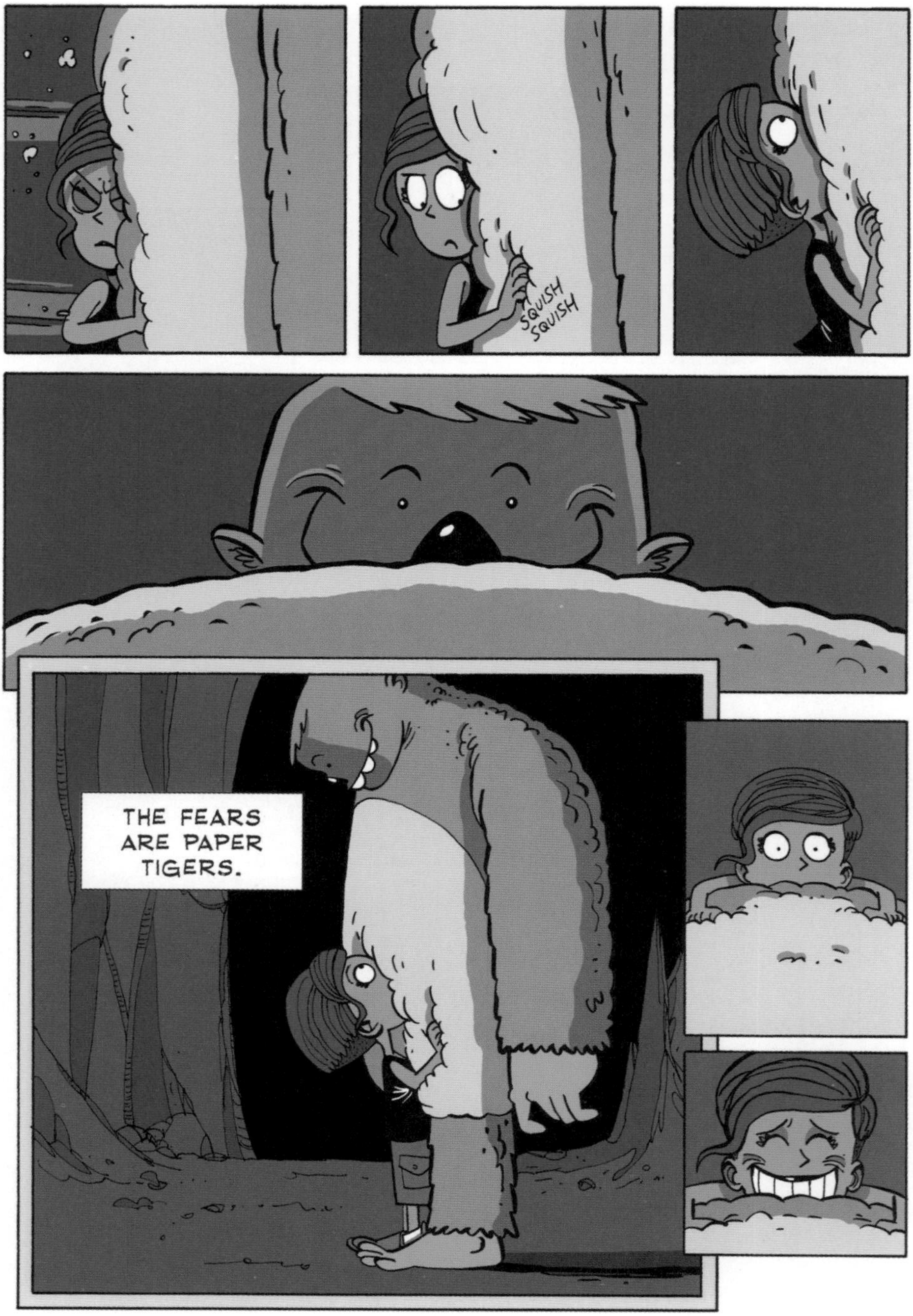
SQUISH
SQUISH
THE FEARS ARE PAPER TIGERS.

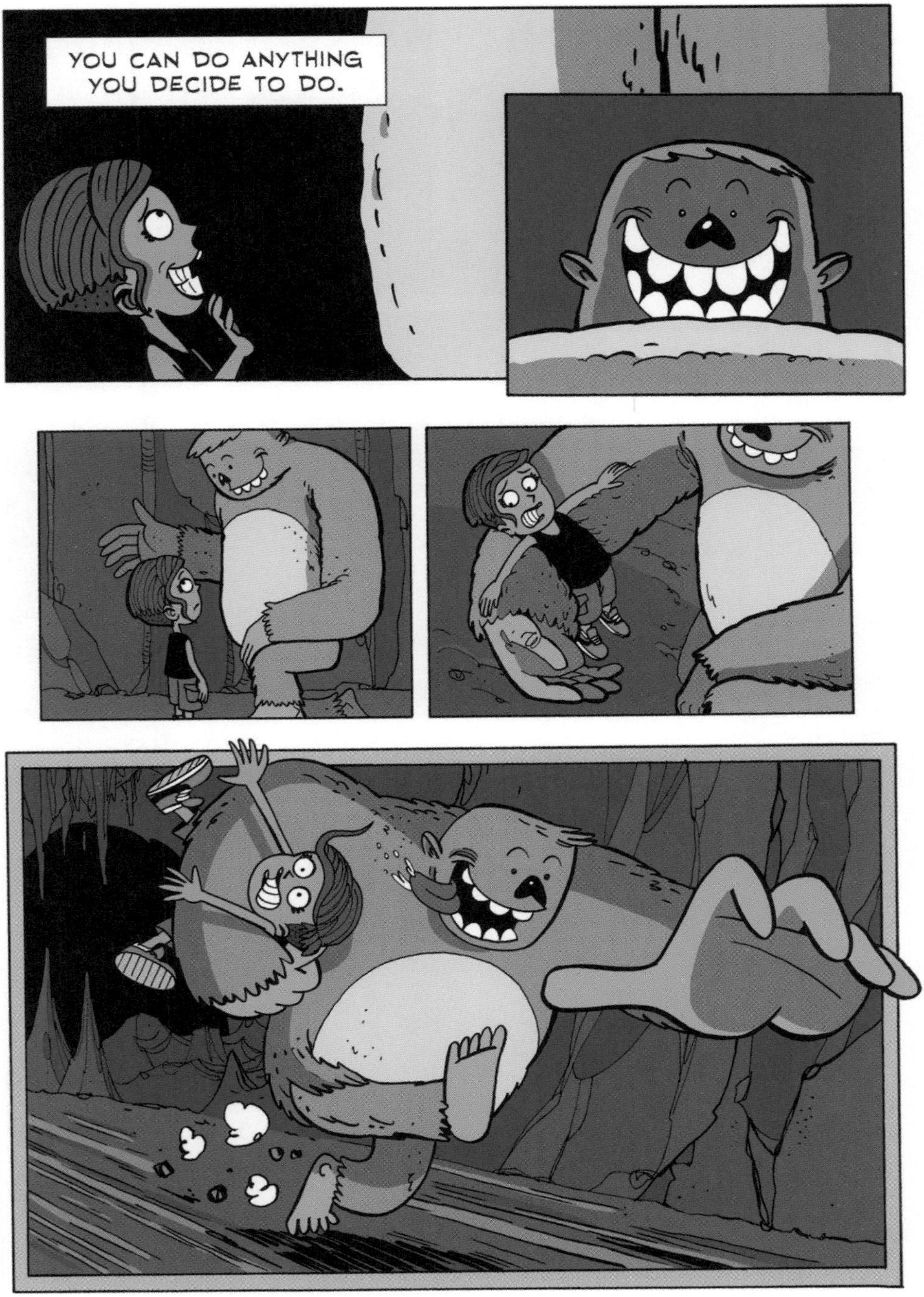
YOU CAN DO ANYTHING
YOU DECIDE TO DO.

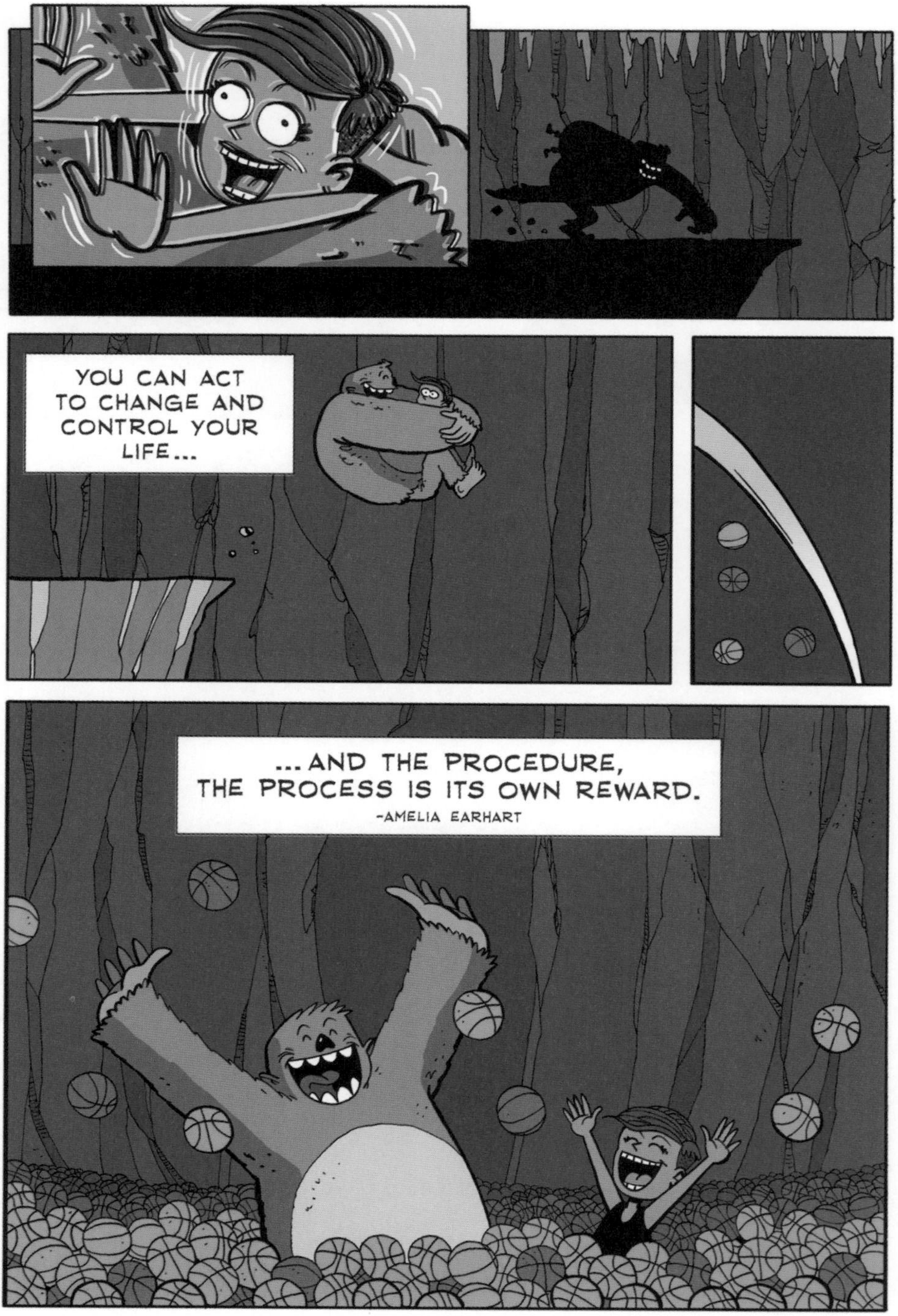
YOU CAN ACT TO CHANGE AND CONTROL YOUR LIFE...
...AND THE PROCEDURE, THE PROCESS IS ITS OWN REWARD.
-AMELIA EARHART

ON THE MINDLESS MENACE OF VIOLENCE Robert F. Kennedy

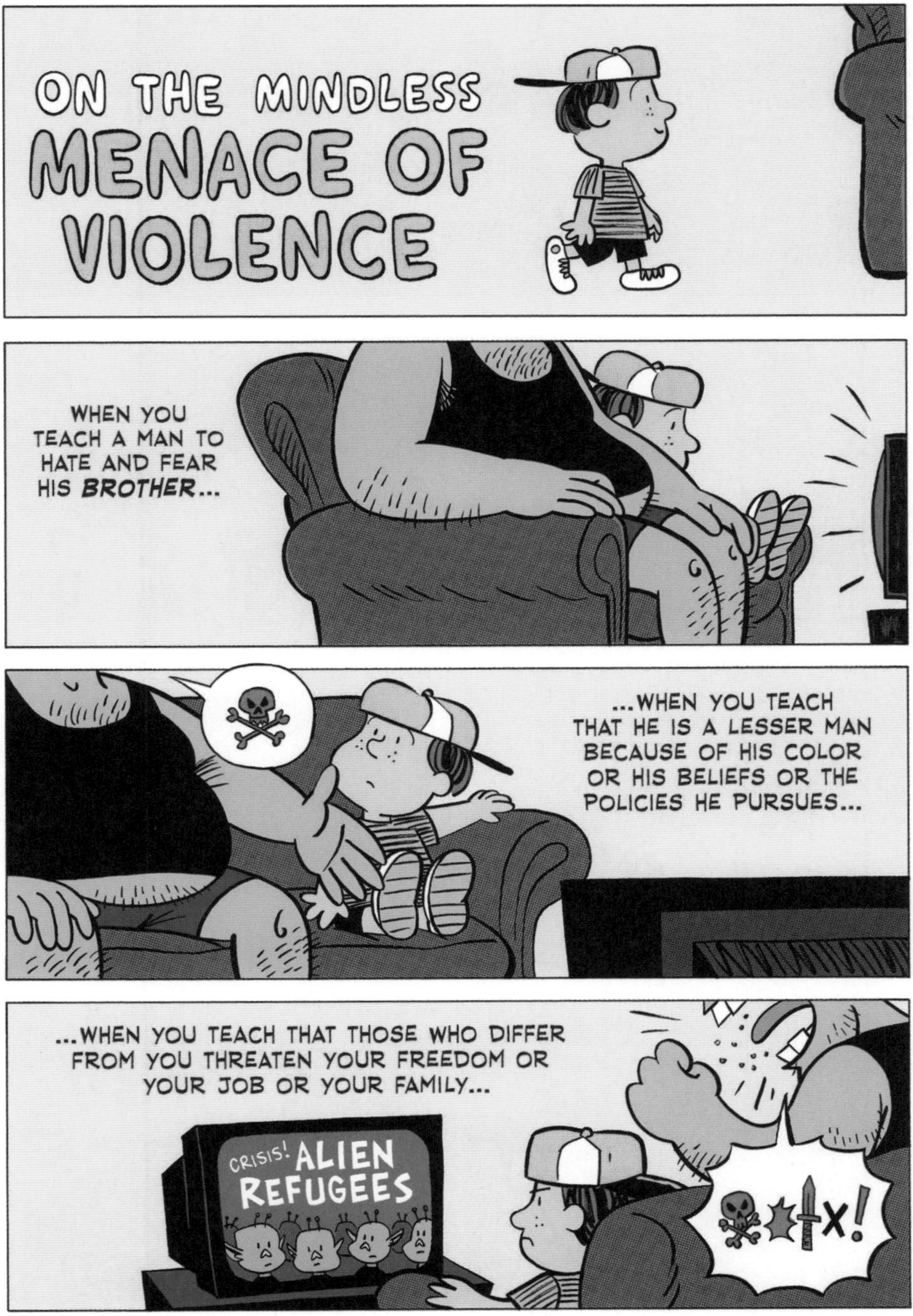
ON THE MINDLESS MENACE OF VIOLENCE
WHEN YOU TEACH A MAN TO HATE AND FEAR HIS ***BROTHER***...
...WHEN YOU TEACH THAT HE IS A LESSER MAN BECAUSE OF HIS COLOR OR HIS BELIEFS OR THE POLICIES HE PURSUES...
...WHEN YOU TEACH THAT THOSE WHO DIFFER FROM YOU THREATEN YOUR FREEDOM OR YOUR JOB OR YOUR FAMILY...
CRISIS! ALIEN REFUGEES
X!

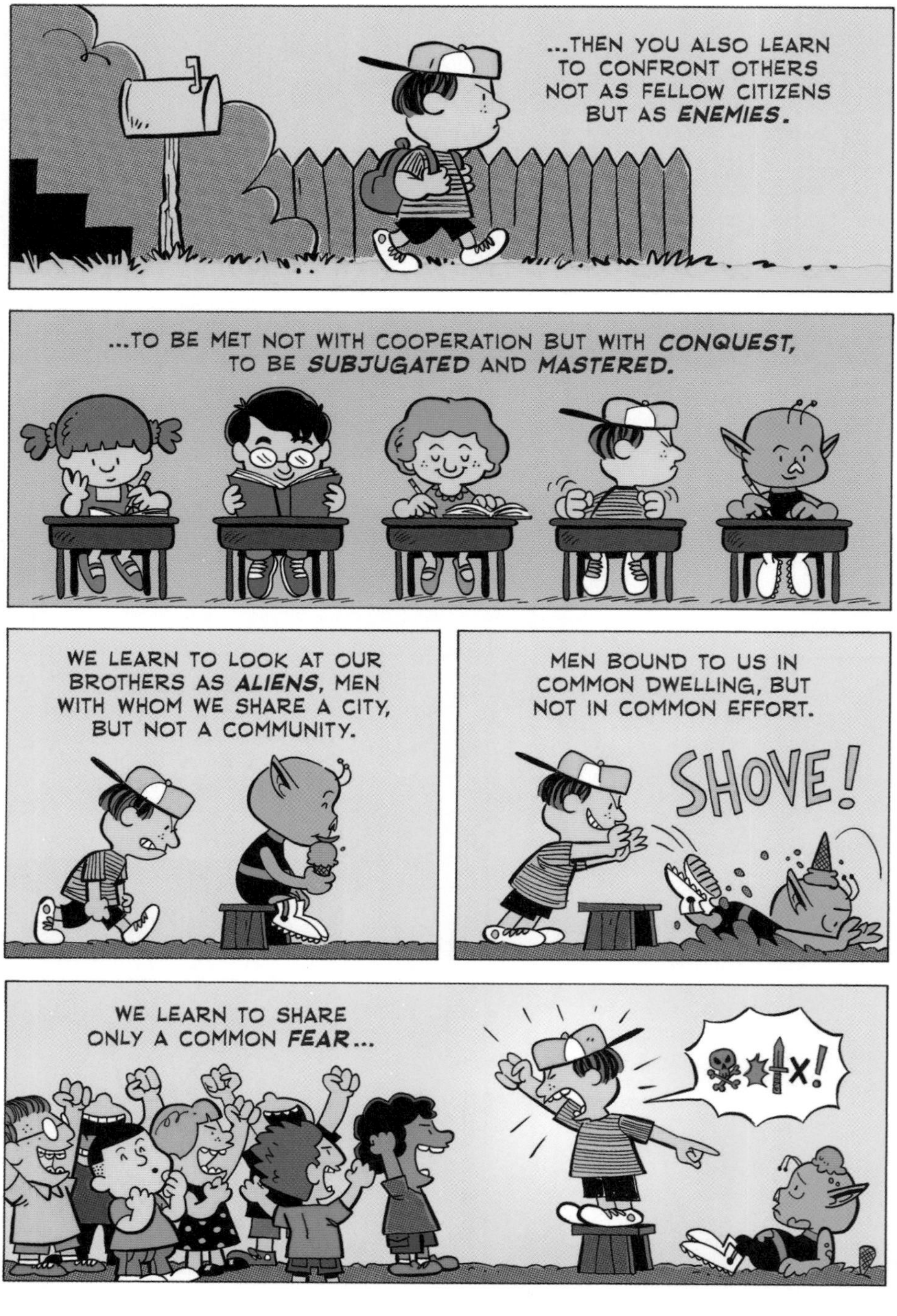
...THEN YOU ALSO LEARN TO CONFRONT OTHERS NOT AS FELLOW CITIZENS BUT AS *ENEMIES*.
...TO BE MET NOT WITH COOPERATION BUT WITH *CONQUEST*, TO BE *SUBJUGATED* AND *MASTERED*.
WE LEARN TO LOOK AT OUR BROTHERS AS *ALIENS*, MEN WITH WHOM WE SHARE A CITY, BUT NOT A COMMUNITY.
MEN BOUND TO US IN COMMON DWELLING, BUT NOT IN COMMON EFFORT.
SHOVE!
WE LEARN TO SHARE ONLY A COMMON *FEAR*...

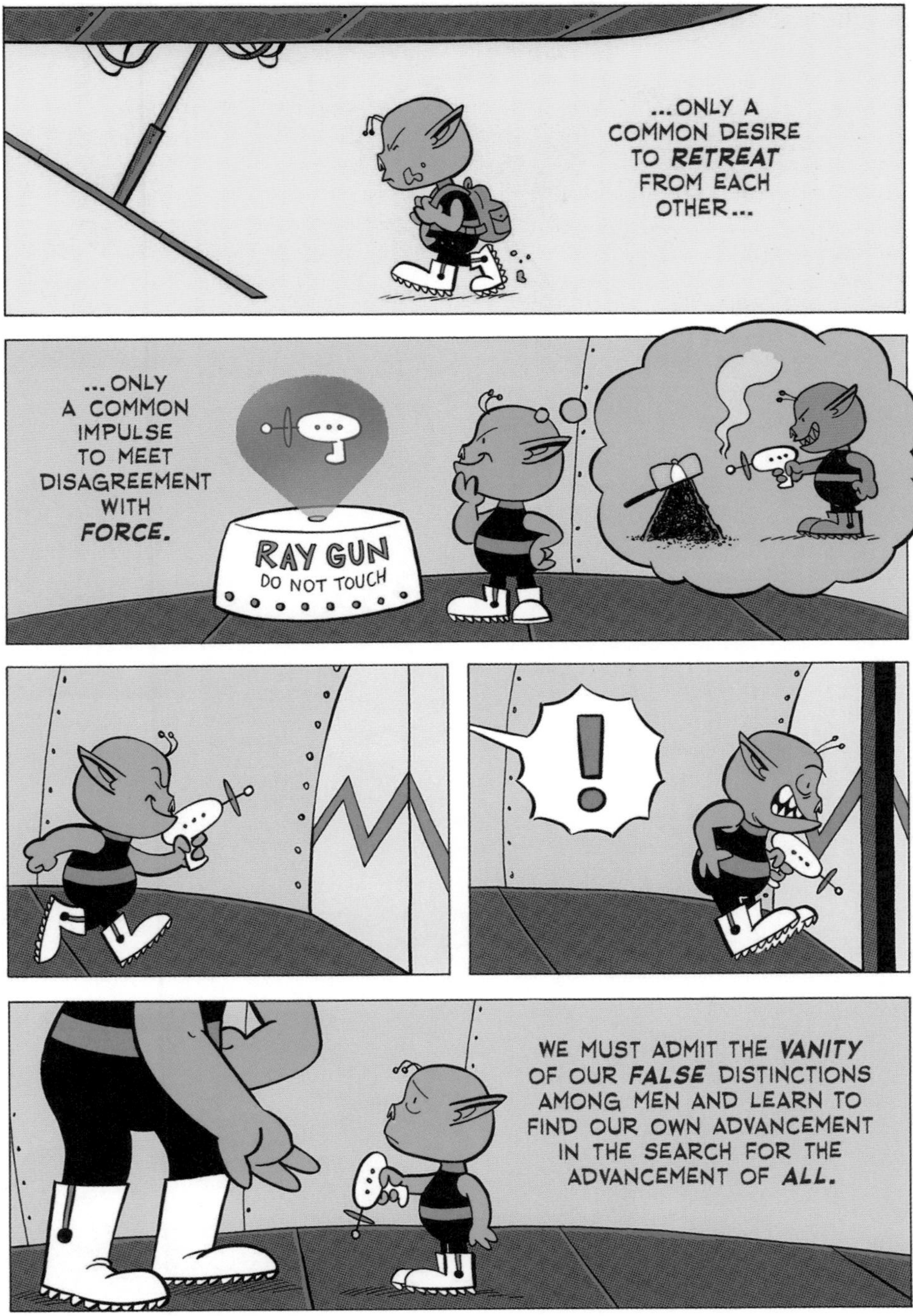
...ONLY A COMMON DESIRE TO RETREAT FROM EACH OTHER...
...ONLY A COMMON IMPULSE TO MEET DISAGREEMENT WITH FORCE.
RAY GUN
DO NOT TOUCH
!
WE MUST ADMIT THE VANITY OF OUR FALSE DISTINCTIONS AMONG MEN AND LEARN TO FIND OUR OWN ADVANCEMENT IN THE SEARCH FOR THE ADVANCEMENT OF ALL.

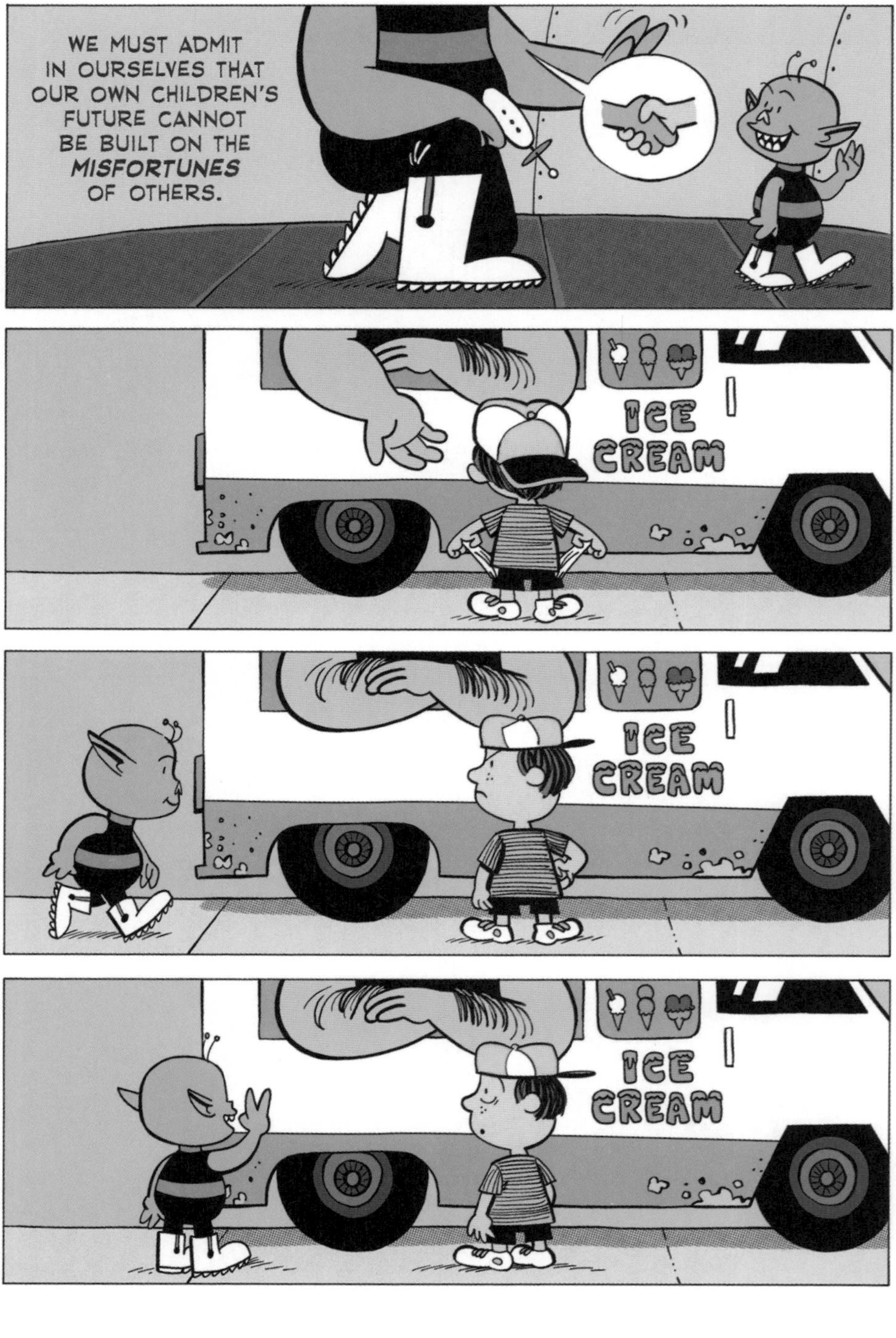
WE MUST ADMIT IN OURSELVES THAT OUR OWN CHILDREN'S FUTURE CANNOT BE BUILT ON THE *MISFORTUNES* OF OTHERS.
ICE CREAM
ICE CREAM
ICE CREAM

WE MUST RECOGNIZE
THAT THIS SHORT LIFE CAN
NEITHER BE ENNOBLED OR
ENRICHED BY *HATRED*
OR *REVENGE.*

- ROBERT F. KENNEDY

AN ASTRONAUT'S ADVICE Chris Hadfield

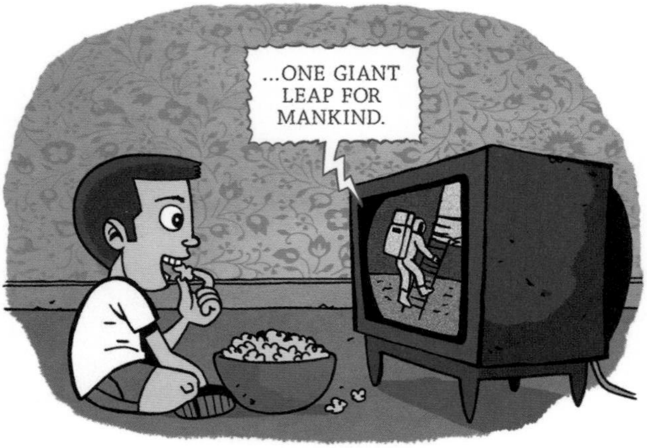
...ONE GIANT LEAP FOR MANKIND.

DECIDE IN YOUR HEART OF HEARTS WHAT REALLY EXCITES AND CHALLENGES YOU...

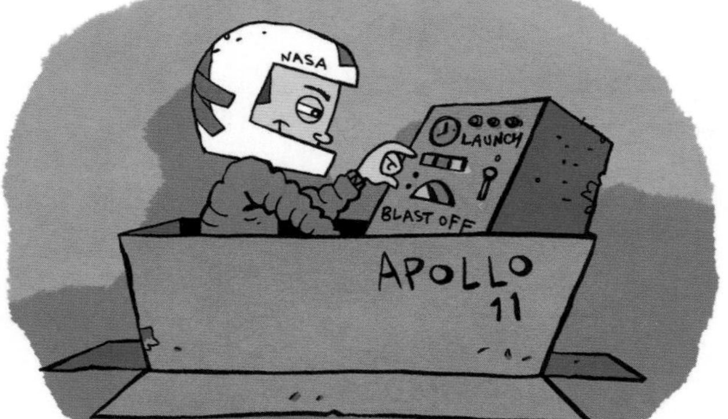
NASA
LAUNCH
BLAST OFF
APOLLO 11

...AND START MOVING YOUR LIFE IN THAT DIRECTION.

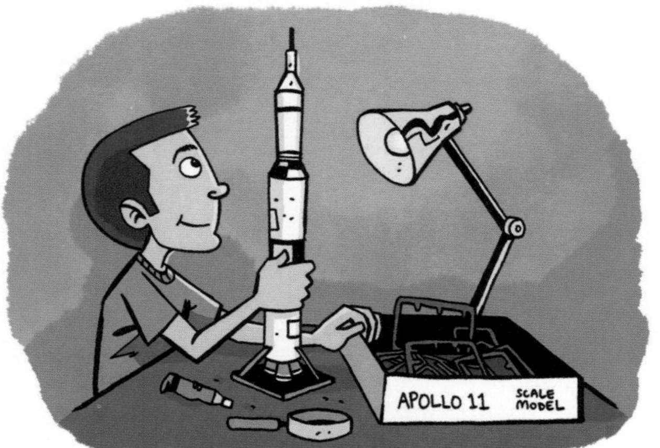
APOLLO 11
SCALE MODEL

EVERY DECISION YOU MAKE, FROM WHAT YOU EAT TO WHAT YOU DO WITH YOUR TIME TONIGHT...

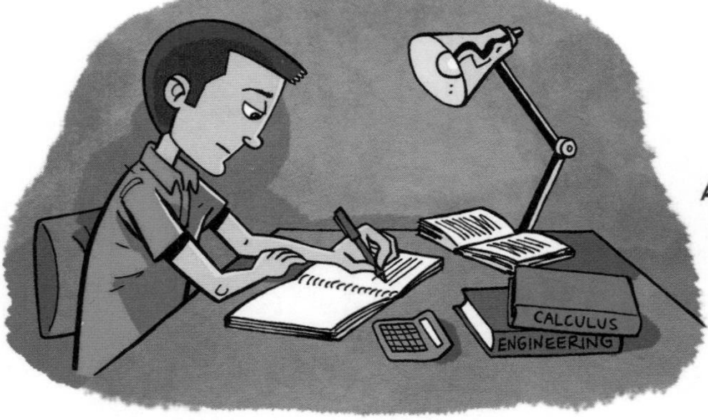
CALCULUS
ENGINEERING

...TURNS YOU INTO WHO YOU ARE TOMORROW, AND THE DAY AFTER THAT.

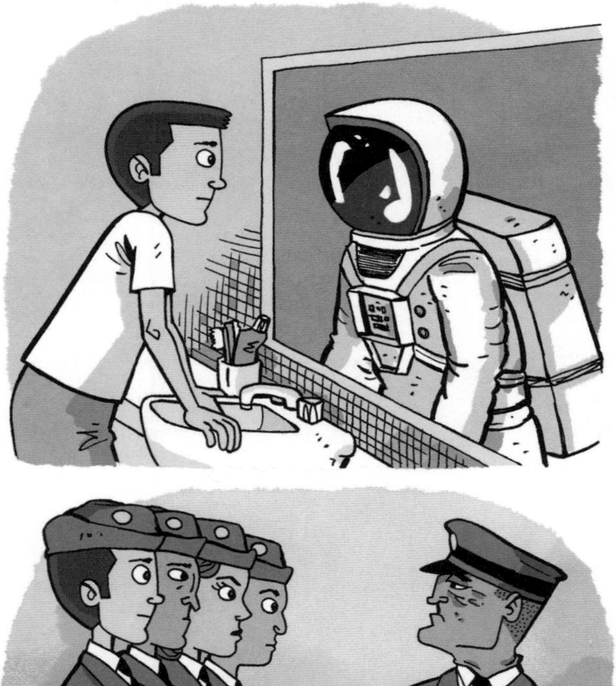

LOOK AT WHO YOU WANT TO BE, AND START SCULPTING YOURSELF INTO THAT PERSON.

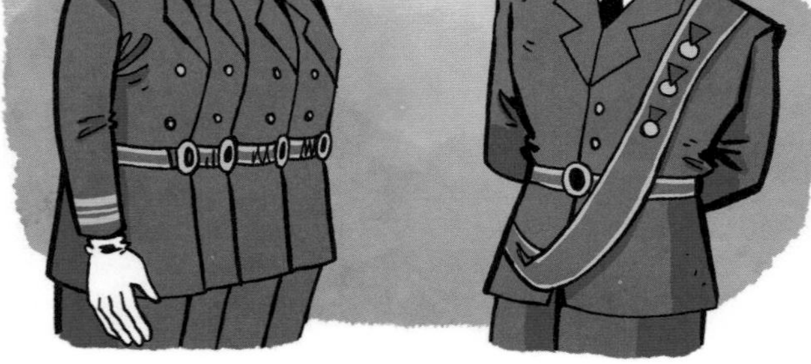

YOU MAY NOT GET EXACTLY WHERE YOU THOUGHT YOU'D BE...

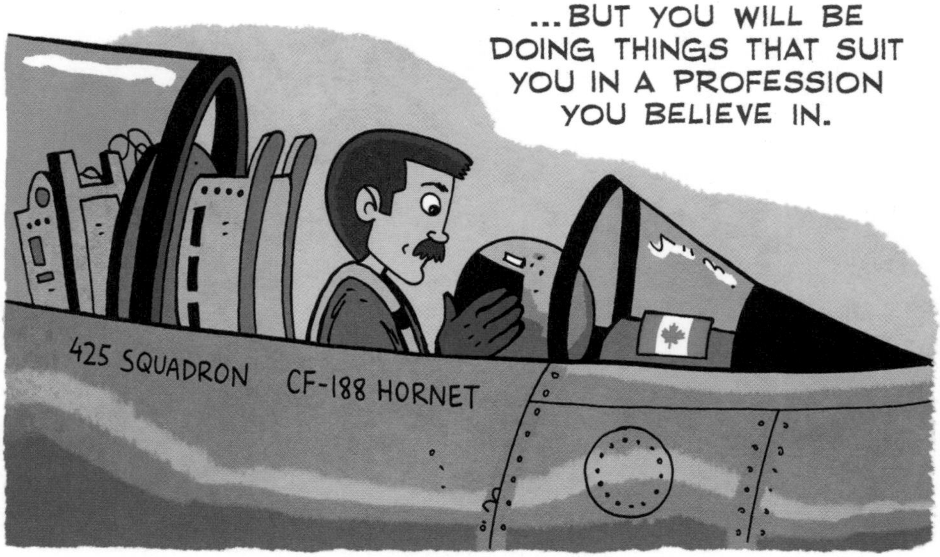
...BUT YOU WILL BE DOING THINGS THAT SUIT YOU IN A PROFESSION YOU BELIEVE IN.
425 SQUADRON
CF-188 HORNET

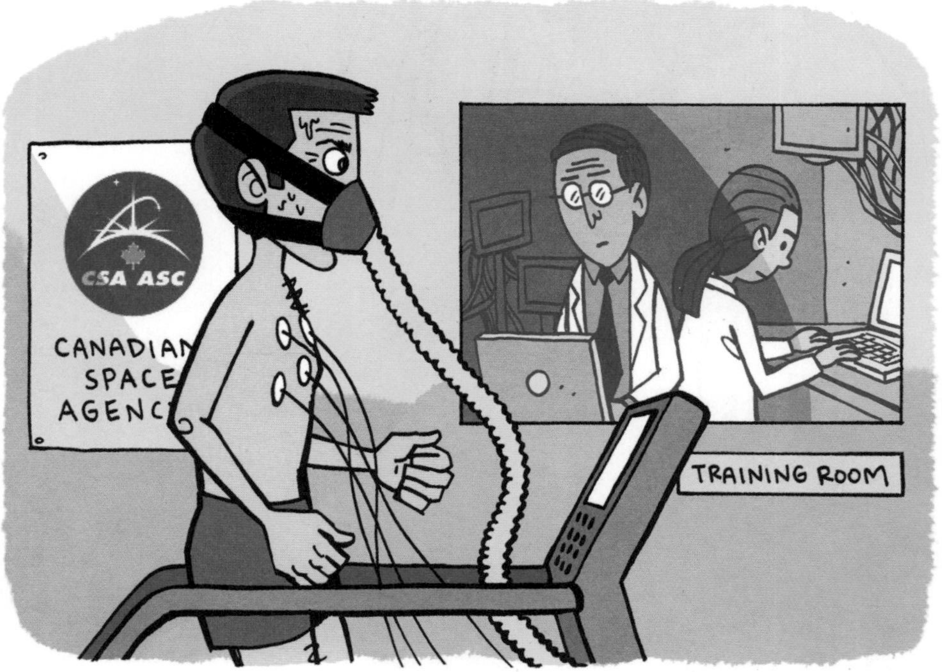
CSA ASC
CANADIAN
SPACE
AGENC
TRAINING ROOM

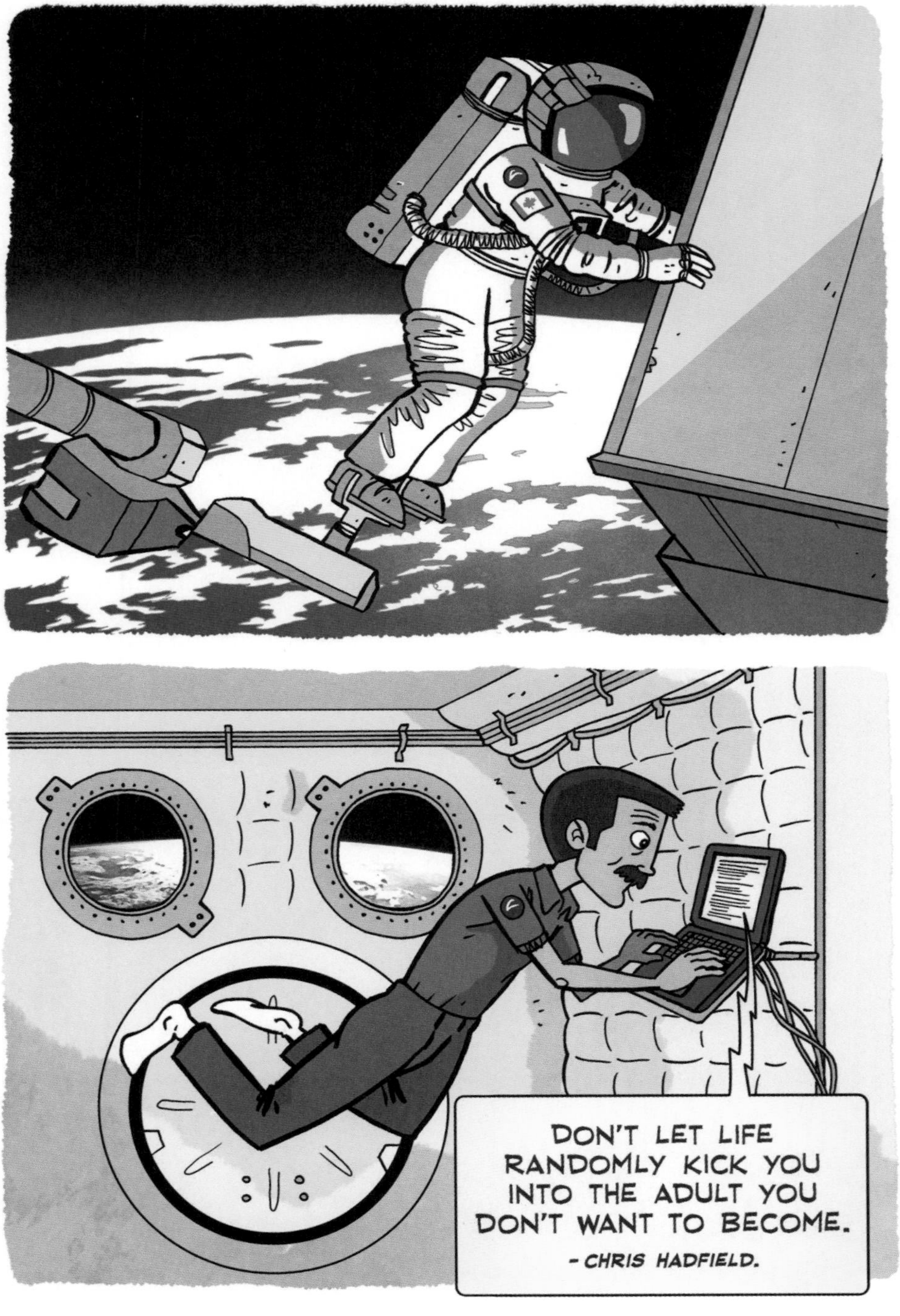
DON'T LET LIFE RANDOMLY KICK YOU INTO THE ADULT YOU DON'T WANT TO BECOME.
- CHRIS HADFIELD.

MAKE GIFTS FOR PEOPLE John Green

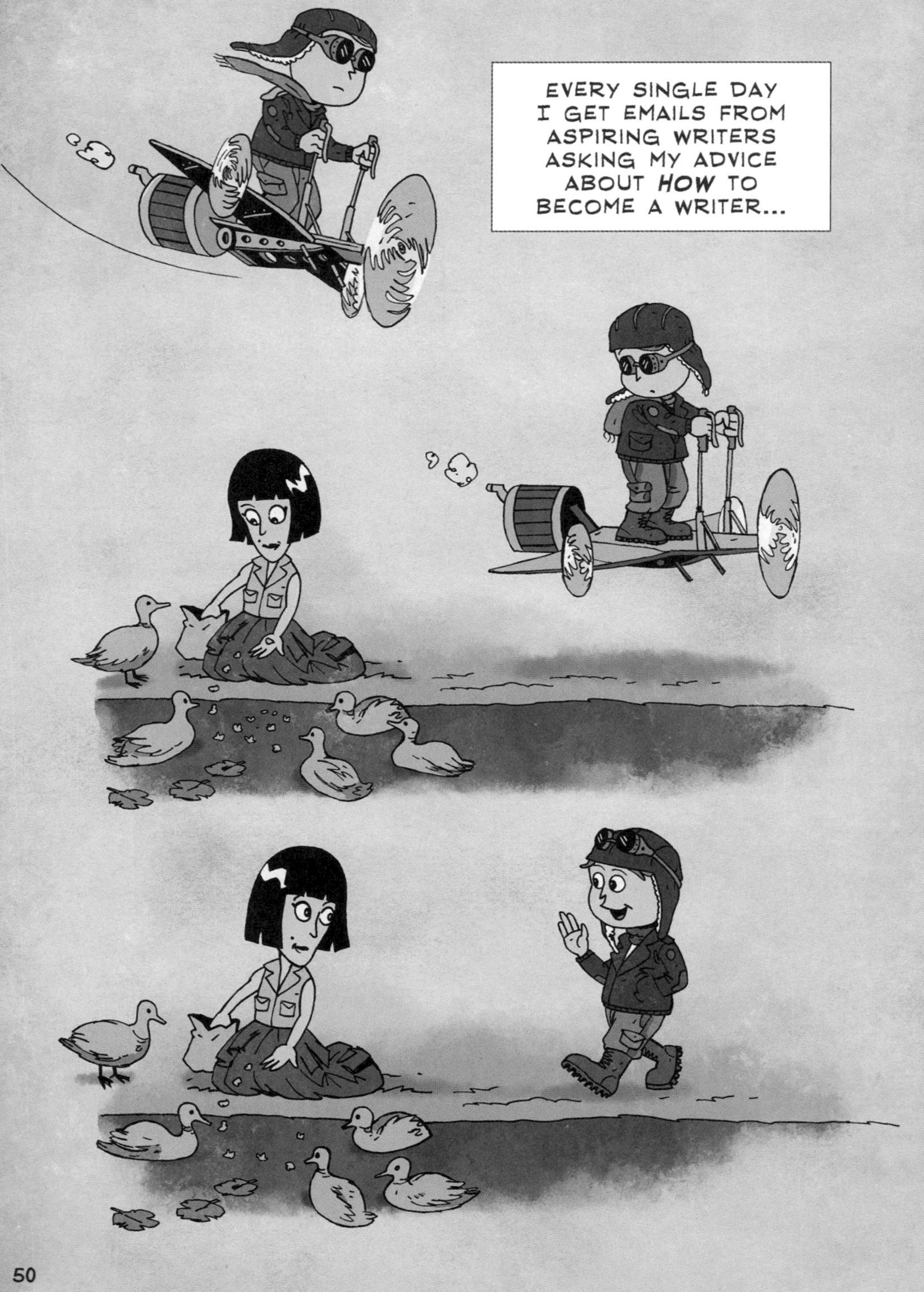
EVERY SINGLE DAY I GET EMAILS FROM ASPIRING WRITERS ASKING MY ADVICE ABOUT *HOW* TO BECOME A WRITER...

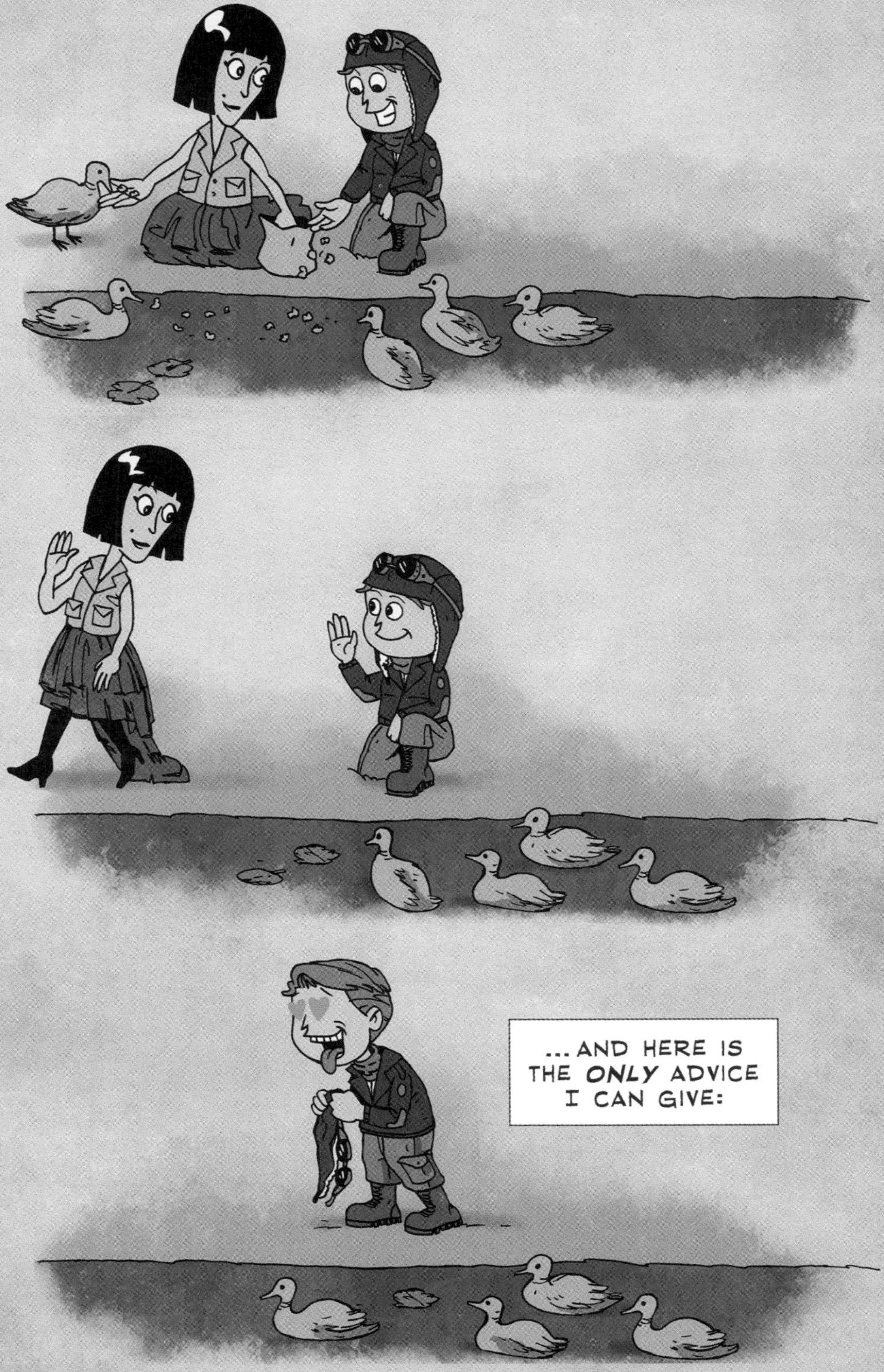
...AND HERE IS THE *ONLY* ADVICE I CAN GIVE:

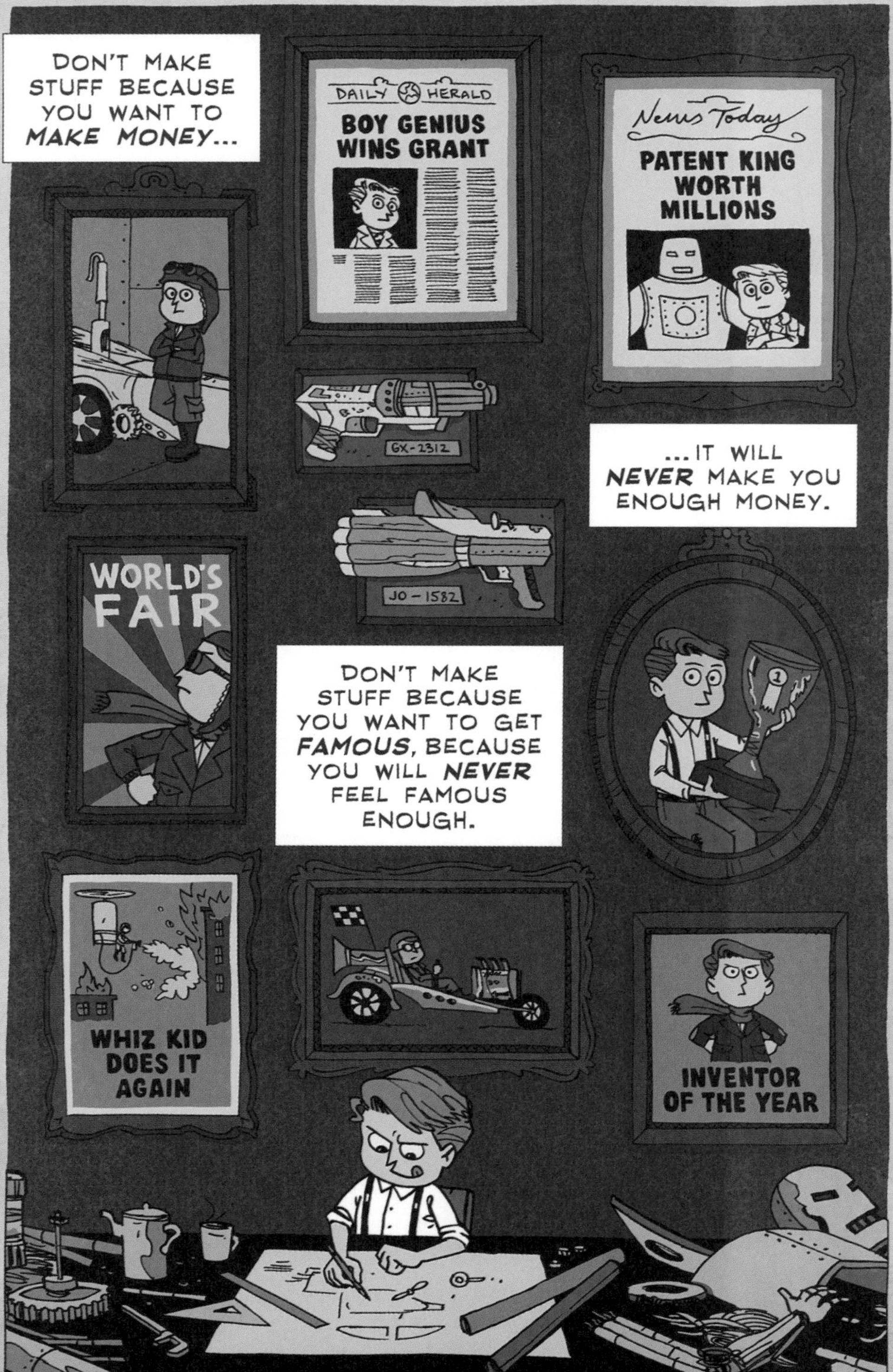
DON'T MAKE STUFF BECAUSE YOU WANT TO *MAKE MONEY*...
DAILY HERALD
BOY GENIUS WINS GRANT
News Today
PATENT KING WORTH MILLIONS
GX-2312
...IT WILL *NEVER* MAKE YOU ENOUGH MONEY.
JO – 1582
WORLD'S FAIR
DON'T MAKE STUFF BECAUSE YOU WANT TO GET *FAMOUS*, BECAUSE YOU WILL *NEVER* FEEL FAMOUS ENOUGH.
WHIZ KID DOES IT AGAIN
INVENTOR OF THE YEAR

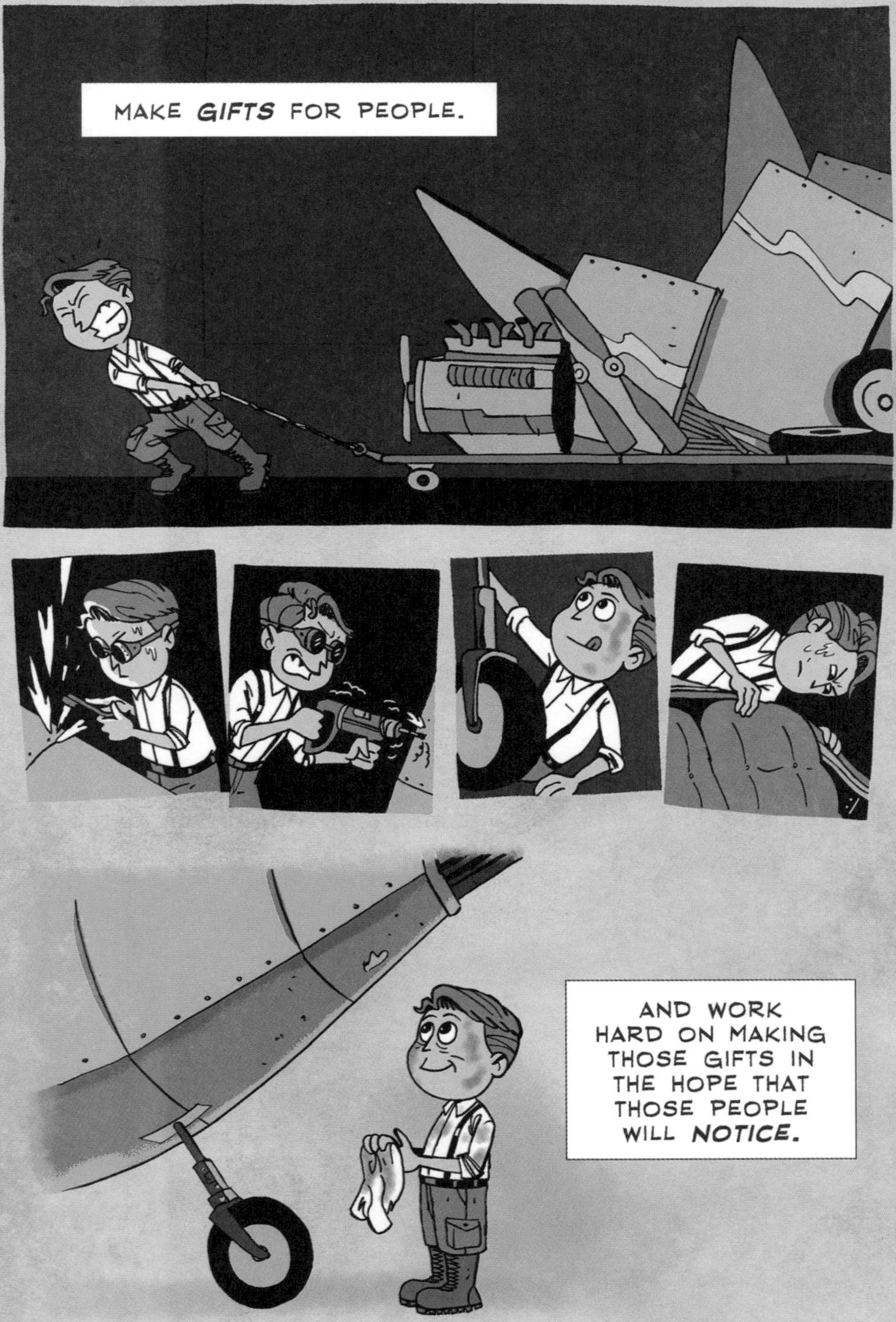
MAKE GIFTS FOR PEOPLE.
AND WORK HARD ON MAKING THOSE GIFTS IN THE HOPE THAT THOSE PEOPLE WILL NOTICE.

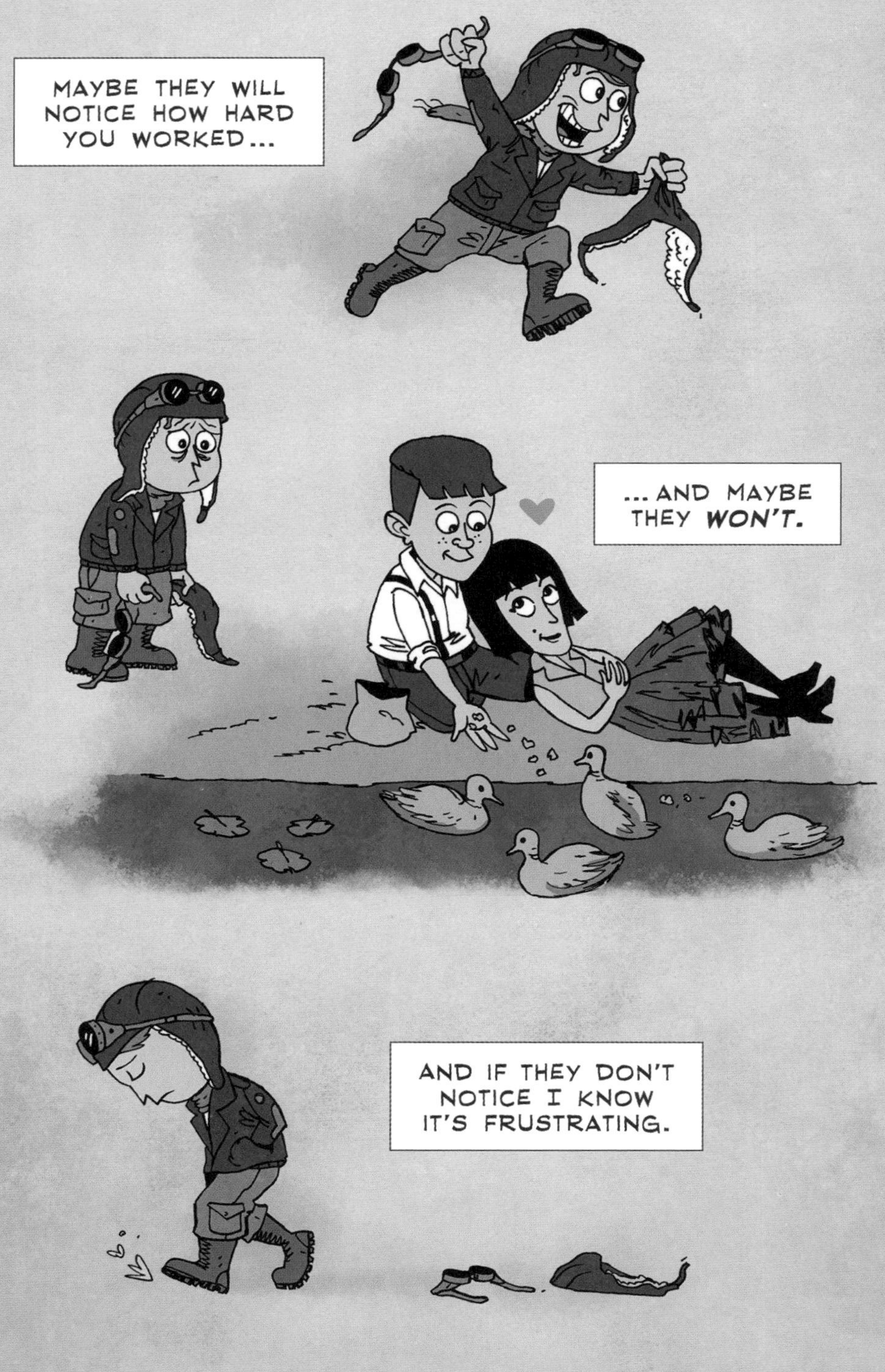

MAYBE THEY WILL NOTICE HOW HARD YOU WORKED...
...AND MAYBE THEY *WON'T.*
AND IF THEY DON'T NOTICE I KNOW IT'S FRUSTRATING.

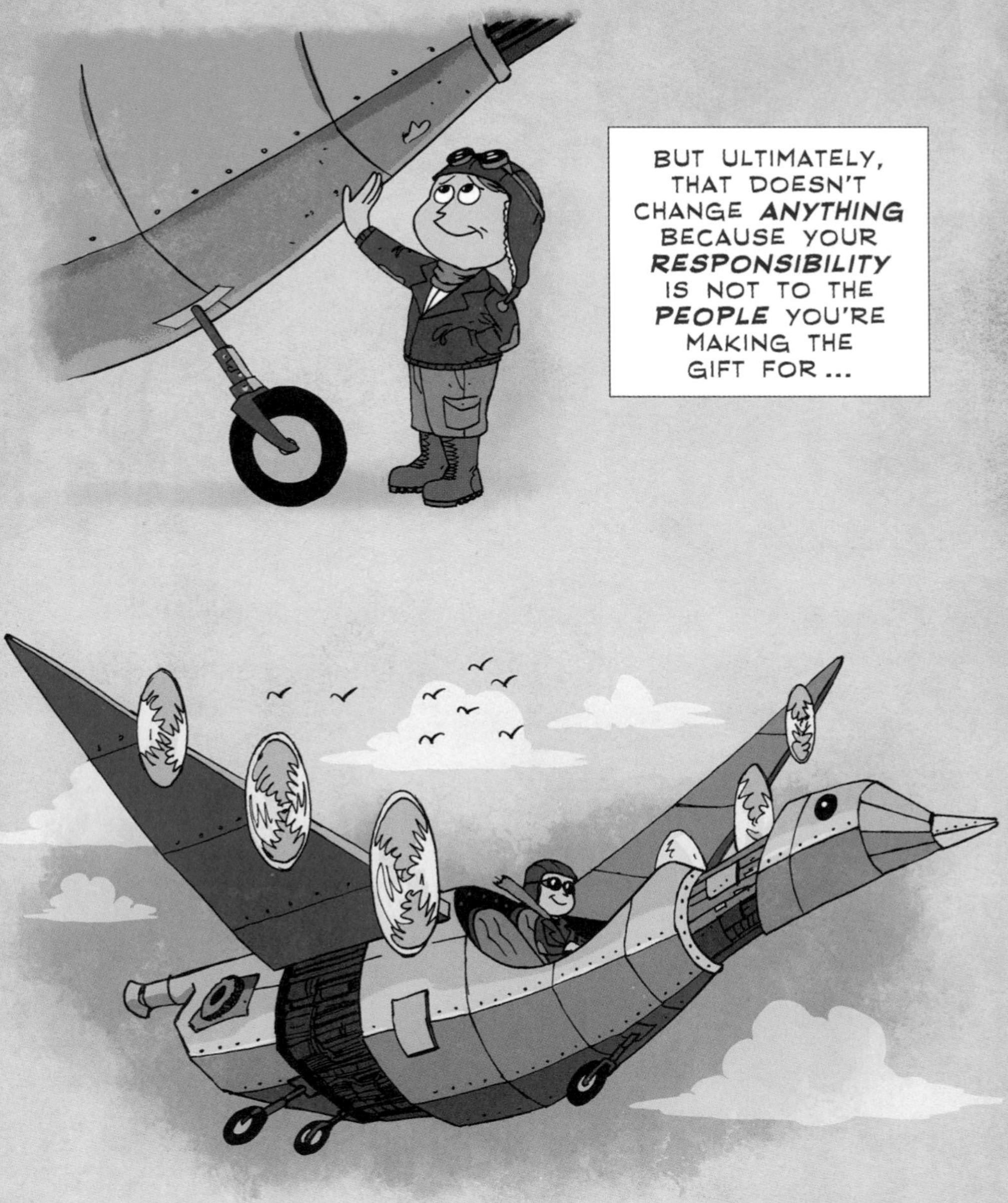
BUT ULTIMATELY, THAT DOESN'T CHANGE ***ANYTHING*** BECAUSE YOUR ***RESPONSIBILITY*** IS NOT TO THE ***PEOPLE*** YOU'RE MAKING THE GIFT FOR...
...BUT TO THE GIFT ITSELF.
-JOHN GREEN

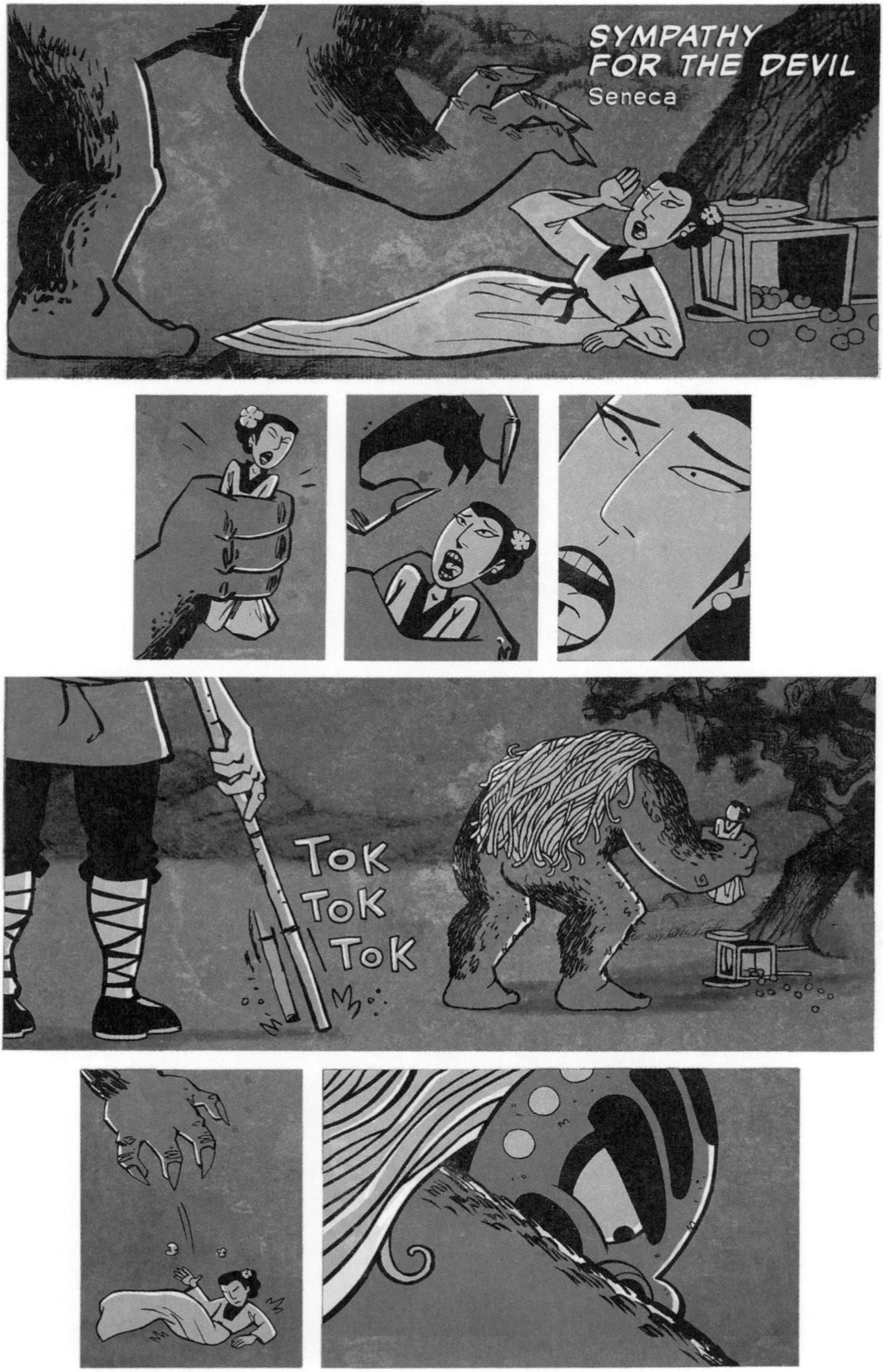
SYMPATHY FOR THE DEVIL
Seneca
TOK
TOK
TOK

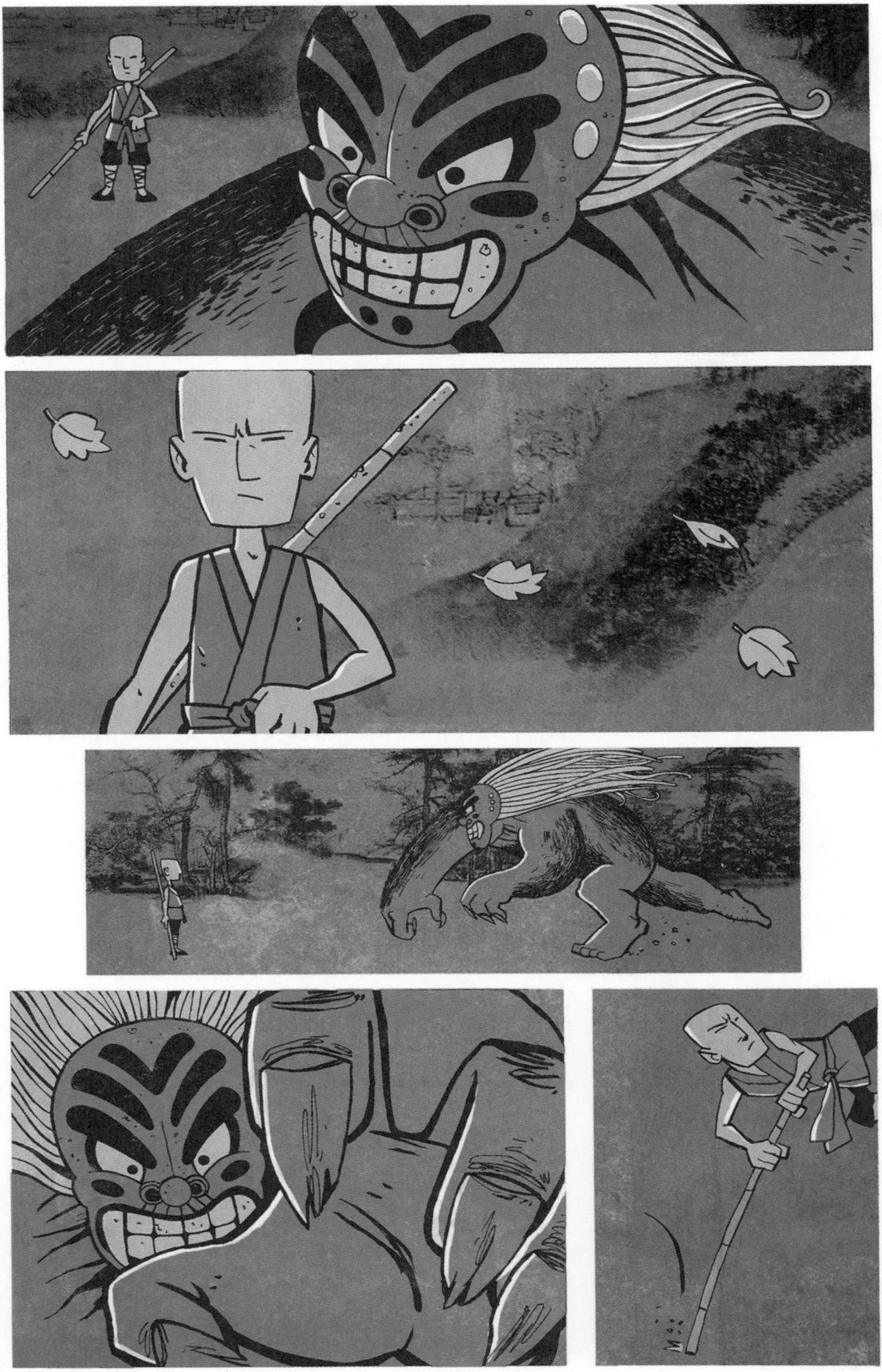

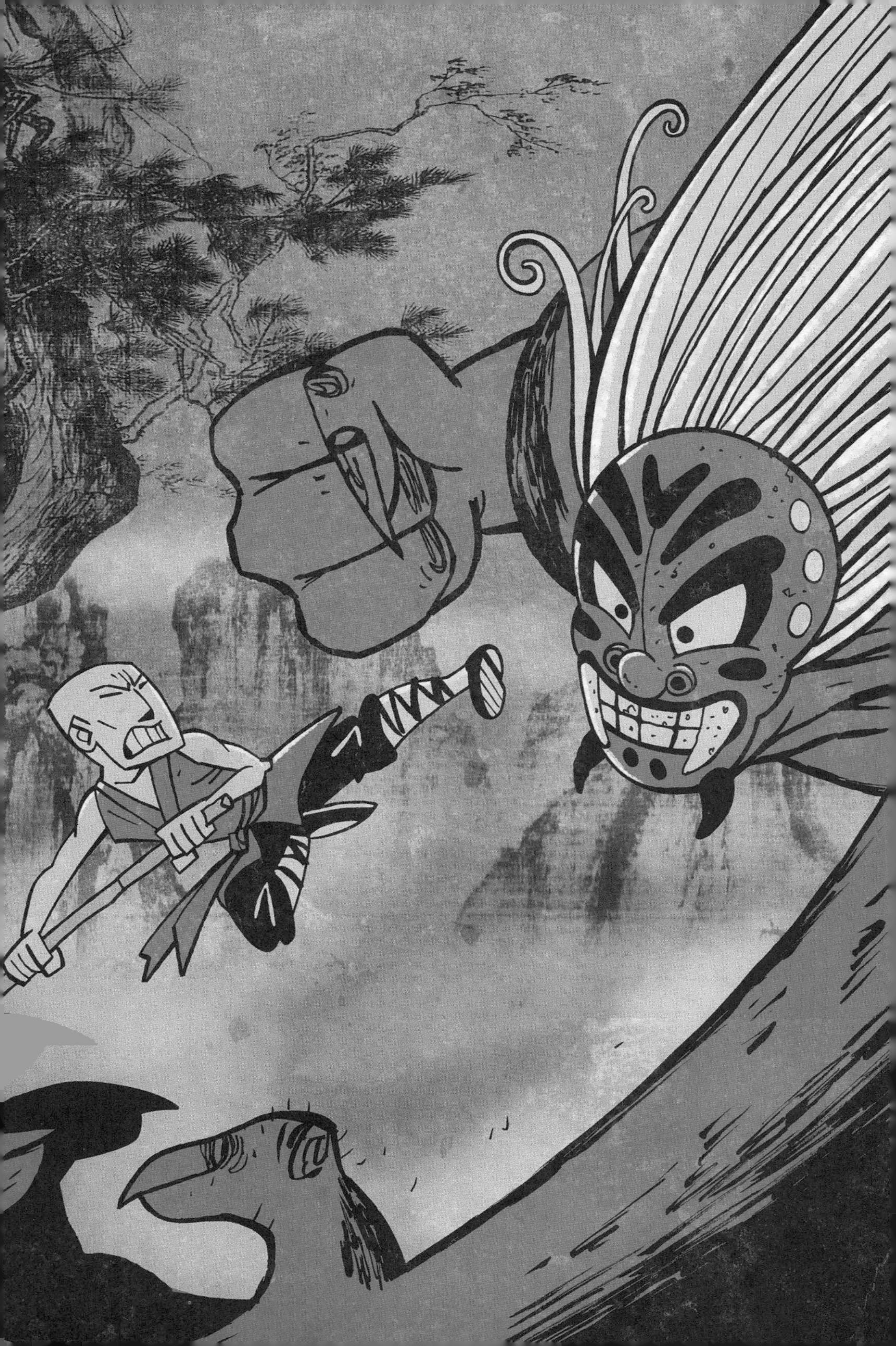

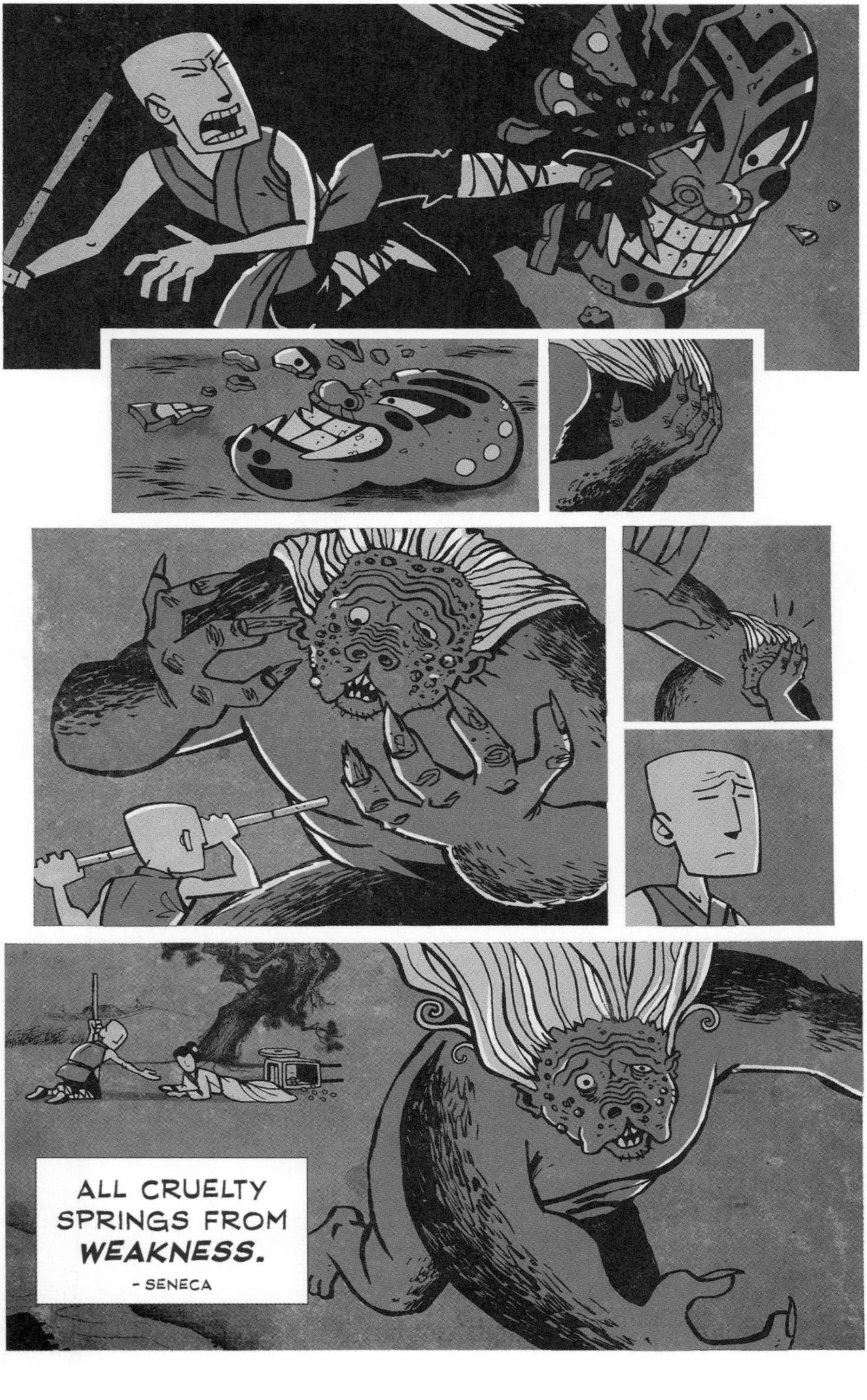
ALL CRUELTY SPRINGS FROM WEAKNESS.
- SENECA

NEVER YIELD TO FORCE Winston Churchill

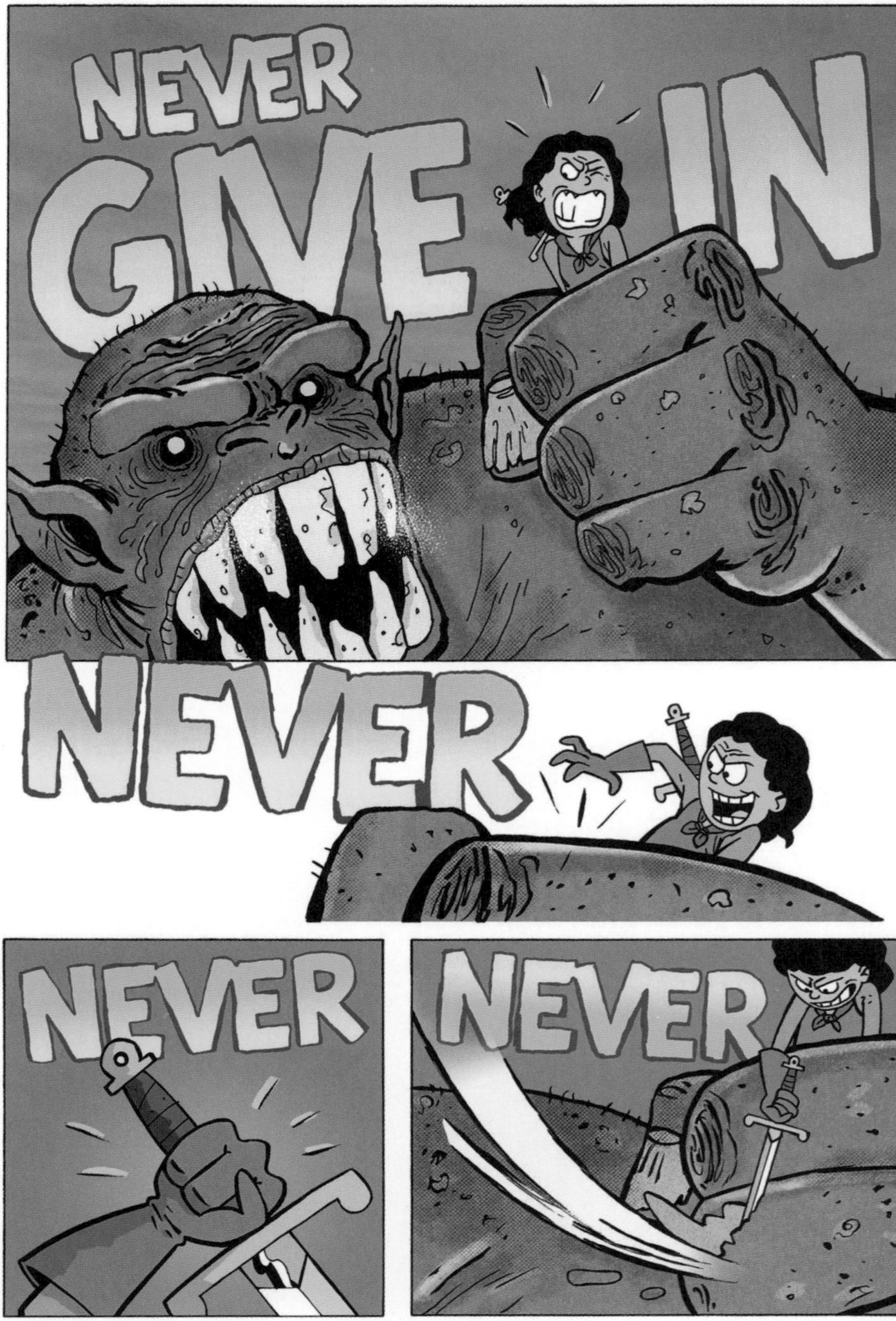
NEVER
GIVE IN
NEVER
NEVER
NEVER

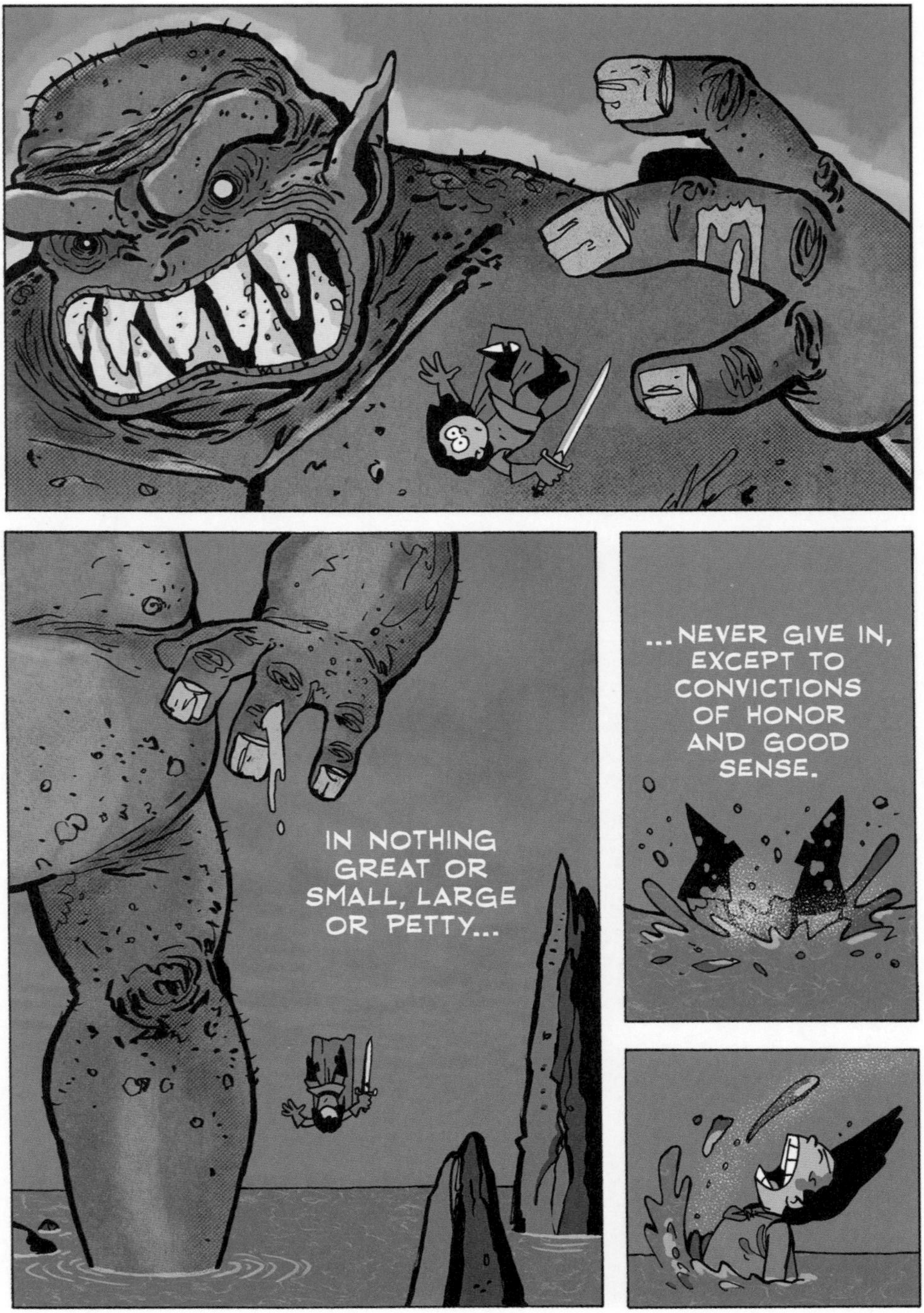
IN NOTHING GREAT OR SMALL, LARGE OR PETTY...
...NEVER GIVE IN, EXCEPT TO CONVICTIONS OF HONOR AND GOOD SENSE.

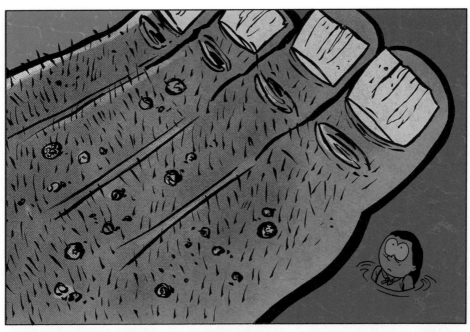

NEVER
YIELD TO
FORCE.

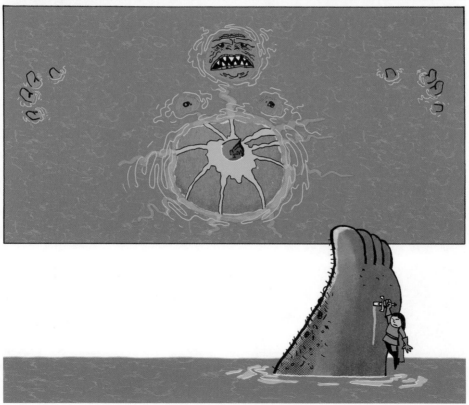

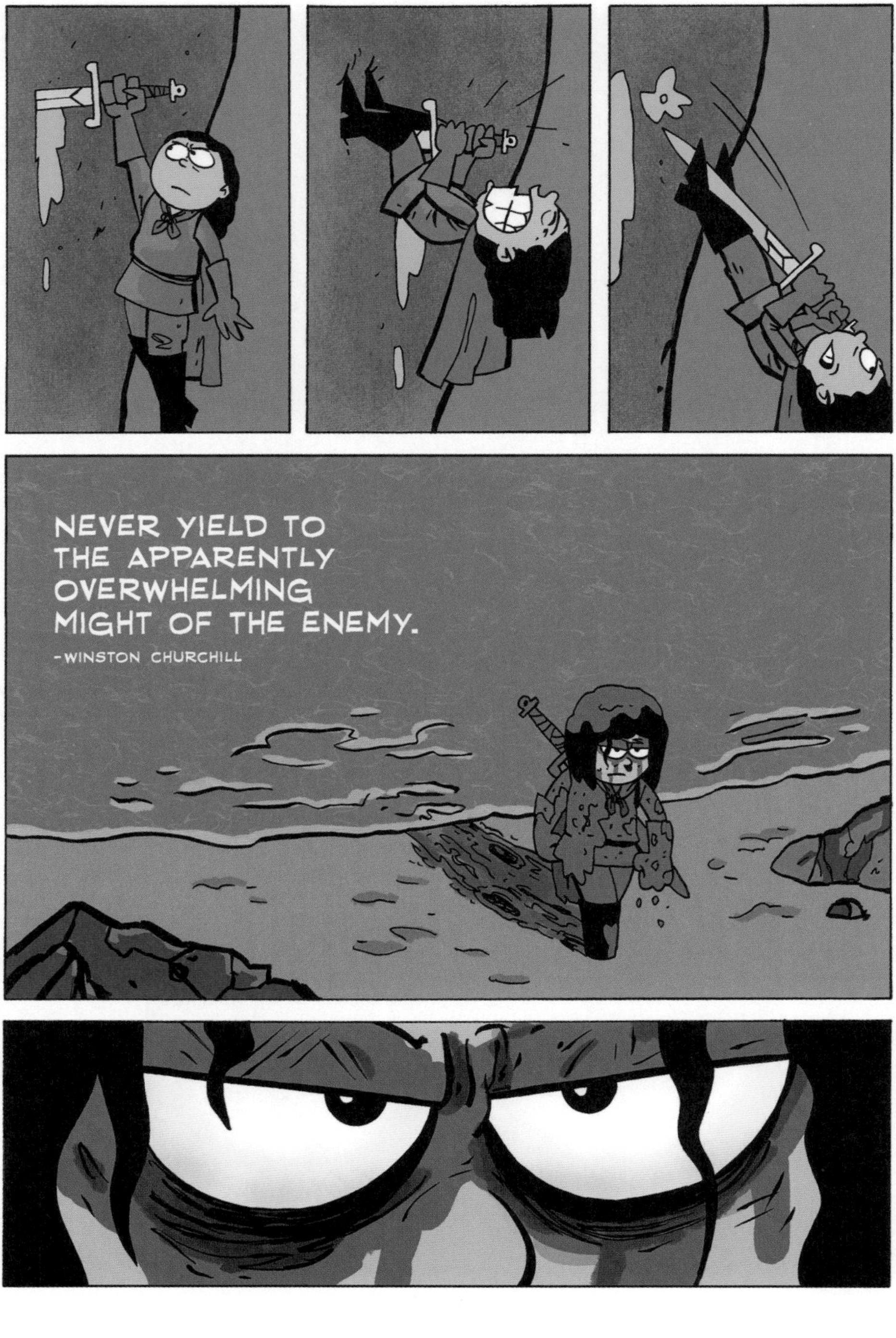
NEVER YIELD TO
THE APPARENTLY
OVERWHELMING
MIGHT OF THE ENEMY.
-WINSTON CHURCHILL

FULL BODY EDUCATION Sir Ken Robinson

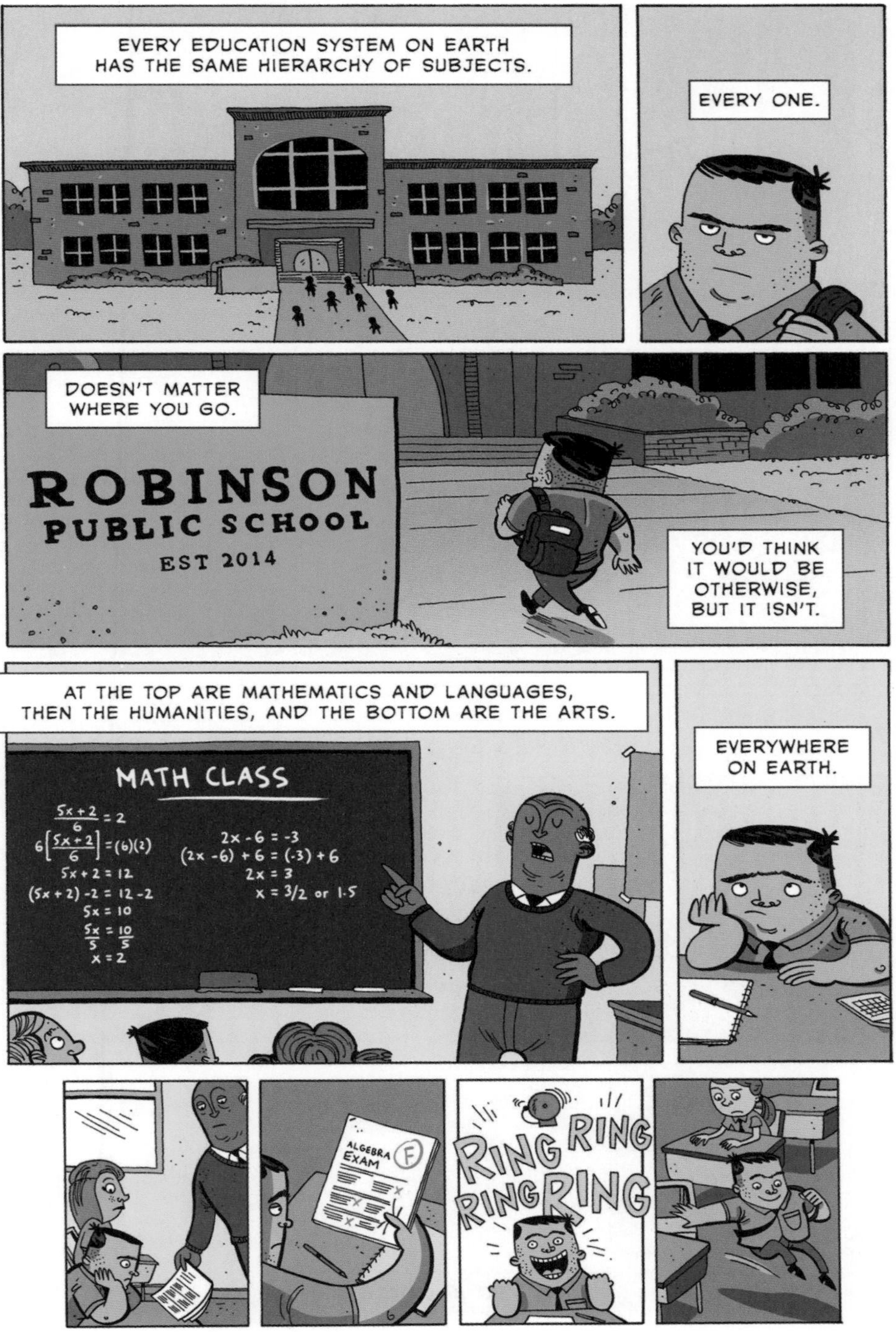
EVERY EDUCATION SYSTEM ON EARTH HAS THE SAME HIERARCHY OF SUBJECTS.
EVERY ONE.
DOESN'T MATTER WHERE YOU GO.
ROBINSON
PUBLIC SCHOOL
EST 2014
YOU'D THINK IT WOULD BE OTHERWISE, BUT IT ISN'T.
AT THE TOP ARE MATHEMATICS AND LANGUAGES, THEN THE HUMANITIES, AND THE BOTTOM ARE THE ARTS.
MATH CLASS
5x + 2 / 6 = 2
6[5x + 2 / 6] = (6)(2)
5x + 2 = 12
(5x + 2) -2 = 12 -2
5x = 10
5x / 5 = 10 / 5
x = 2
2x - 6 = -3
(2x - 6) + 6 = (-3) + 6
2x = 3
x = 3/2 or 1.5
EVERYWHERE ON EARTH.
ALGEBRA EXAM
F
RING RING
RING RING

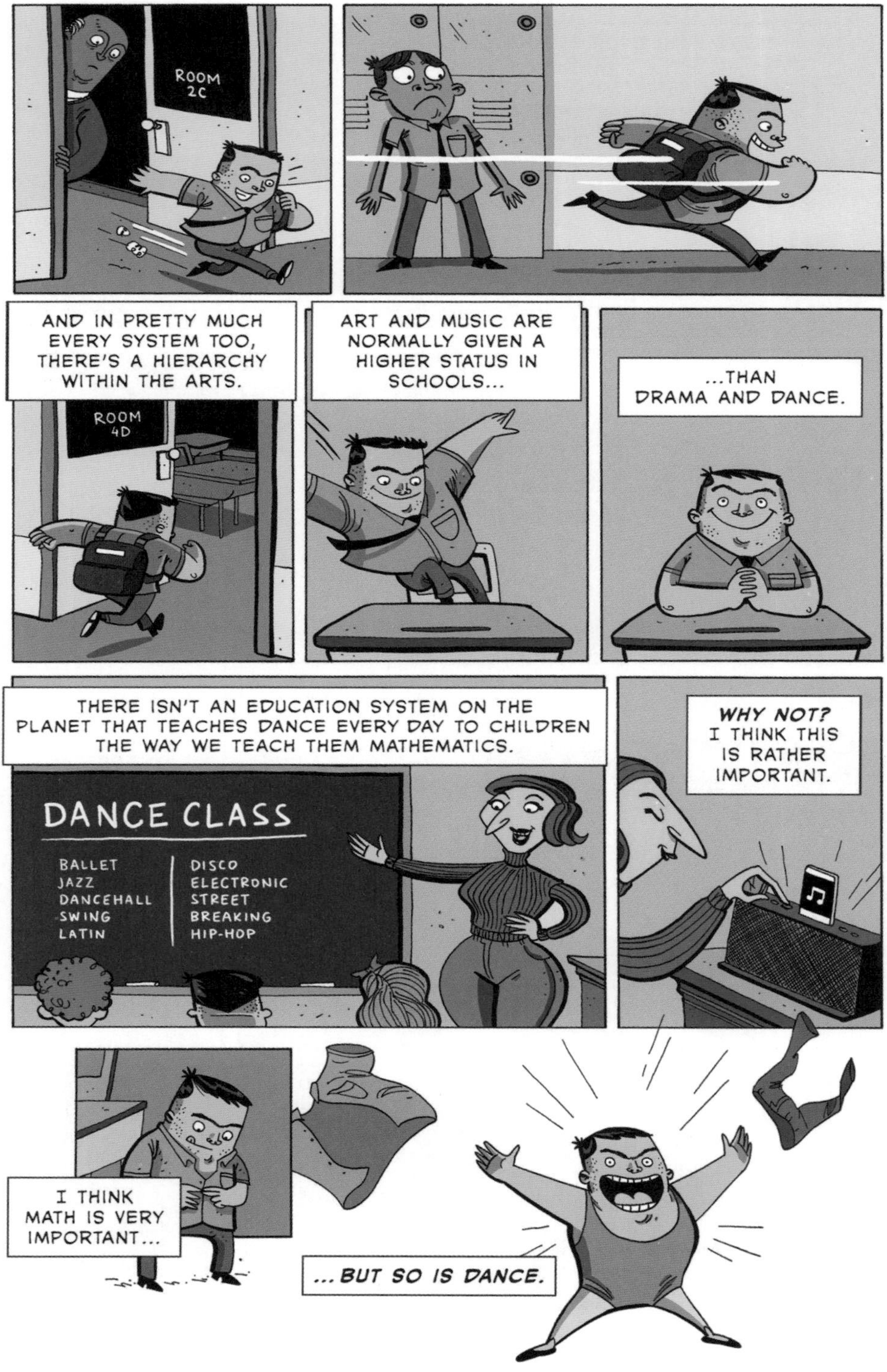
ROOM 2C
AND IN PRETTY MUCH EVERY SYSTEM TOO, THERE'S A HIERARCHY WITHIN THE ARTS.
ROOM 4D
ART AND MUSIC ARE NORMALLY GIVEN A HIGHER STATUS IN SCHOOLS...
...THAN DRAMA AND DANCE.
THERE ISN'T AN EDUCATION SYSTEM ON THE PLANET THAT TEACHES DANCE EVERY DAY TO CHILDREN THE WAY WE TEACH THEM MATHEMATICS.
DANCE CLASS
BALLET
JAZZ
DANCEHALL
SWING
LATIN
DISCO
ELECTRONIC
STREET
BREAKING
HIP-HOP
WHY NOT? I THINK THIS IS RATHER IMPORTANT.
I THINK MATH IS VERY IMPORTANT...
...BUT SO IS DANCE.

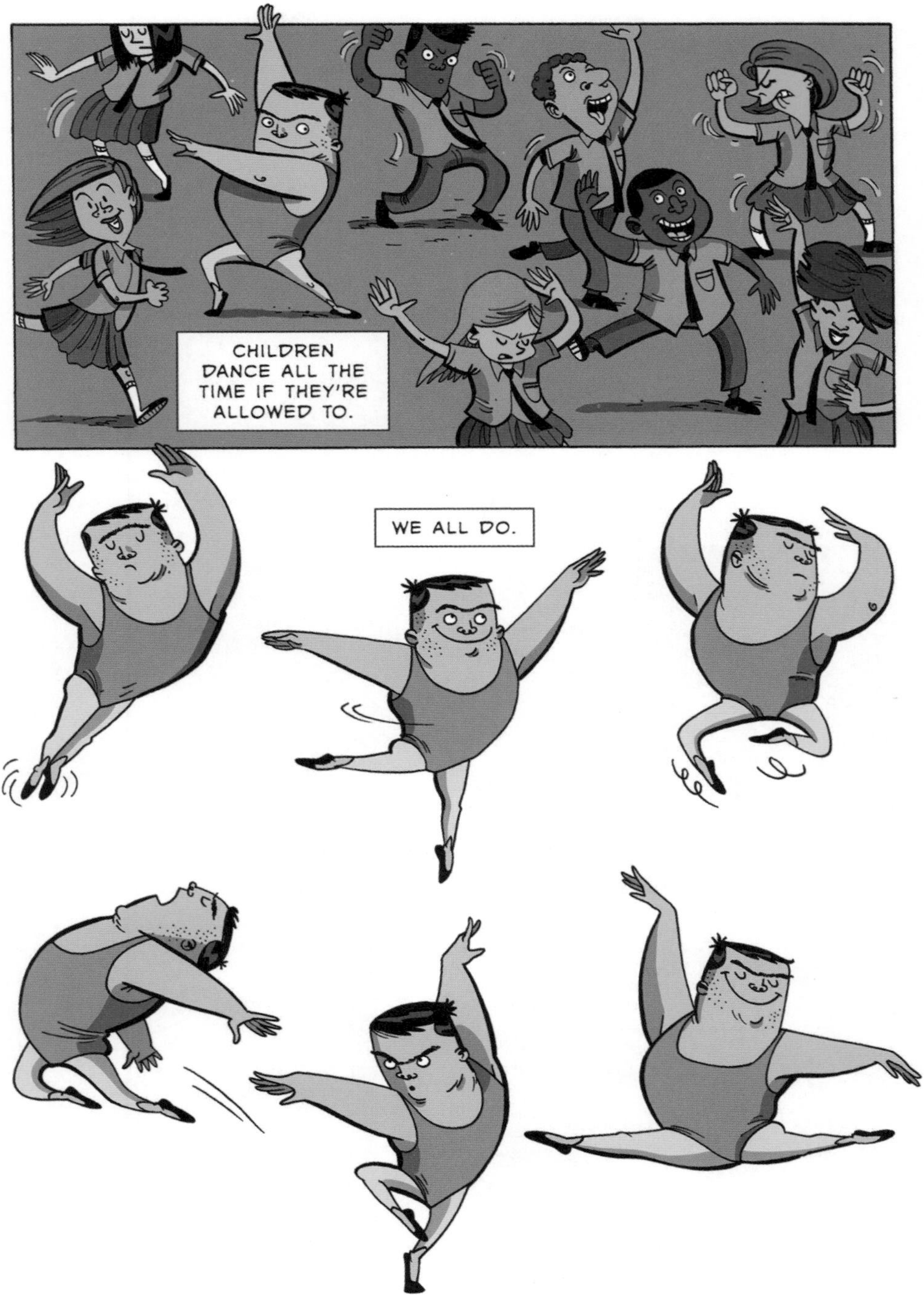
CHILDREN DANCE ALL THE TIME IF THEY'RE ALLOWED TO.
WE ALL DO.

WE ALL HAVE BODIES, DON'T WE?
DID I MISS A MEETING?
HIGH PRIORITY
MATH
SCIENCE
LANGUAGES
HUMANITIES
LOW PRIORITY
ART
MUSIC
DANCE
BOARD OF EDUCATION
TRUTHFULLY, WHAT HAPPENS IS, AS CHILDREN GROW UP, WE START TO EDUCATE THEM PROGRESSIVELY FROM THE WAIST UP.
EDUCATION GUIDELINES OF 1892
AND THEN WE FOCUS ON THEIR HEADS...
...AND SLIGHTLY TO ONE SIDE.

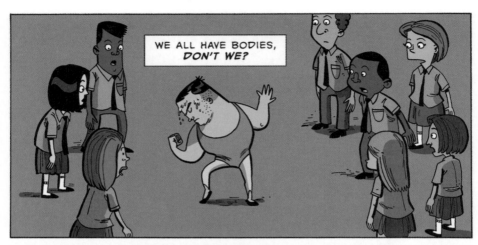

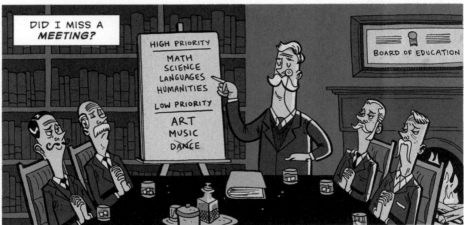

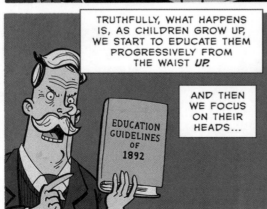

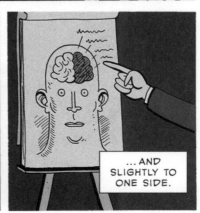

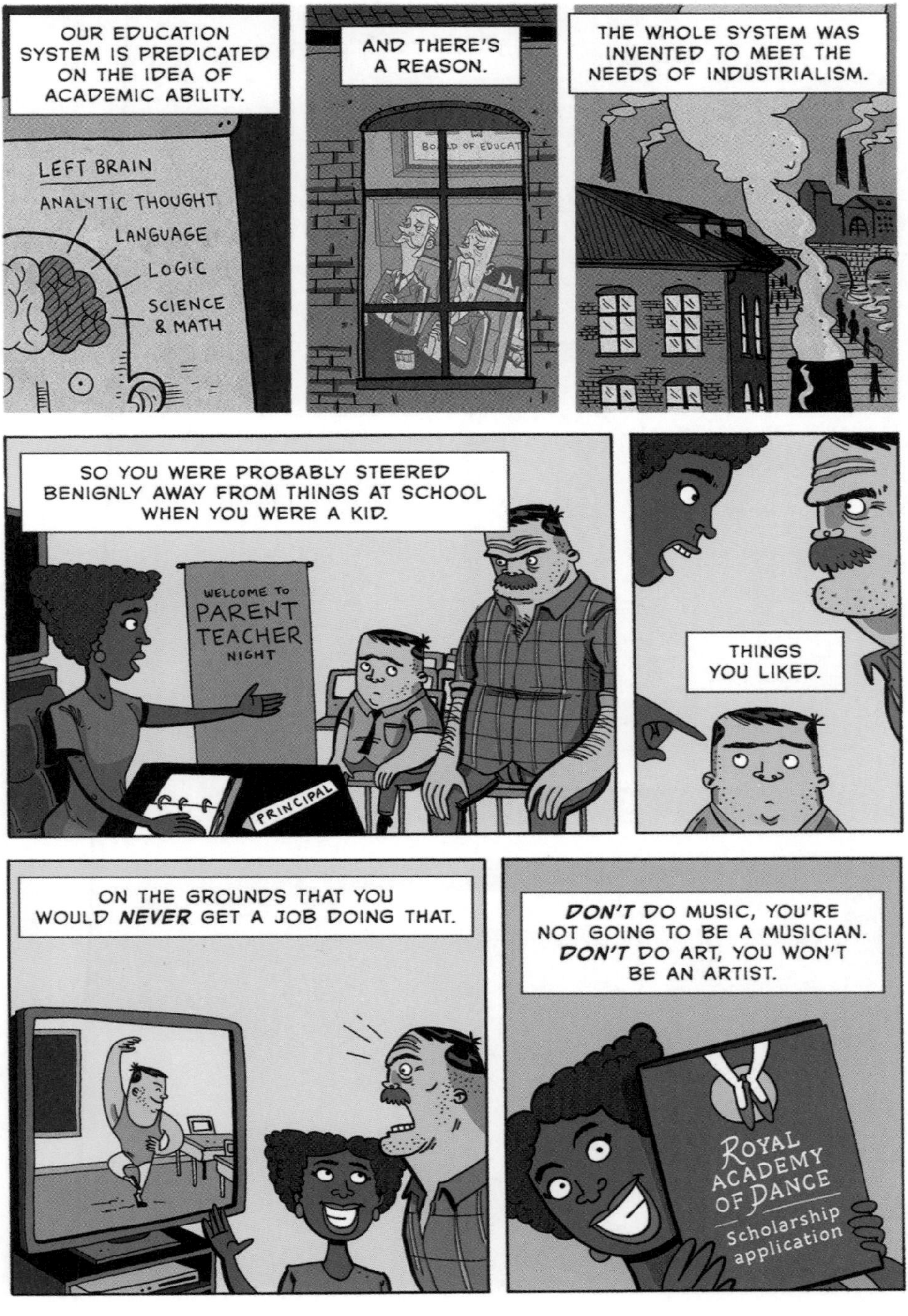
OUR EDUCATION SYSTEM IS PREDICATED ON THE IDEA OF ACADEMIC ABILITY.
LEFT BRAIN
ANALYTIC THOUGHT
LANGUAGE
LOGIC
SCIENCE & MATH
AND THERE'S A REASON.
THE WHOLE SYSTEM WAS INVENTED TO MEET THE NEEDS OF INDUSTRIALISM.
SO YOU WERE PROBABLY STEERED BENIGNLY AWAY FROM THINGS AT SCHOOL WHEN YOU WERE A KID.
WELCOME TO PARENT TEACHER NIGHT
PRINCIPAL
THINGS YOU LIKED.
ON THE GROUNDS THAT YOU WOULD NEVER GET A JOB DOING THAT.
DON'T DO MUSIC, YOU'RE NOT GOING TO BE A MUSICIAN. DON'T DO ART, YOU WON'T BE AN ARTIST.
ROYAL ACADEMY OF DANCE
Scholarship application

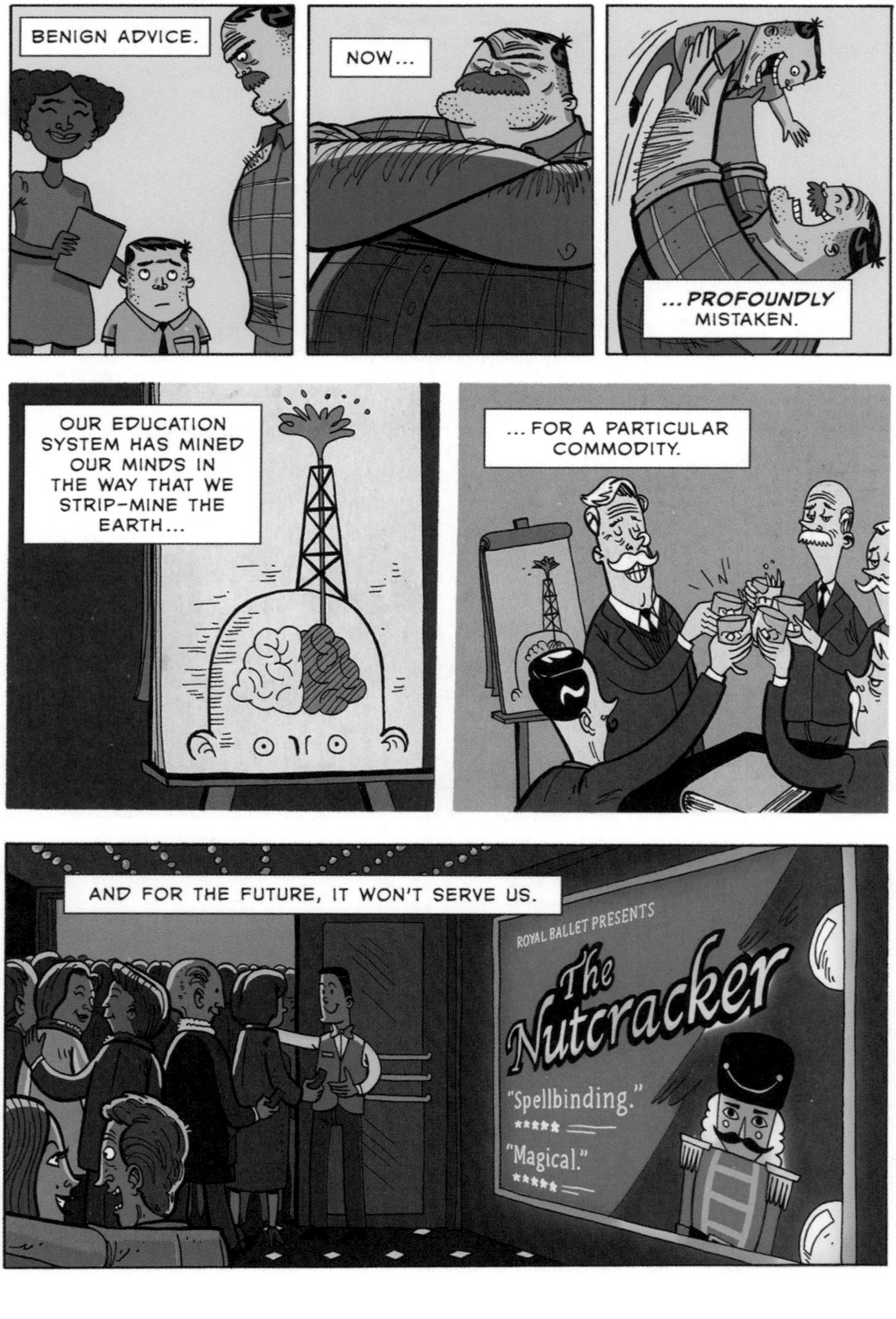
BENIGN ADVICE.
NOW...
...PROFOUNDLY MISTAKEN.
OUR EDUCATION SYSTEM HAS MINED OUR MINDS IN THE WAY THAT WE STRIP-MINE THE EARTH...
...FOR A PARTICULAR COMMODITY.
AND FOR THE FUTURE, IT WON'T SERVE US.
ROYAL BALLET PRESENTS
The Nutcracker
"Spellbinding."
"Magical."

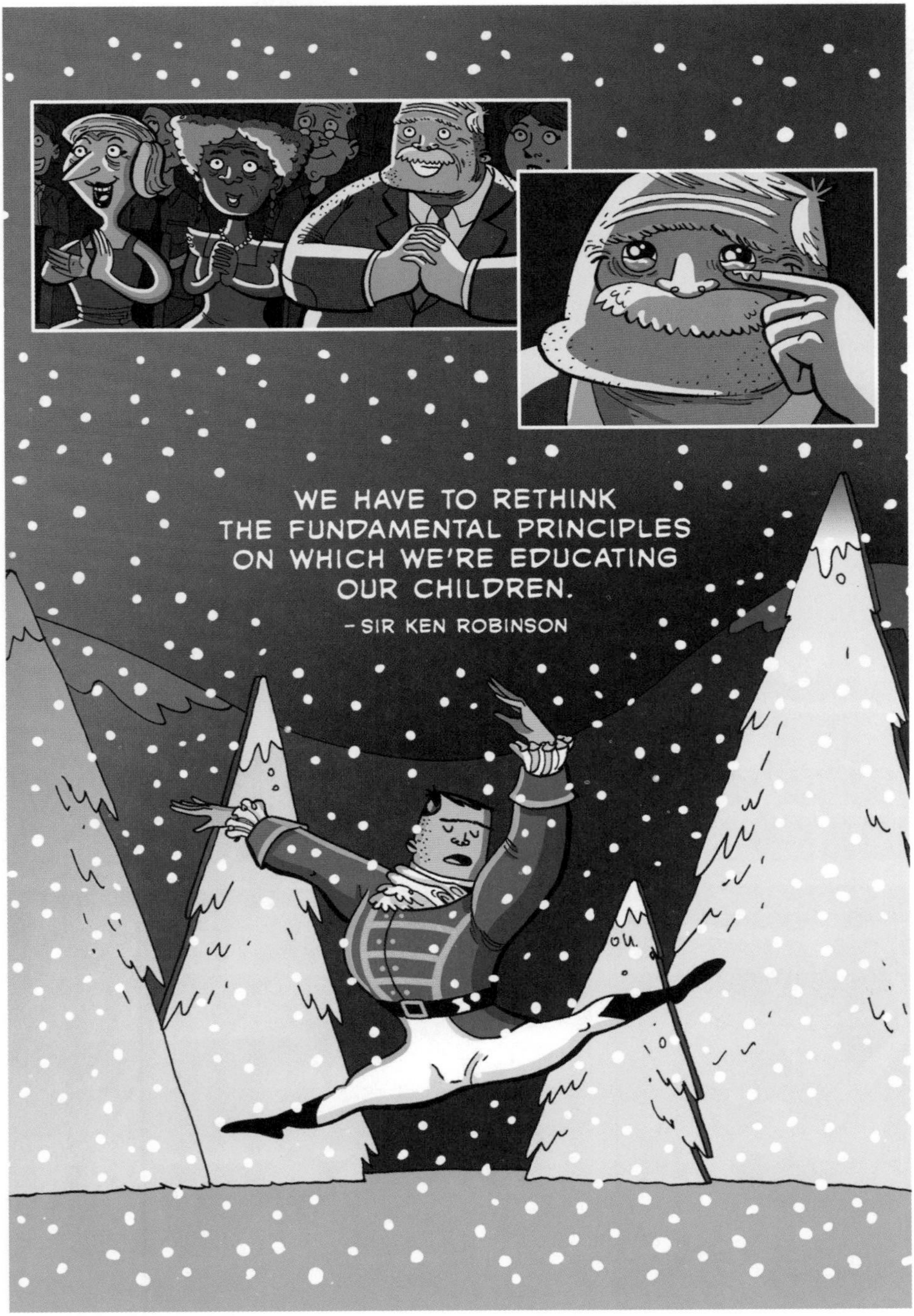
WE HAVE TO RETHINK THE FUNDAMENTAL PRINCIPLES ON WHICH WE'RE EDUCATING OUR CHILDREN.
-SIR KEN ROBINSON

LIFE IS NOT EASY Marie Curie

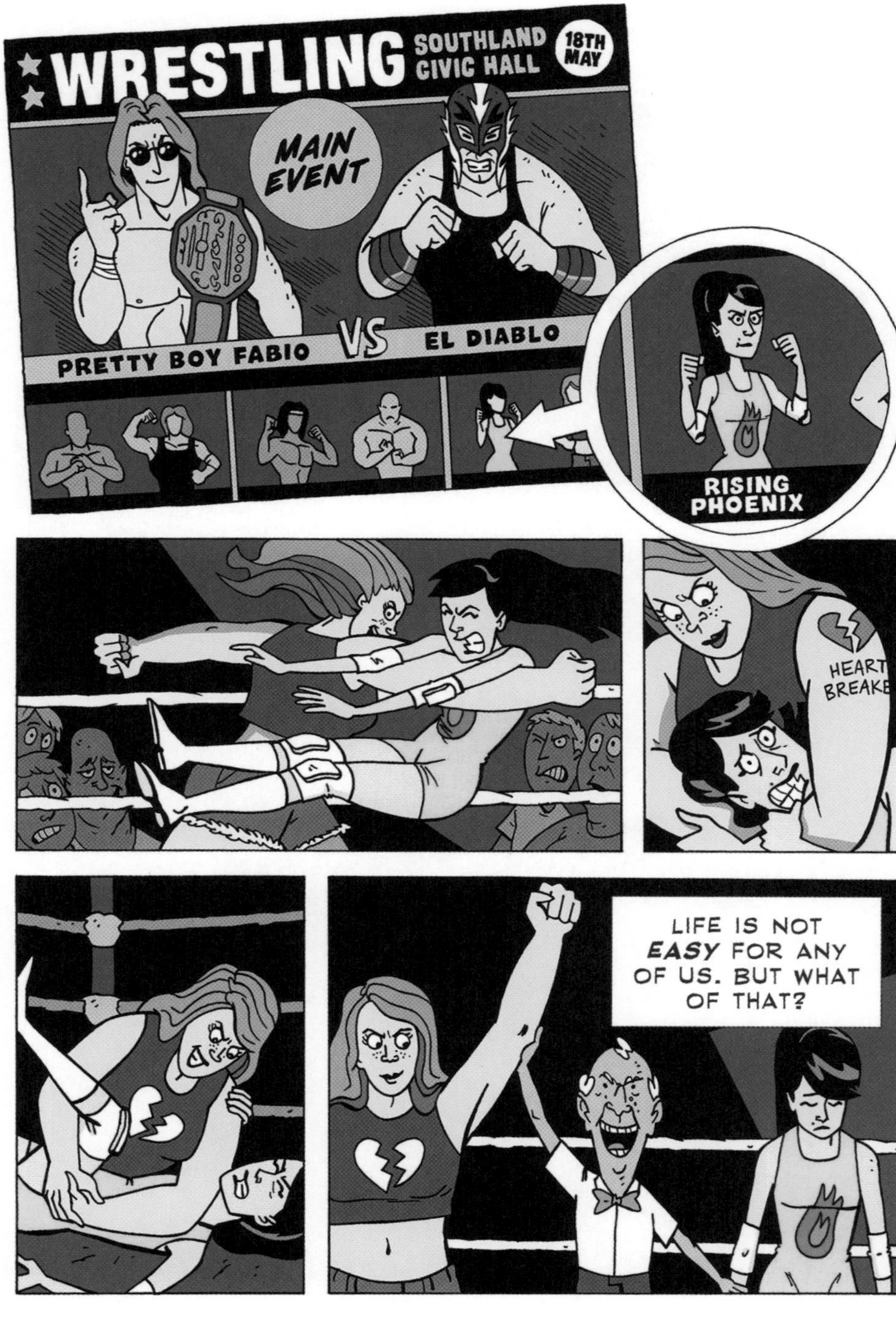

WRESTLING
SOUTHLAND CIVIC HALL
18TH MAY
MAIN EVENT
PRETTY BOY FABIO
VS
EL DIABLO
RISING PHOENIX
HEART BREAKE
LIFE IS NOT *EASY* FOR ANY OF US. BUT WHAT OF THAT?

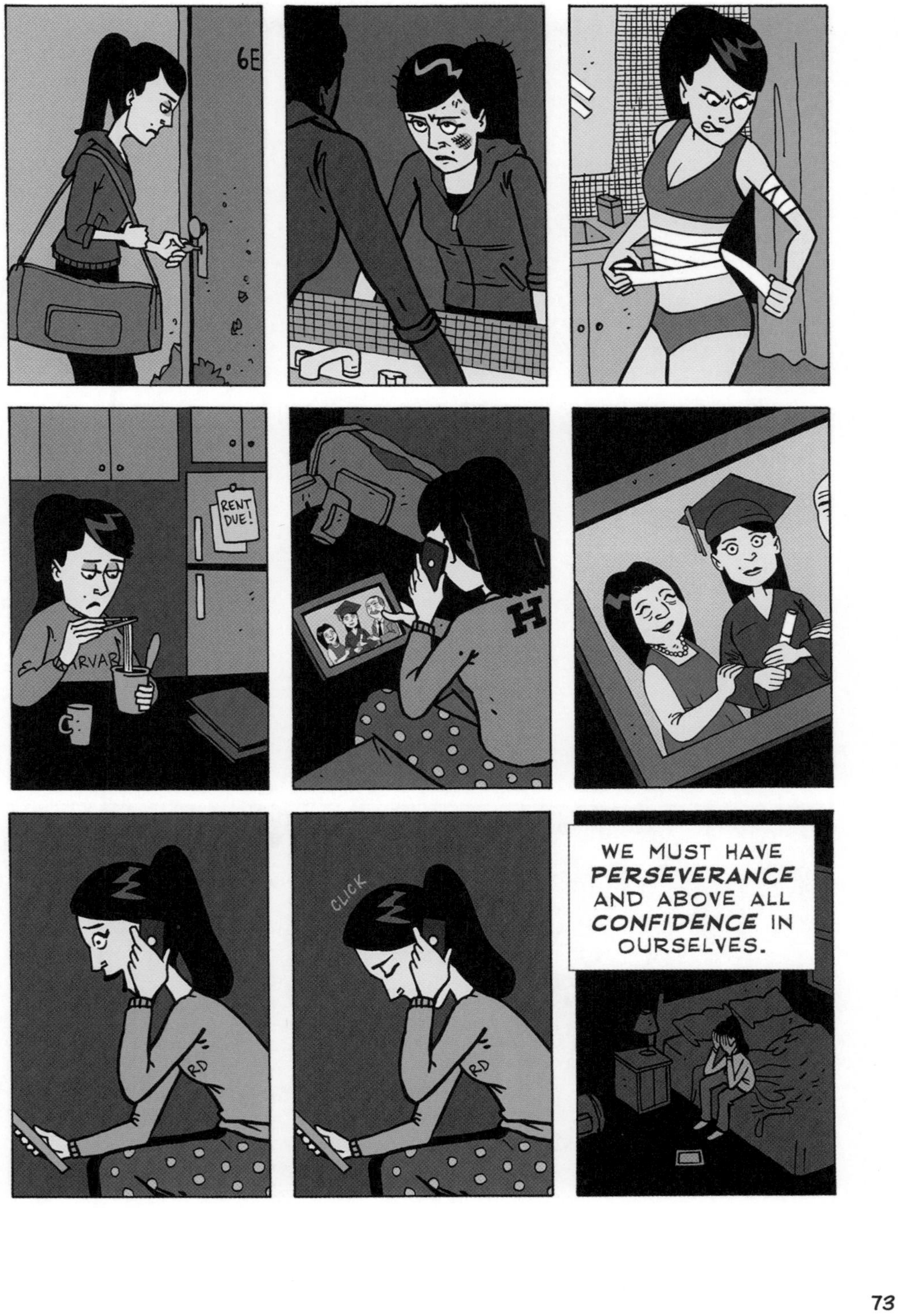
6E
RENT DUE!
RVAR
H
CLICK
RD
RD
WE MUST HAVE **PERSEVERANCE** AND ABOVE ALL **CONFIDENCE** IN OURSELVES.

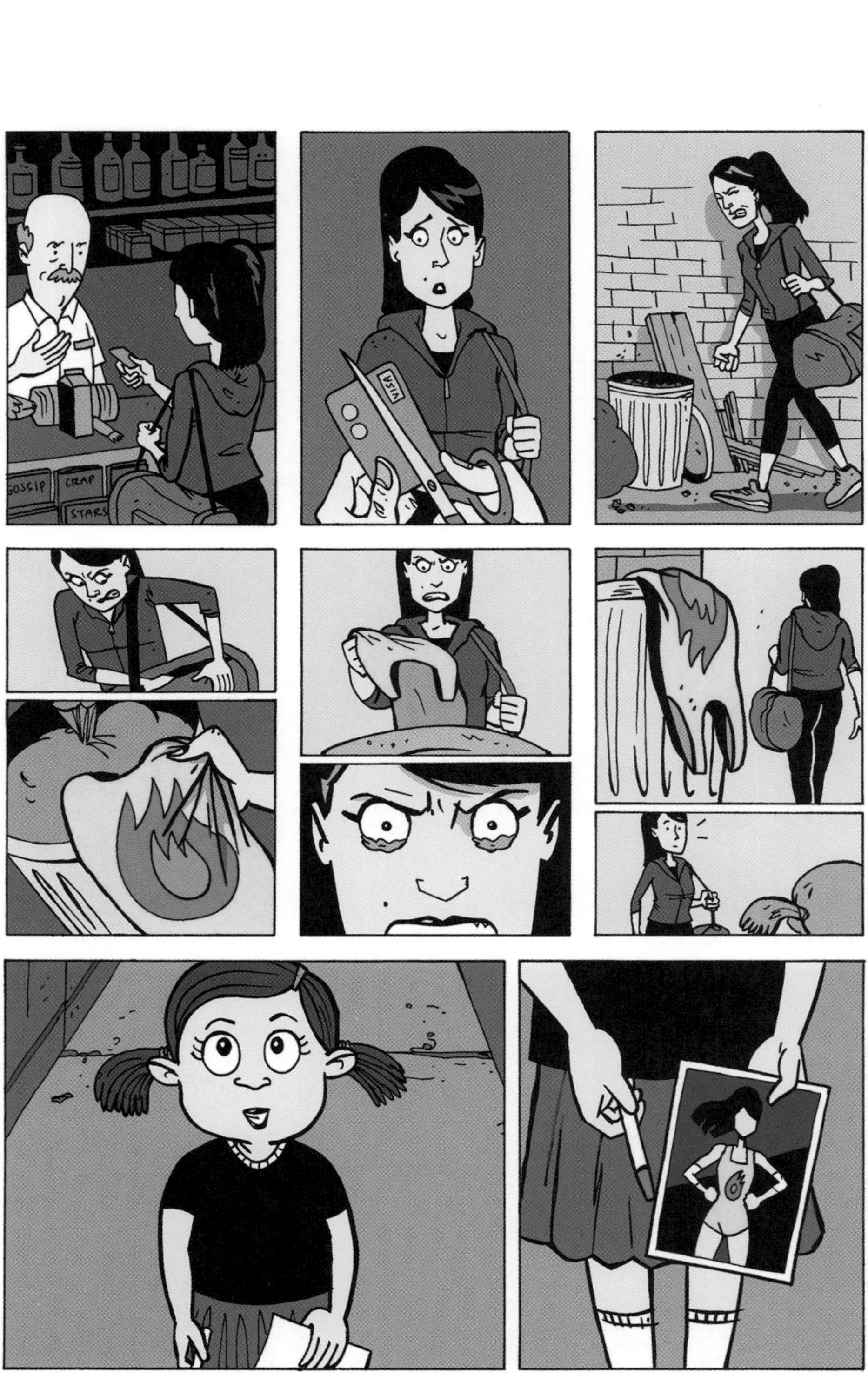
GOSSIP
CRAP
STARS
VISA

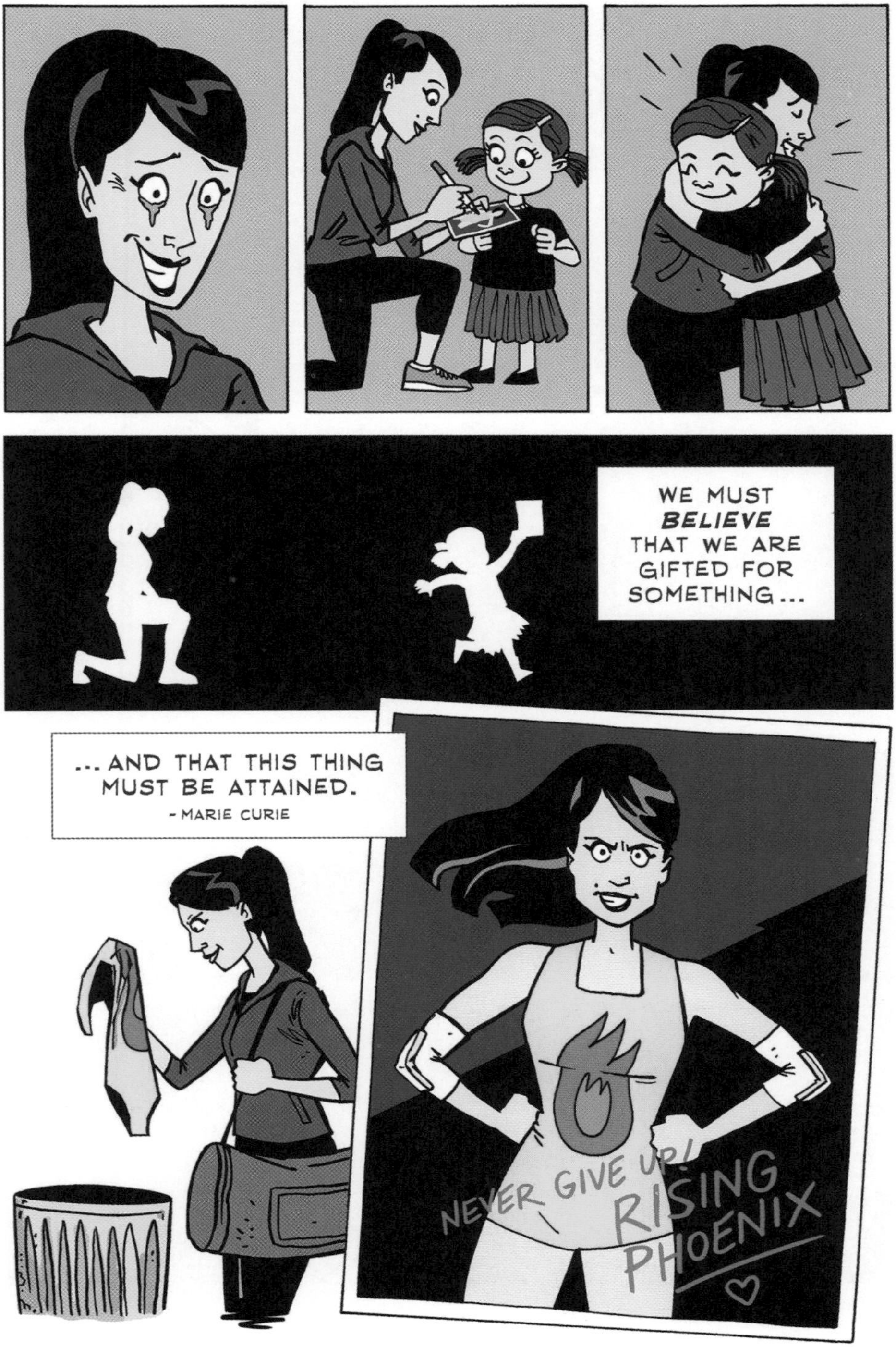
WE MUST
BELIEVE
THAT WE ARE
GIFTED FOR
SOMETHING...
...AND THAT THIS THING
MUST BE ATTAINED.
- MARIE CURIE
NEVER GIVE UP!
RISING
PHOENIX

WE ARE ALL HUMAN BEINGS The Dalai Lama

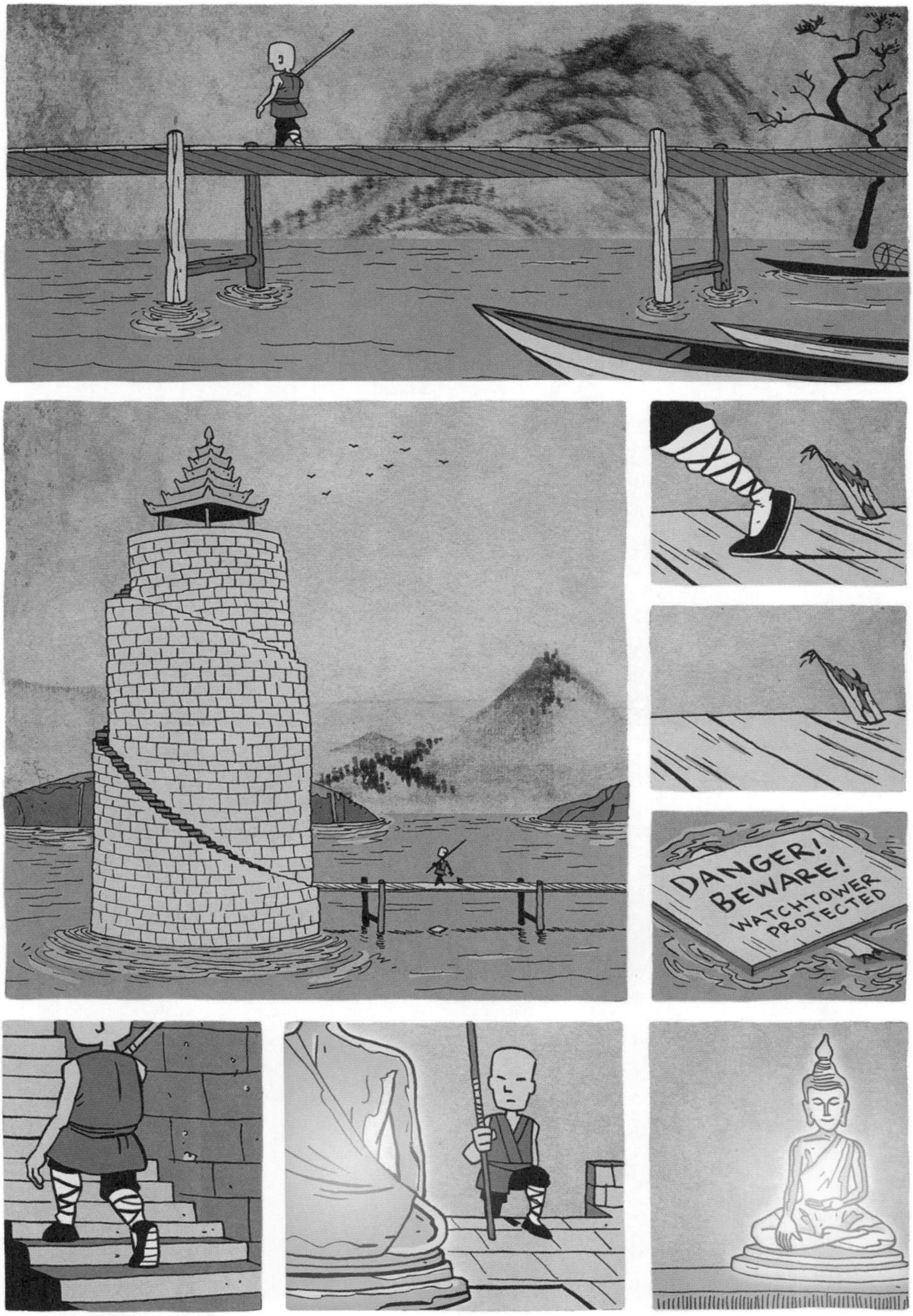
DANGER!
BEWARE!
WATCHTOWER
PROTECTED

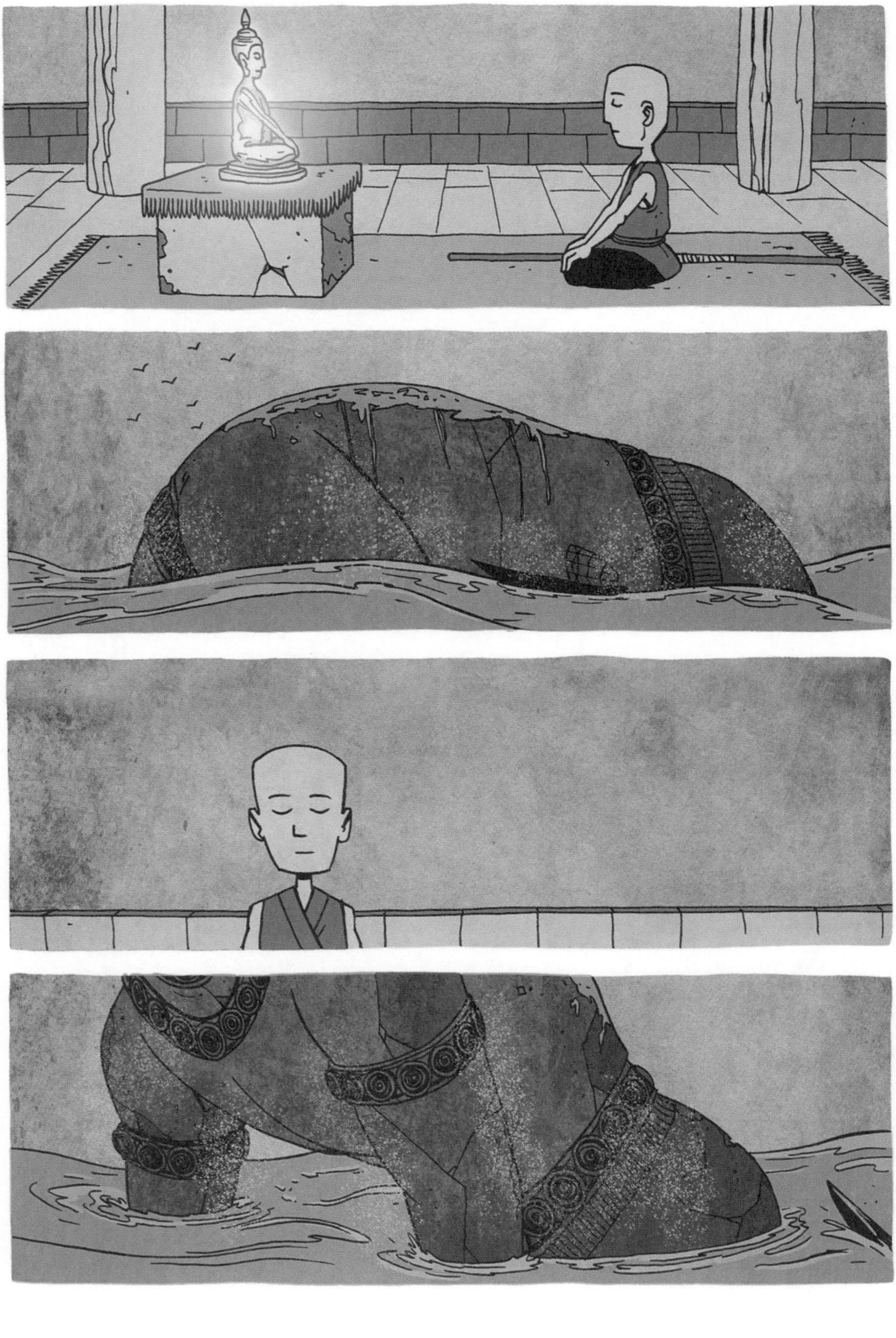

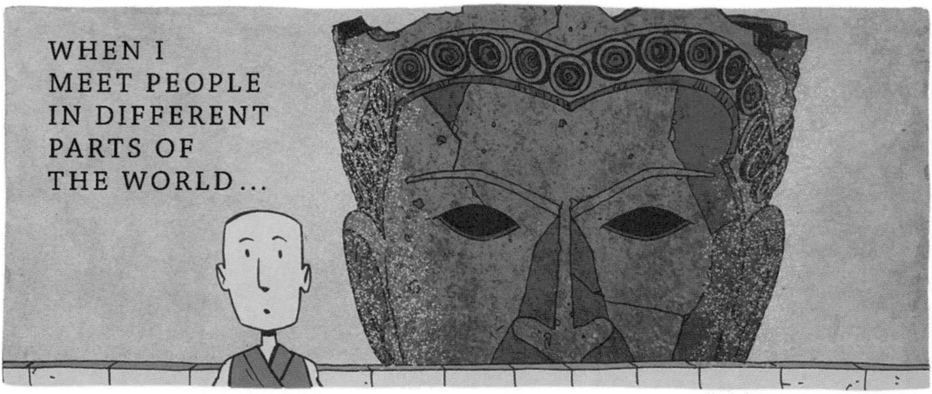
WHEN I
MEET PEOPLE
IN DIFFERENT
PARTS OF
THE WORLD...

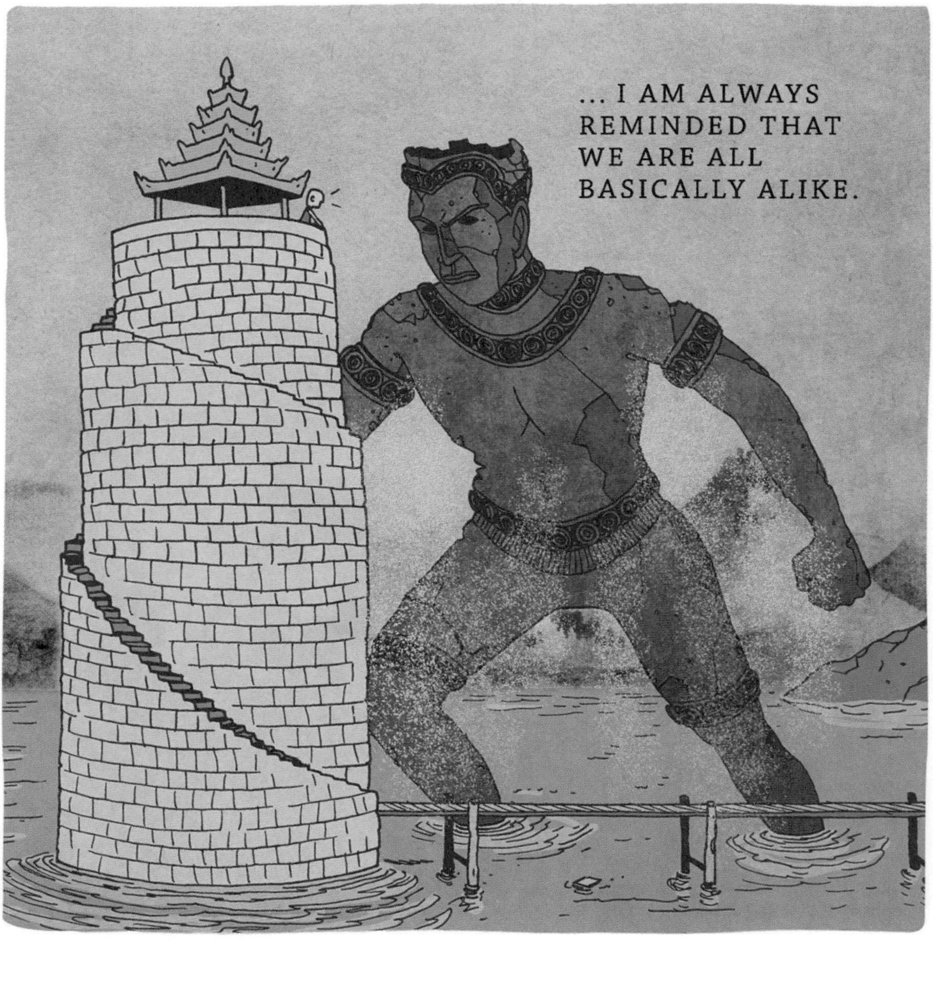
...I AM ALWAYS
REMINDED THAT
WE ARE ALL
BASICALLY ALIKE.

WE ARE ALL
HUMAN BEINGS.

MAYBE WE
HAVE DIFFERENT
CLOTHES...

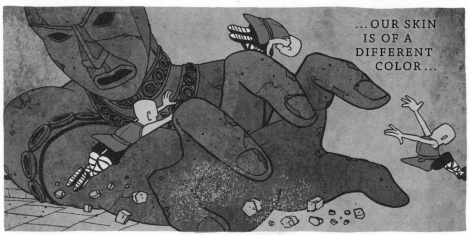

...OUR SKIN
IS OF A
DIFFERENT
COLOR...

...OR
WE SPEAK
DIFFERENT
LANGUAGES.

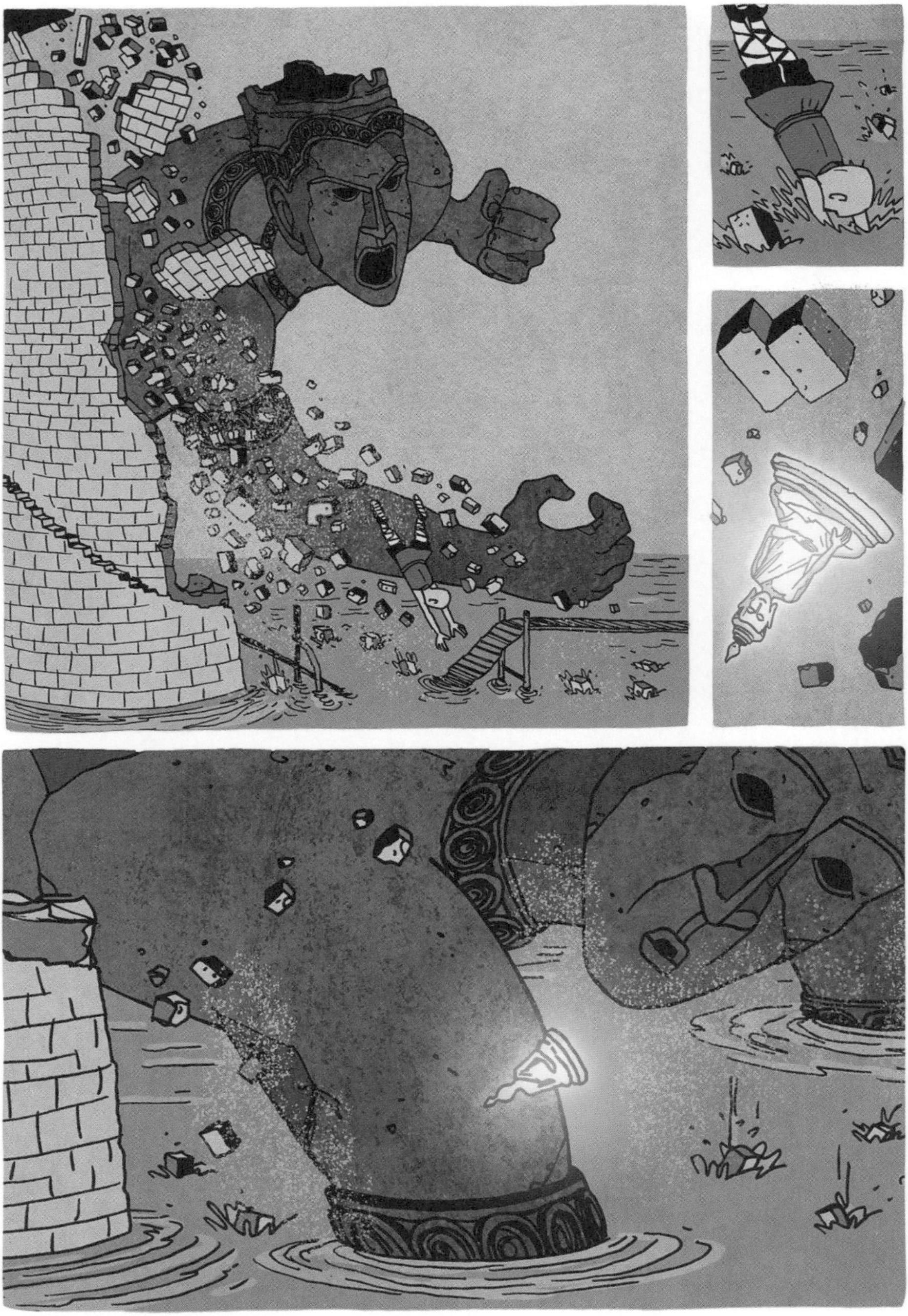

BUT
BASICALLY,
WE ARE
THE SAME
HUMAN
BEINGS.

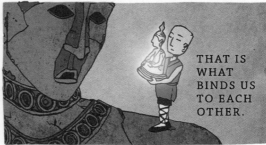

THAT IS
WHAT
BINDS US
TO EACH
OTHER.

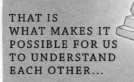

THAT IS
WHAT MAKES IT
POSSIBLE FOR US
TO UNDERSTAND
EACH OTHER...

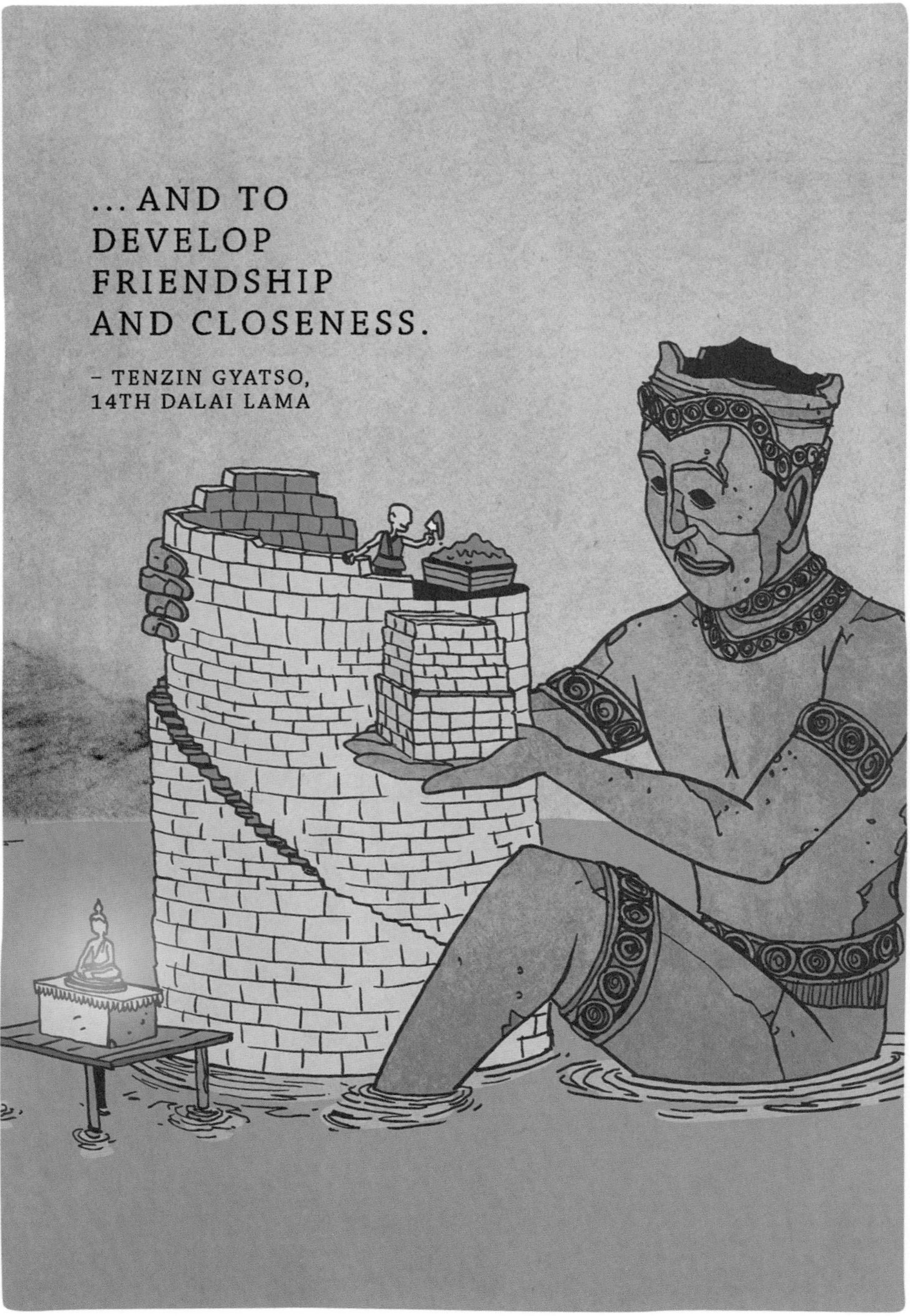
...AND TO DEVELOP FRIENDSHIP AND CLOSENESS.
– TENZIN GYATSO, 14TH DALAI LAMA

THE STONECUTTER Jacob A. Riis

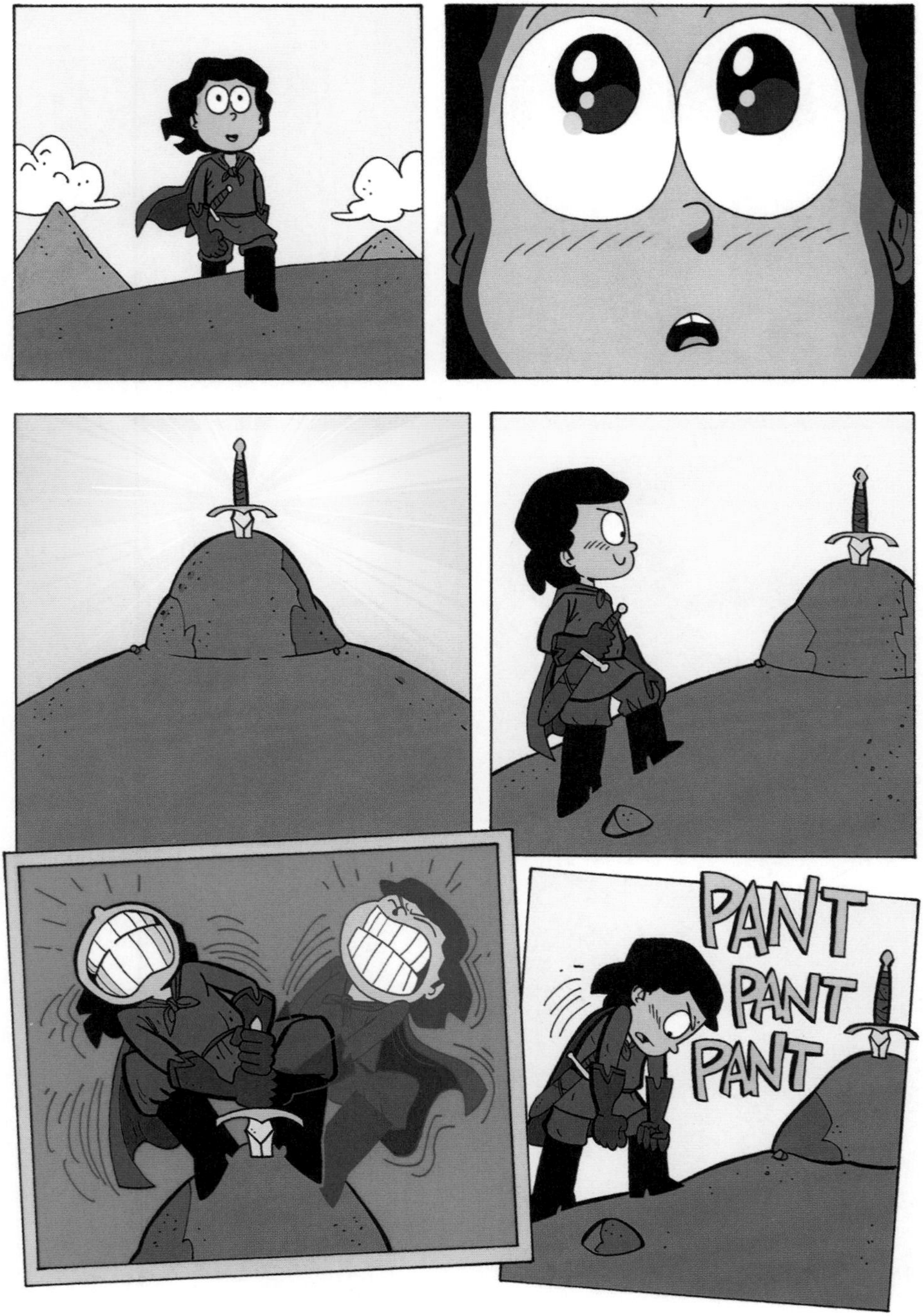
PANT
PANT
PANT

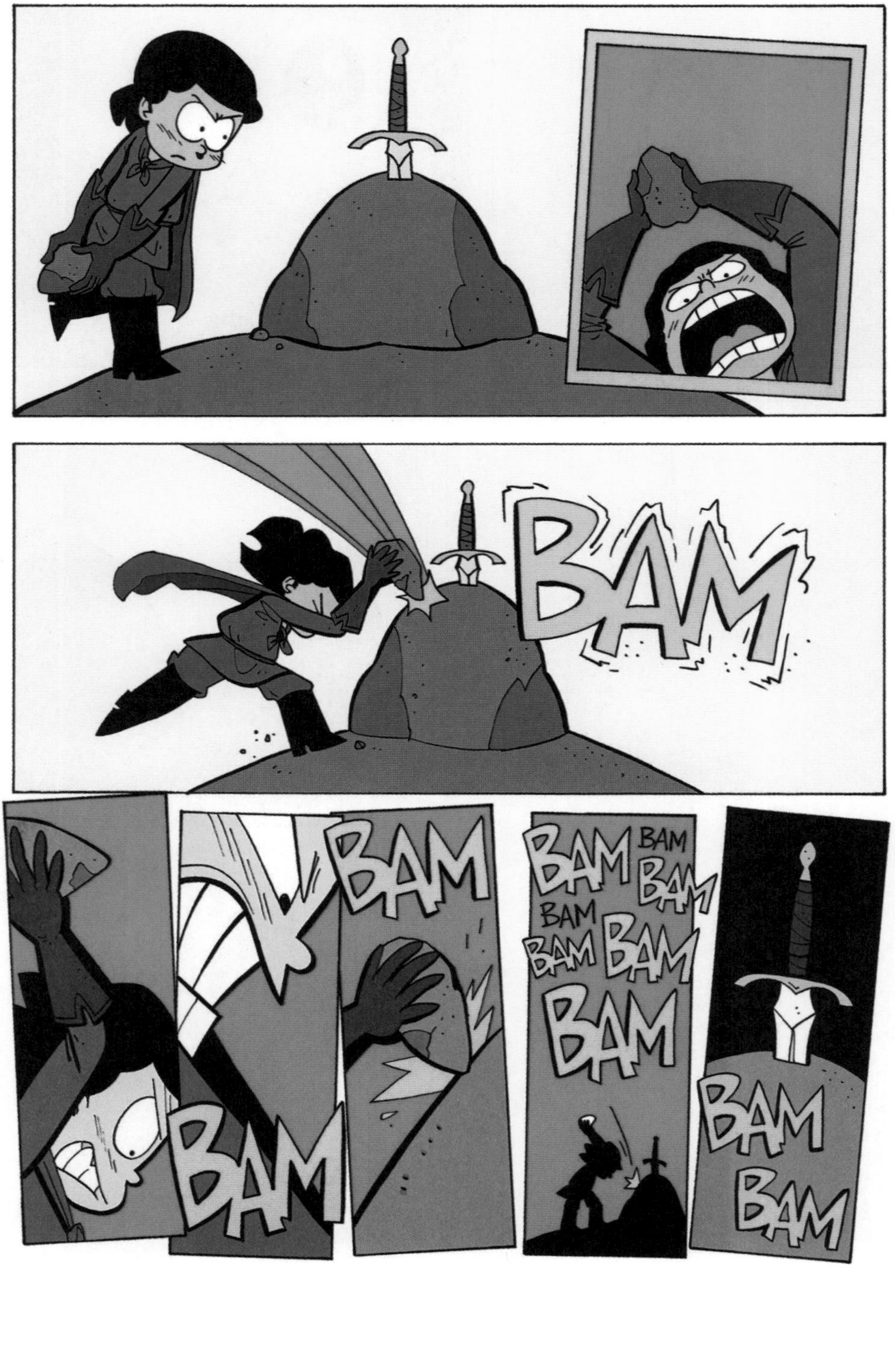
BAM
BAM
BAM
BAM BAM
BAM
BAM
BAM BAM
BAM
BAM
BAM

WHEN NOTHING SEEMS TO HELP, I WOULD GO AND LOOK AT A STONECUTTER HAMMERING AWAY AT HIS ROCK PERHAPS A HUNDRED TIMES WITHOUT AS MUCH AS A CRACK SHOWING IN IT.

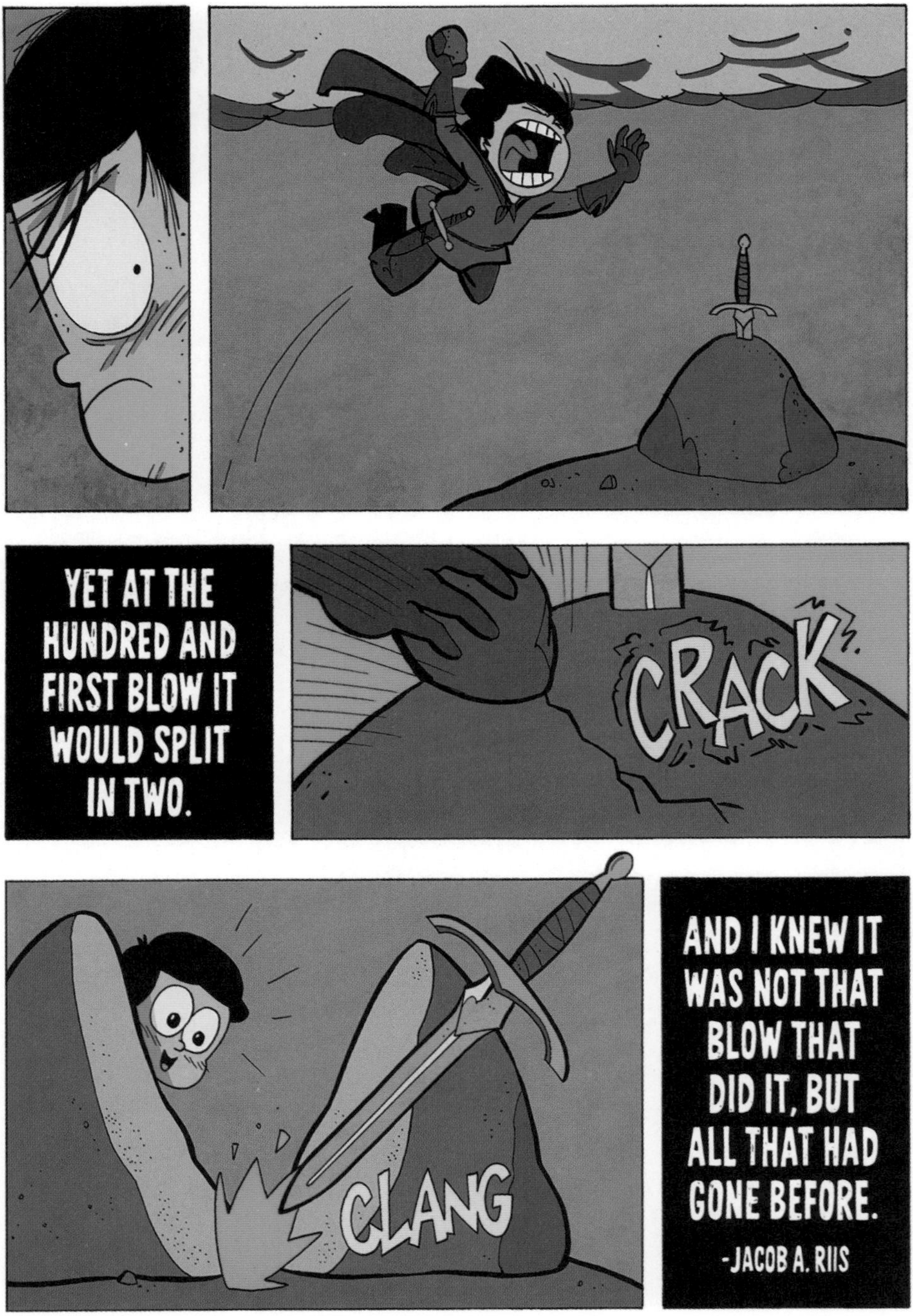
YET AT THE HUNDRED AND FIRST BLOW IT WOULD SPLIT IN TWO.
CRACK
CLANG
AND I KNEW IT WAS NOT THAT BLOW THAT DID IT, BUT ALL THAT HAD GONE BEFORE.
-JACOB A. RIIS

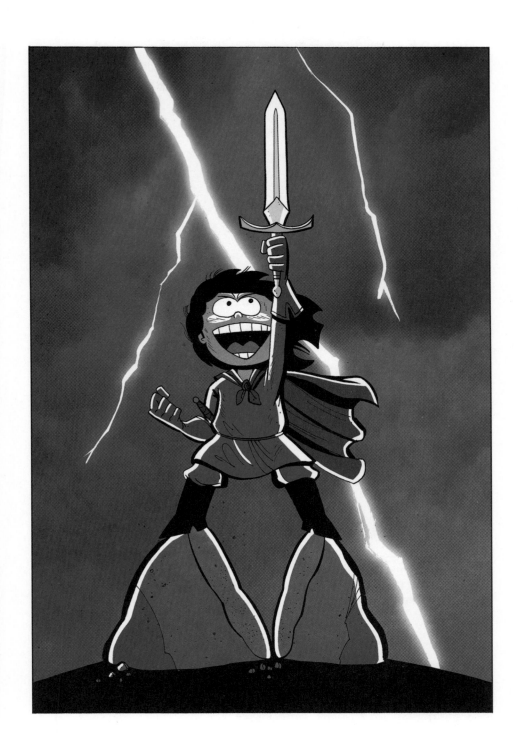

NATURE LOVES COURAGE

Terence McKenna

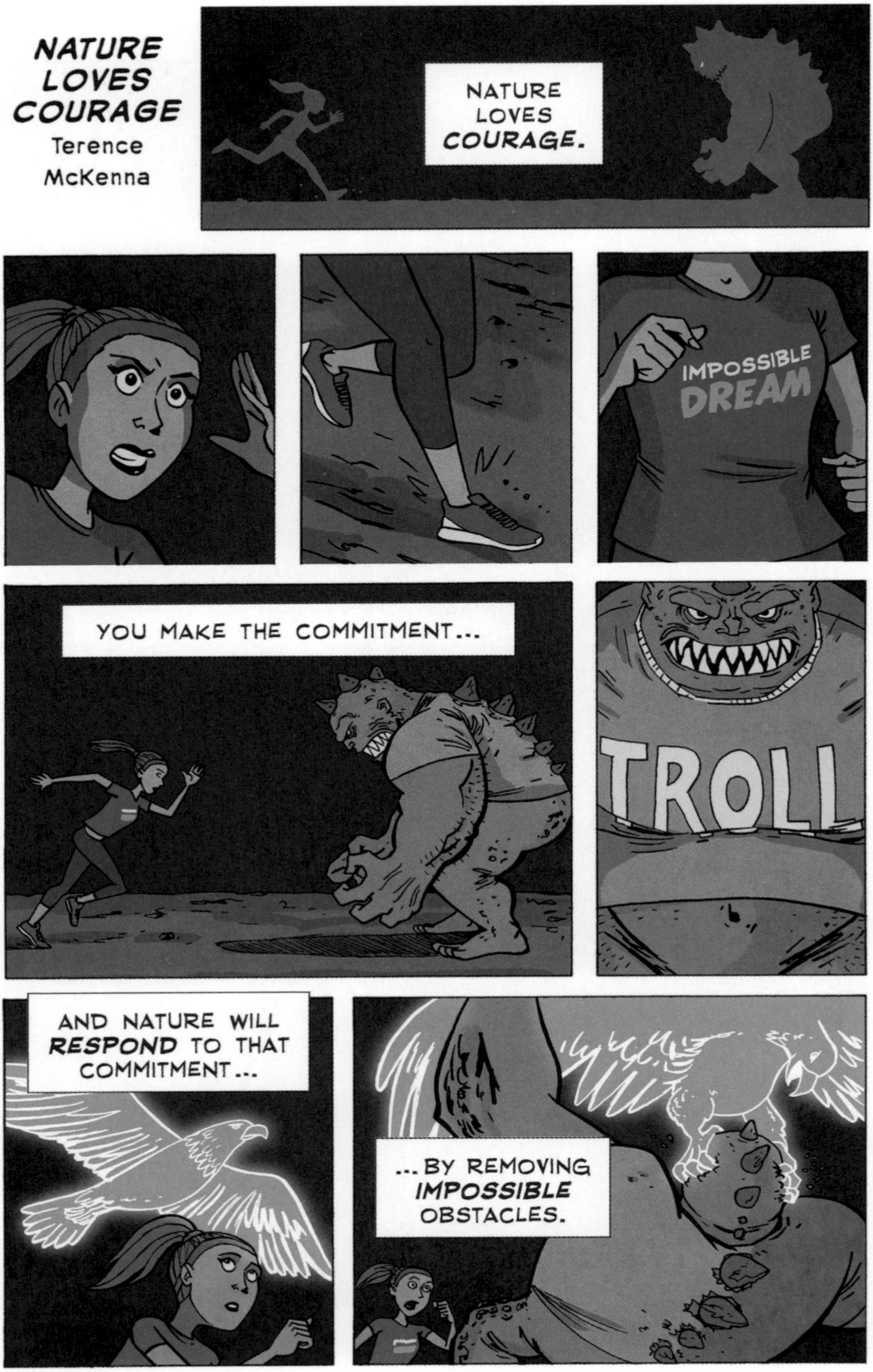
NATURE LOVES *COURAGE*.
IMPOSSIBLE DREAM
YOU MAKE THE COMMITMENT...
TROLL
AND NATURE WILL *RESPOND* TO THAT COMMITMENT...
...BY REMOVING *IMPOSSIBLE* OBSTACLES.

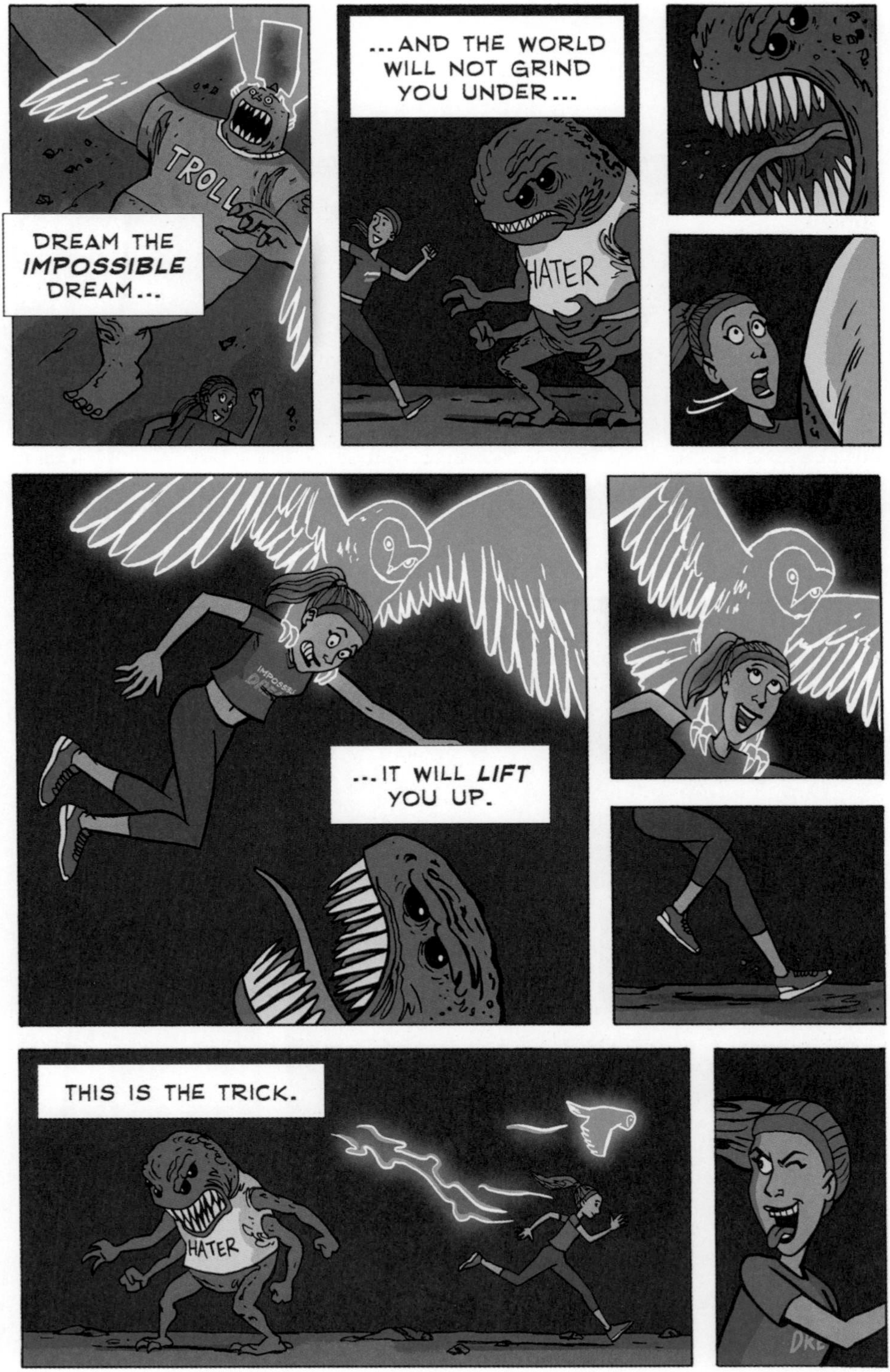
TROLL
DREAM THE IMPOSSIBLE DREAM...
...AND THE WORLD WILL NOT GRIND YOU UNDER...
HATER
IMPOSSIBLE
...IT WILL LIFT YOU UP.
THIS IS THE TRICK.
HATER

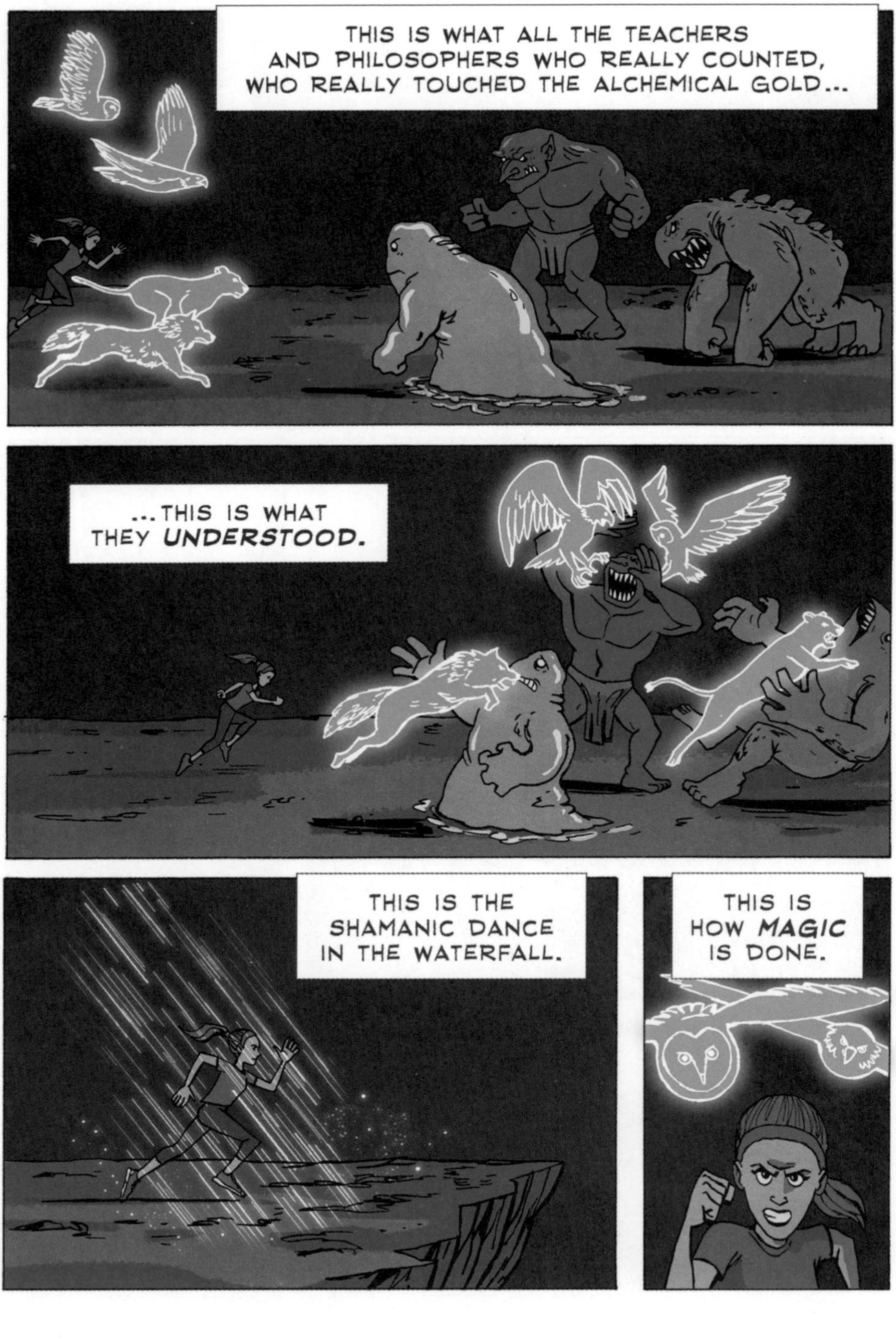
THIS IS WHAT ALL THE TEACHERS AND PHILOSOPHERS WHO REALLY COUNTED, WHO REALLY TOUCHED THE ALCHEMICAL GOLD...
...THIS IS WHAT THEY *UNDERSTOOD.*
THIS IS THE SHAMANIC DANCE IN THE WATERFALL.
THIS IS HOW *MAGIC* IS DONE.

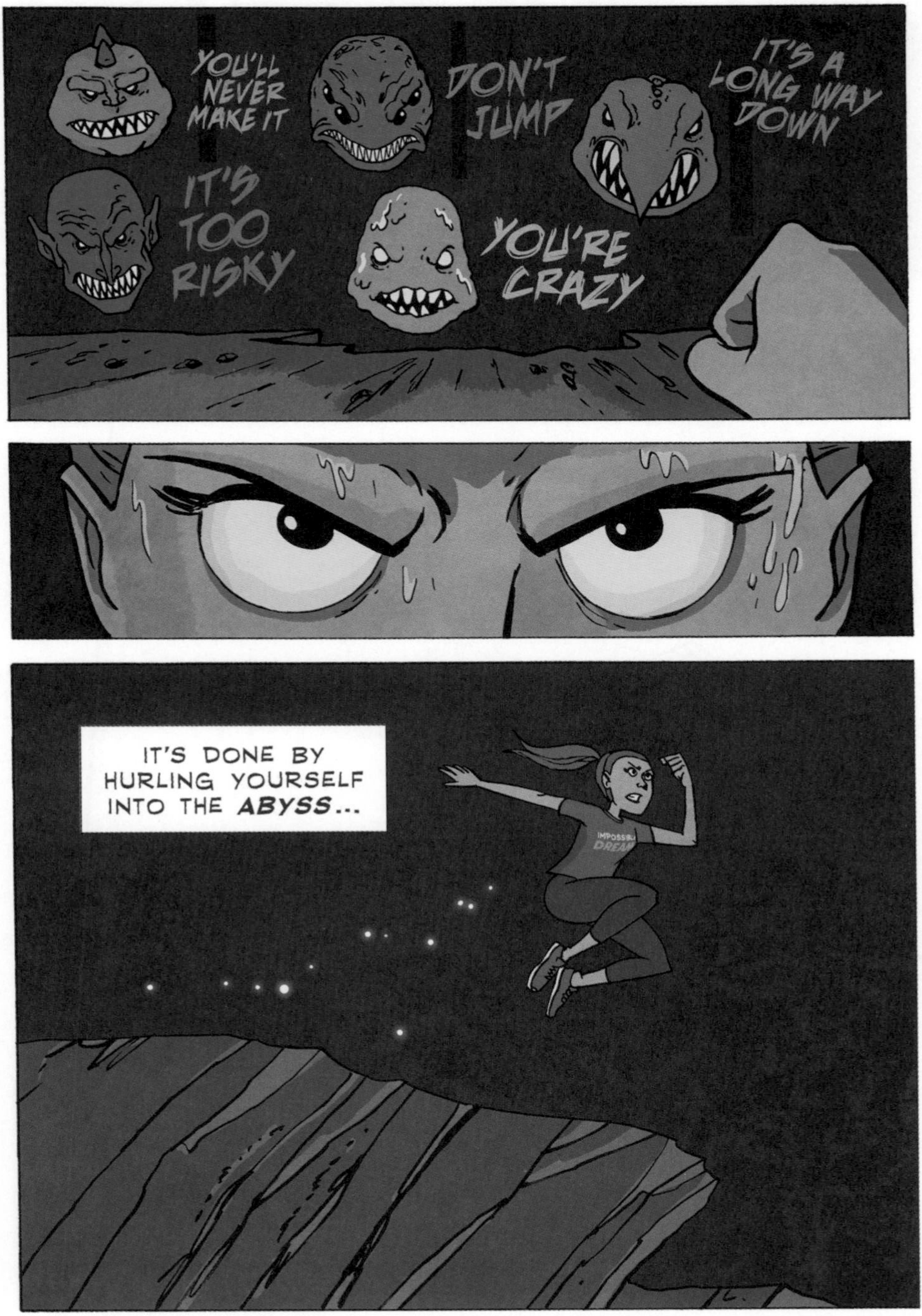
YOU'LL NEVER MAKE IT
DON'T JUMP
IT'S A LONG WAY DOWN
IT'S TOO RISKY
YOU'RE CRAZY
IT'S DONE BY HURLING YOURSELF INTO THE *ABYSS*...

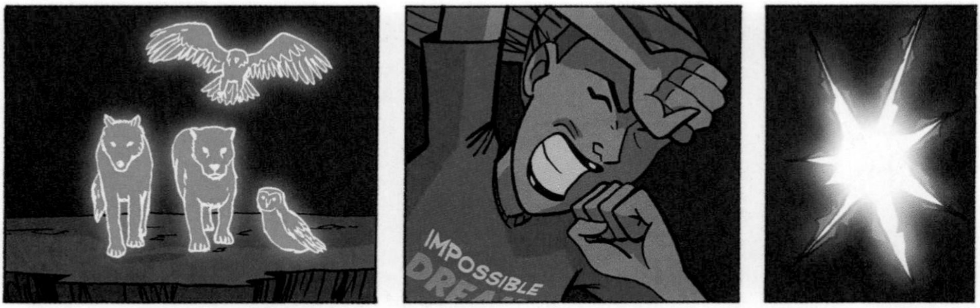
IMPOSSIBLE

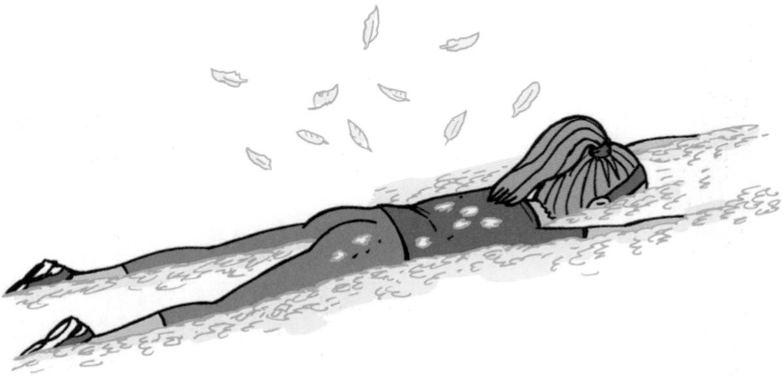

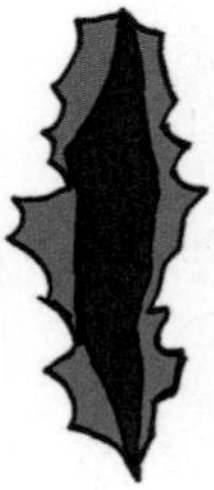

...AND DISCOVERING
IT'S A ***FEATHER BED.***

-TERENCE MCKENNA

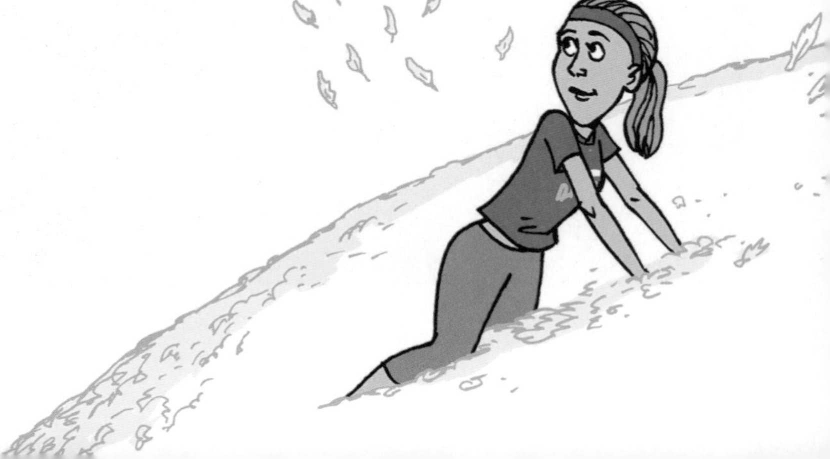

A HEROIC LIFE George Bernard Shaw

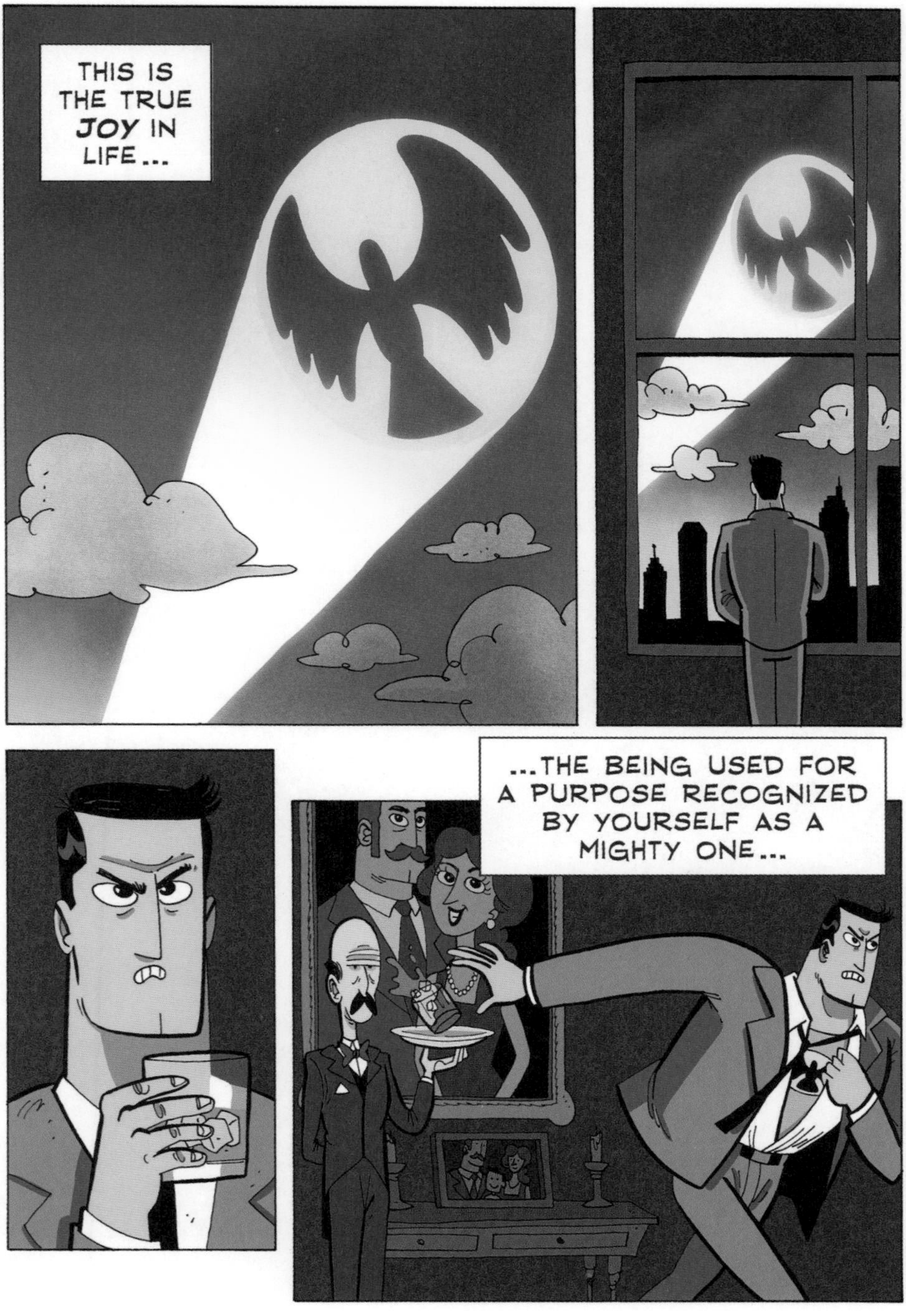
THIS IS THE TRUE JOY IN LIFE...
...THE BEING USED FOR A PURPOSE RECOGNIZED BY YOURSELF AS A MIGHTY ONE...

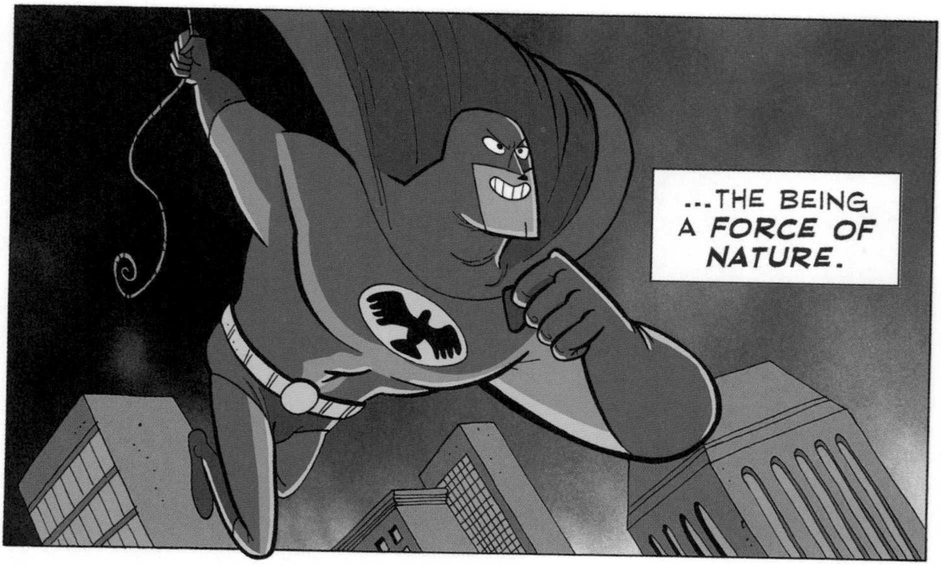
...THE BEING
A FORCE OF
NATURE.

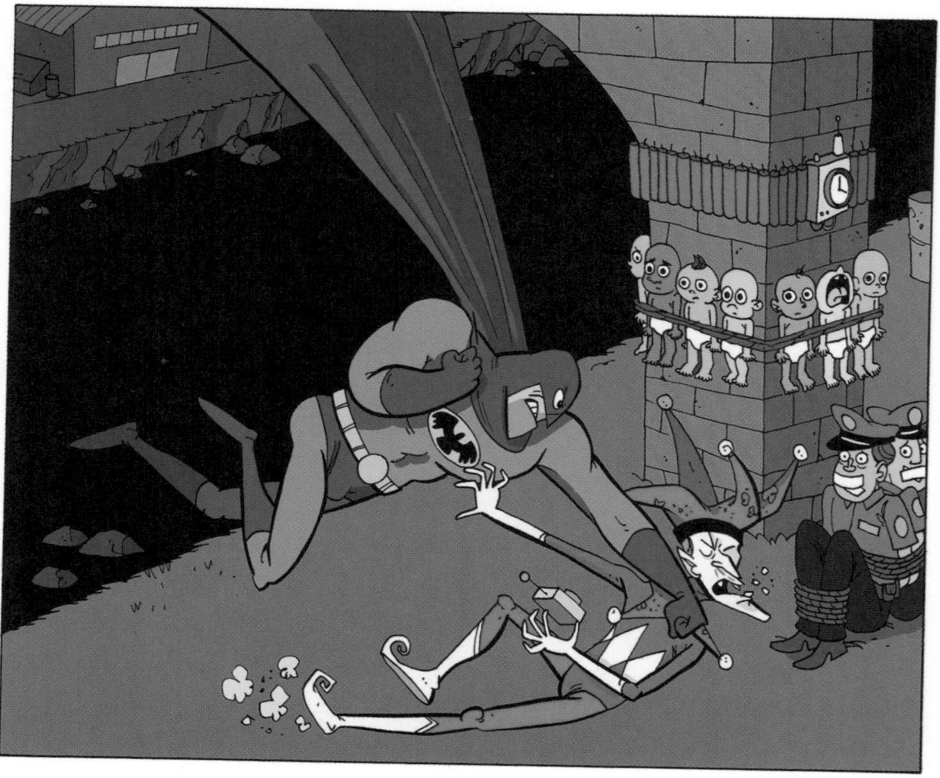

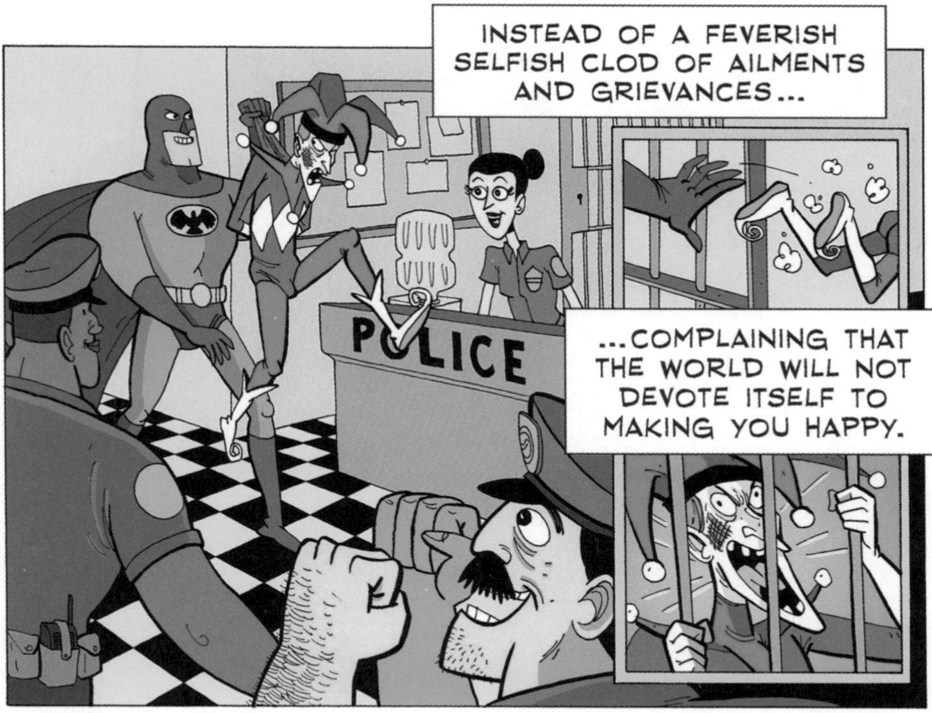
INSTEAD OF A FEVERISH SELFISH CLOD OF AILMENTS AND GRIEVANCES...
POLICE
...COMPLAINING THAT THE WORLD WILL NOT DEVOTE ITSELF TO MAKING YOU HAPPY.

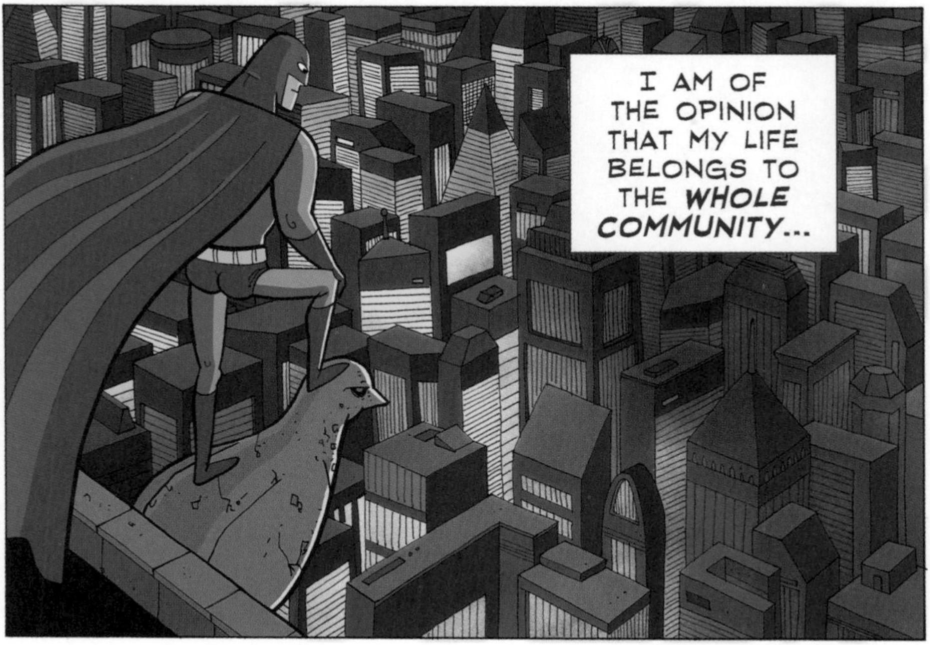
I AM OF THE OPINION THAT MY LIFE BELONGS TO THE *WHOLE COMMUNITY*...

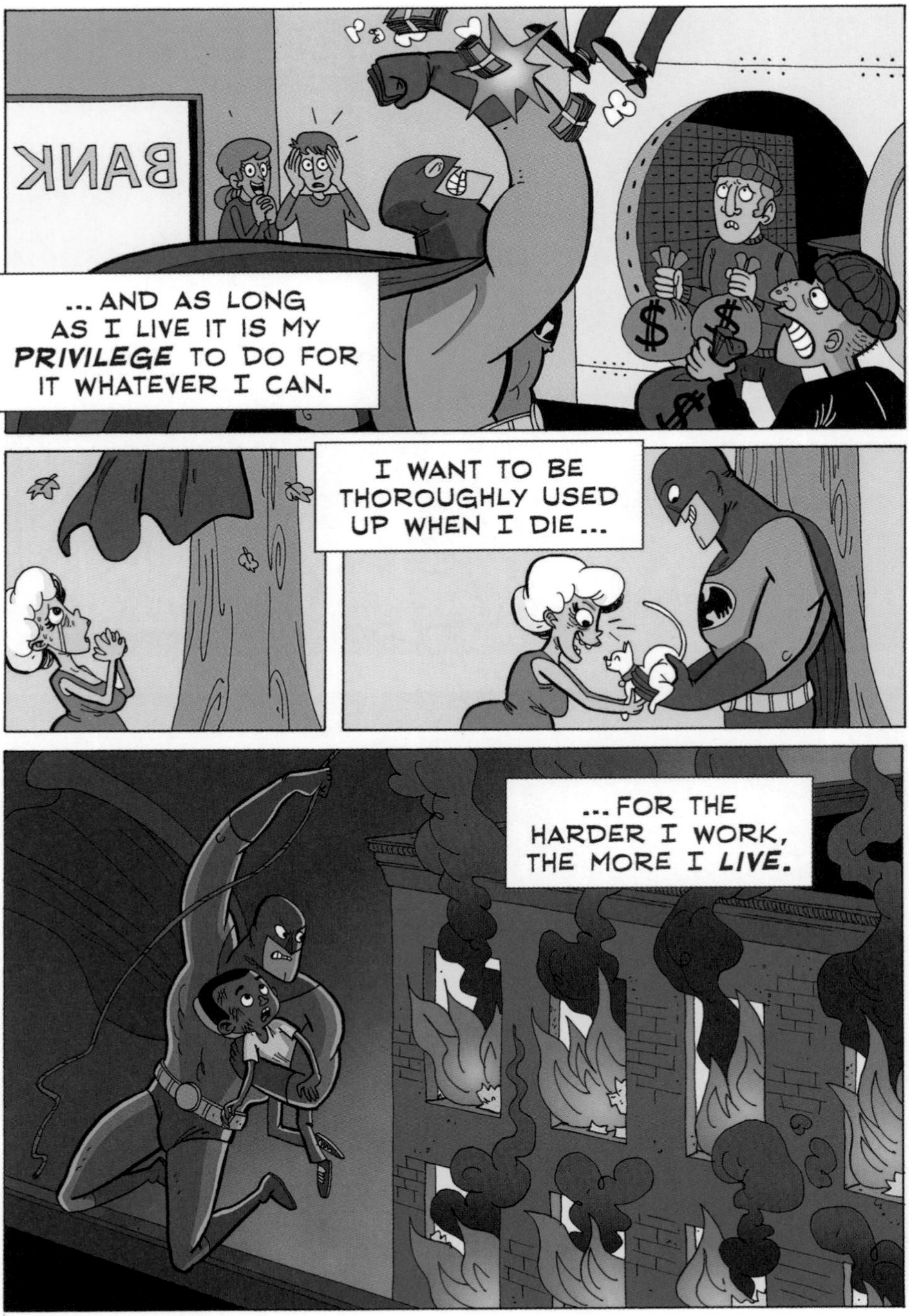
BANK
...AND AS LONG AS I LIVE IT IS MY PRIVILEGE TO DO FOR IT WHATEVER I CAN.
I WANT TO BE THOROUGHLY USED UP WHEN I DIE...
...FOR THE HARDER I WORK, THE MORE I LIVE.

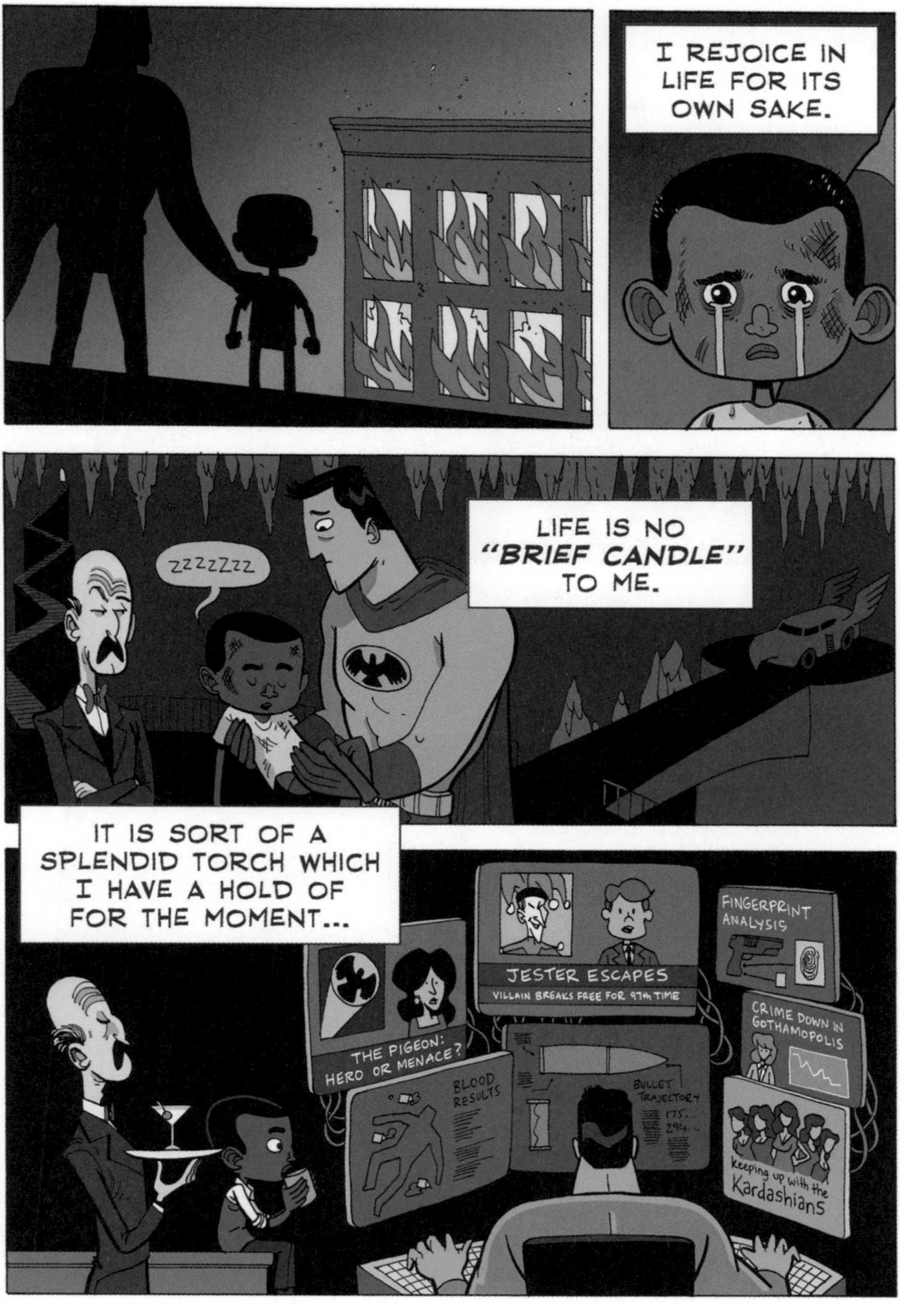
I REJOICE IN LIFE FOR ITS OWN SAKE.
LIFE IS NO "BRIEF CANDLE" TO ME.
ZZZZZZZ
IT IS SORT OF A SPLENDID TORCH WHICH I HAVE A HOLD OF FOR THE MOMENT...
JESTER ESCAPES
VILLAIN BREAKS FREE FOR 97th TIME
FINGERPRINT ANALYSIS
THE PIGEON: HERO OR MENACE?
CRIME DOWN IN GOTHAMOPOLIS
BLOOD RESULTS
BULLET TRAJECTORY
175...
294...
Keeping up with the Kardashians

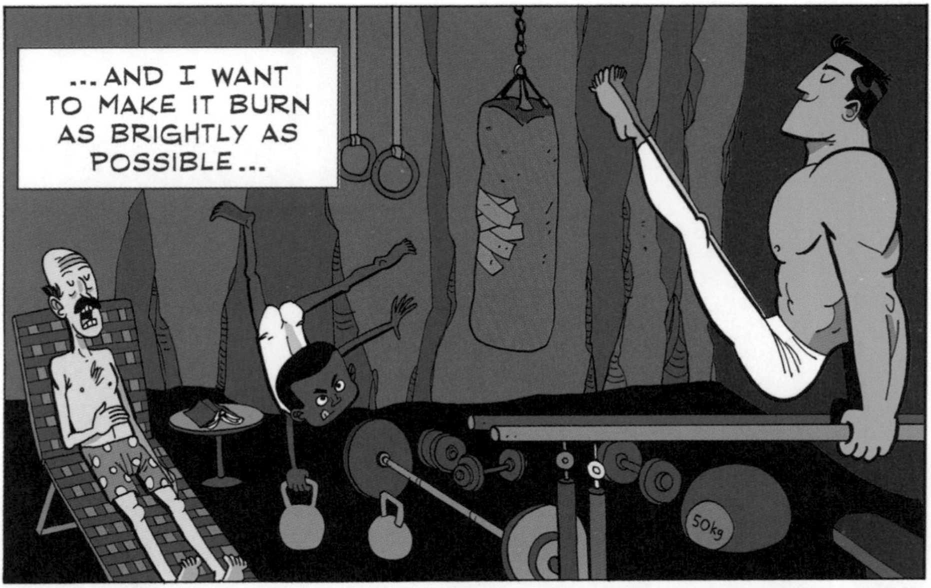
...AND I WANT TO MAKE IT BURN AS BRIGHTLY AS POSSIBLE...
50kg

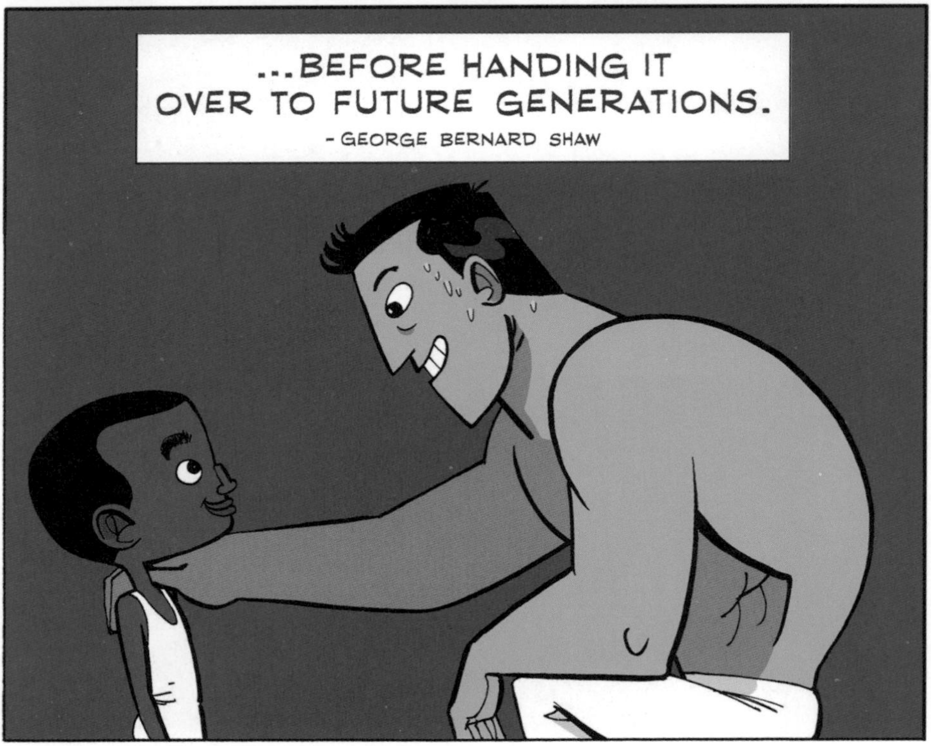
...BEFORE HANDING IT OVER TO FUTURE GENERATIONS.
- GEORGE BERNARD SHAW

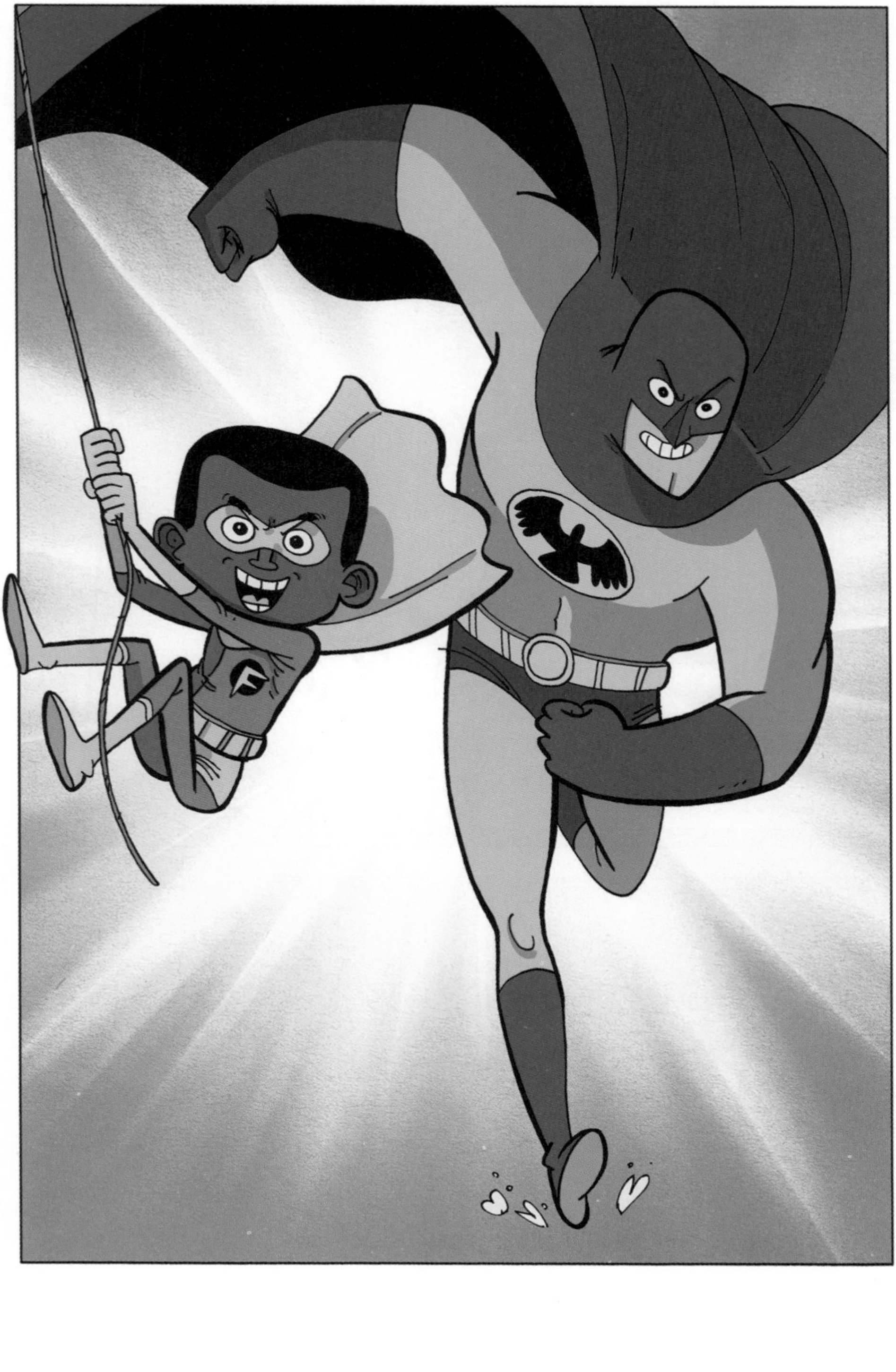

FOLLOWING MY NATURE

Margaret E. Knight

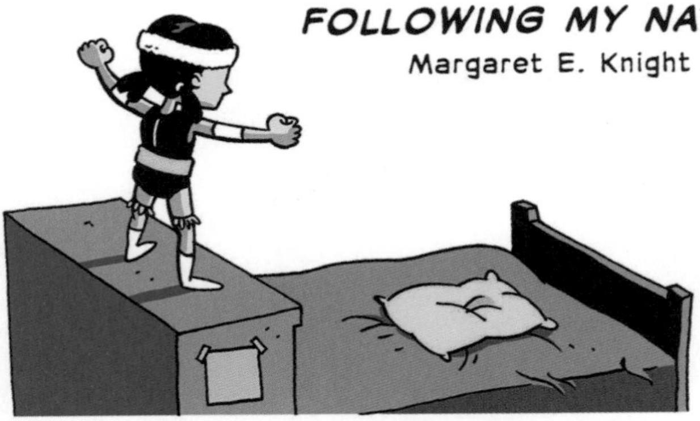

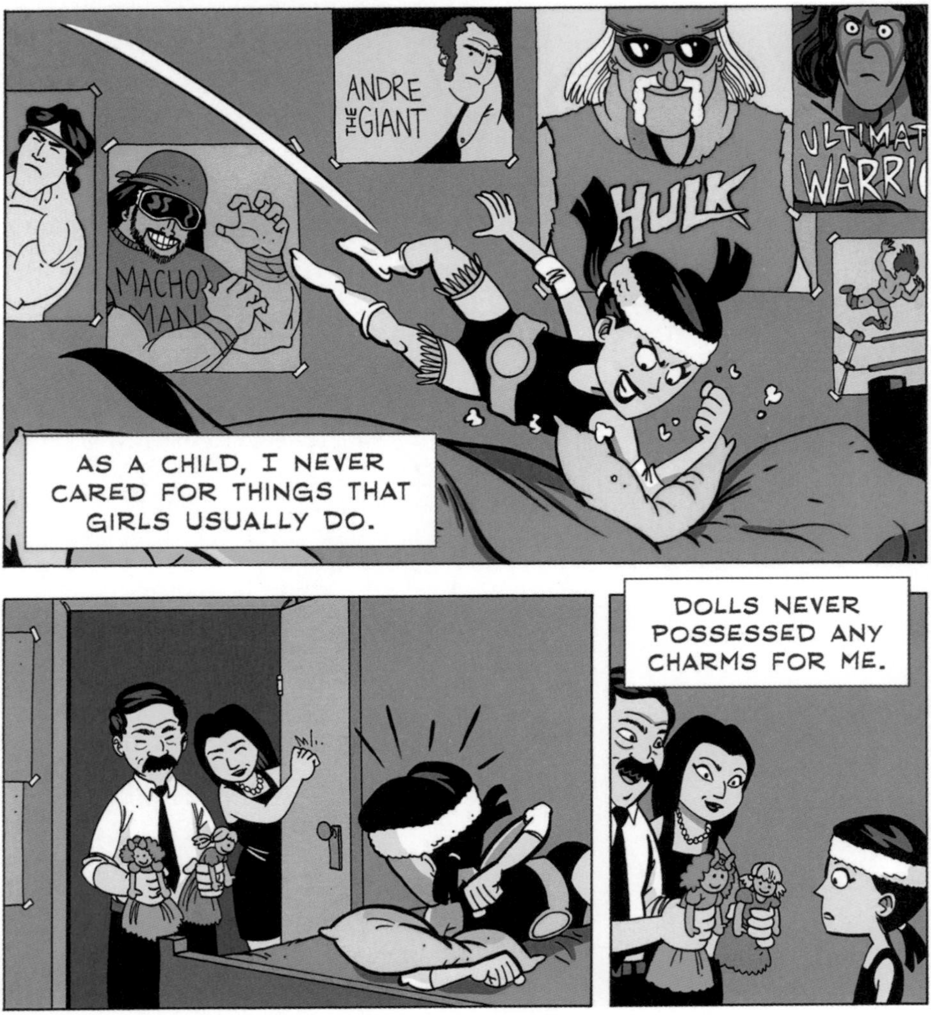
ANDRE THE GIANT
HULK
ULTIMAT
WARRI
MACHO MAN
AS A CHILD, I NEVER CARED FOR THINGS THAT GIRLS USUALLY DO.
DOLLS NEVER POSSESSED ANY CHARMS FOR ME.

I COULDN'T SEE THE SENSE OF CUDDLING BITS OF PORCELAIN WITH SENSELESS FACES.

MY FRIENDS WERE HORRIFIED.

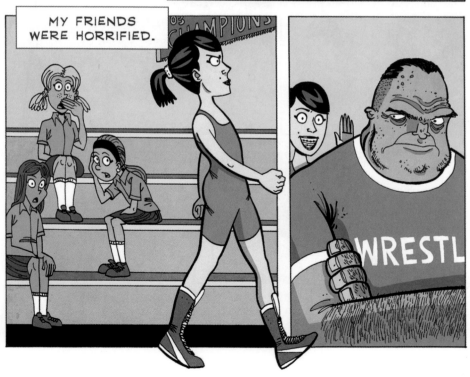

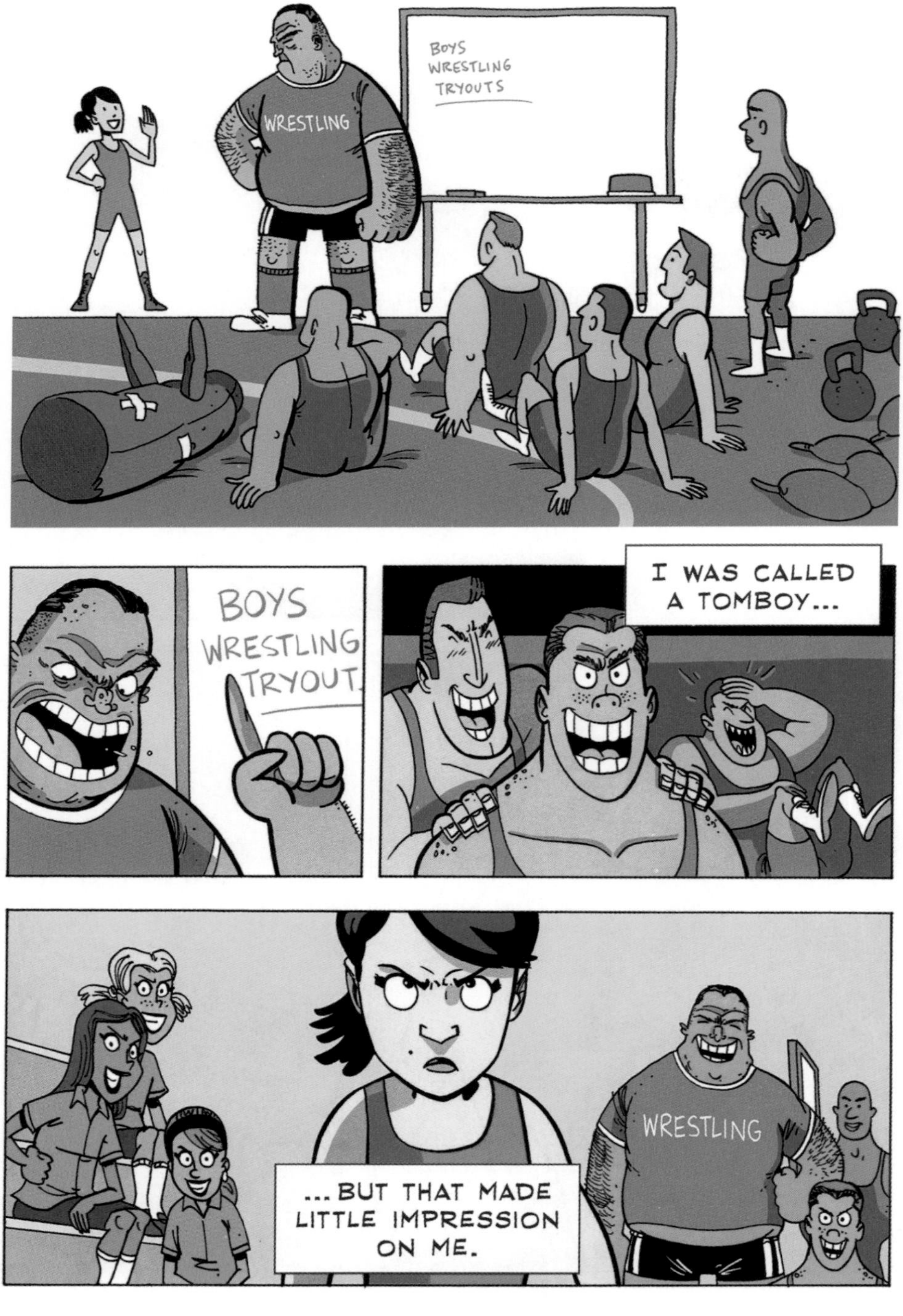
BOYS
WRESTLING
TRYOUTS
WRESTLING
BOYS
WRESTLING
TRYOUT
I WAS CALLED
A TOMBOY...
WRESTLING
...BUT THAT MADE
LITTLE IMPRESSION
ON ME.

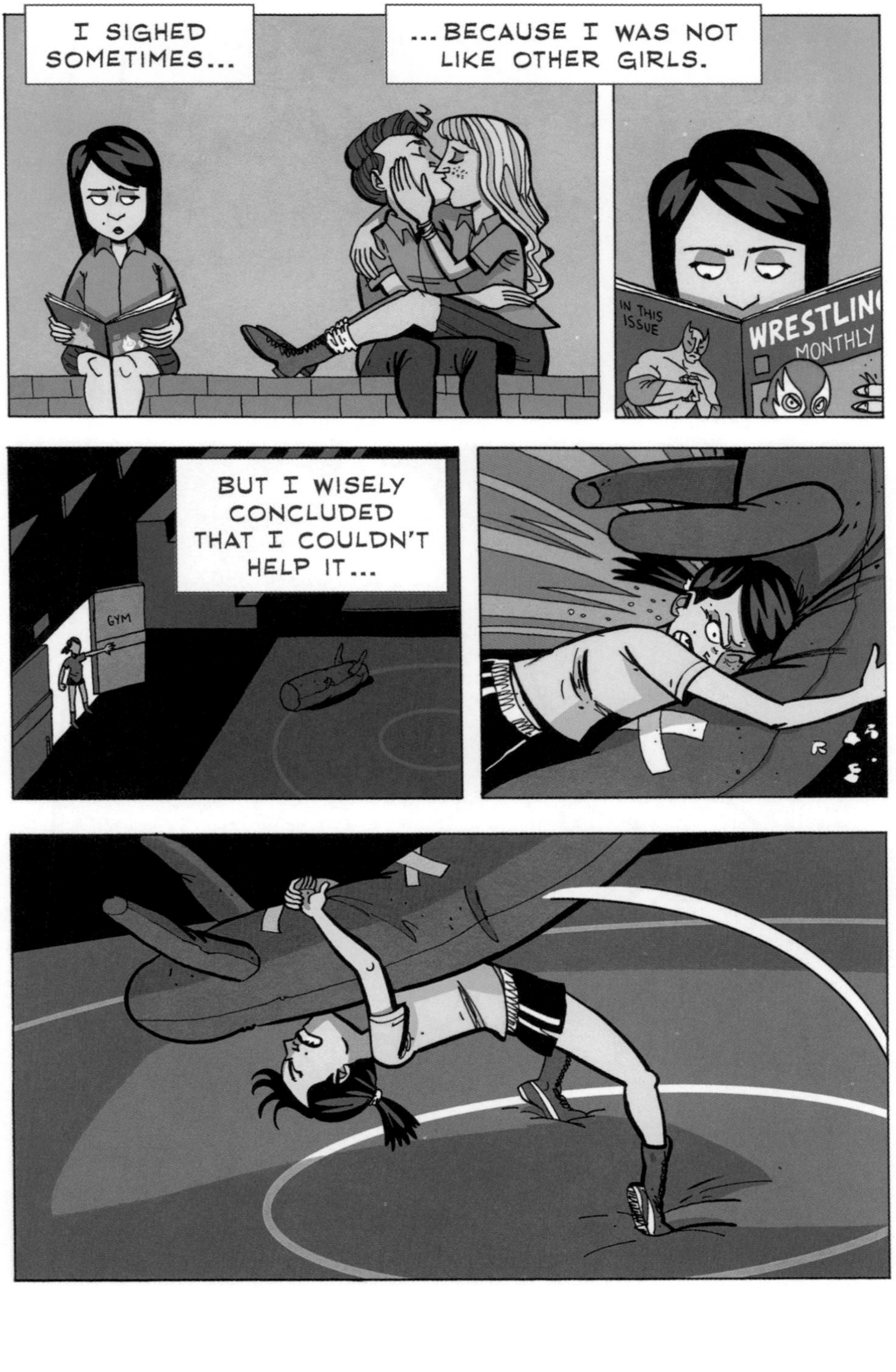
I SIGHED SOMETIMES...
...BECAUSE I WAS NOT LIKE OTHER GIRLS.
IN THIS ISSUE
WRESTLING
MONTHLY
BUT I WISELY CONCLUDED THAT I COULDN'T HELP IT...
GYM

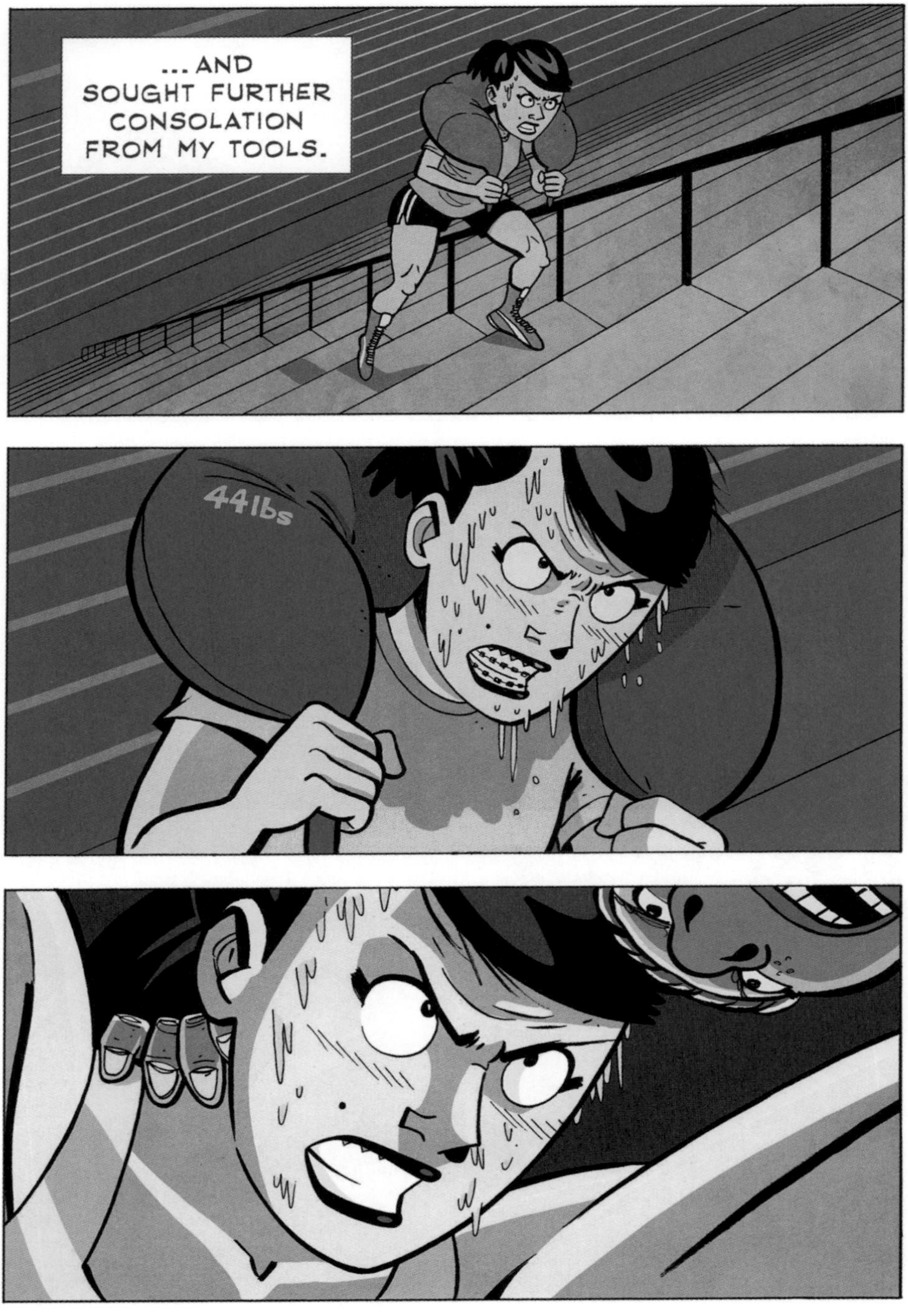
...AND SOUGHT FURTHER CONSOLATION FROM MY TOOLS.
44lbs

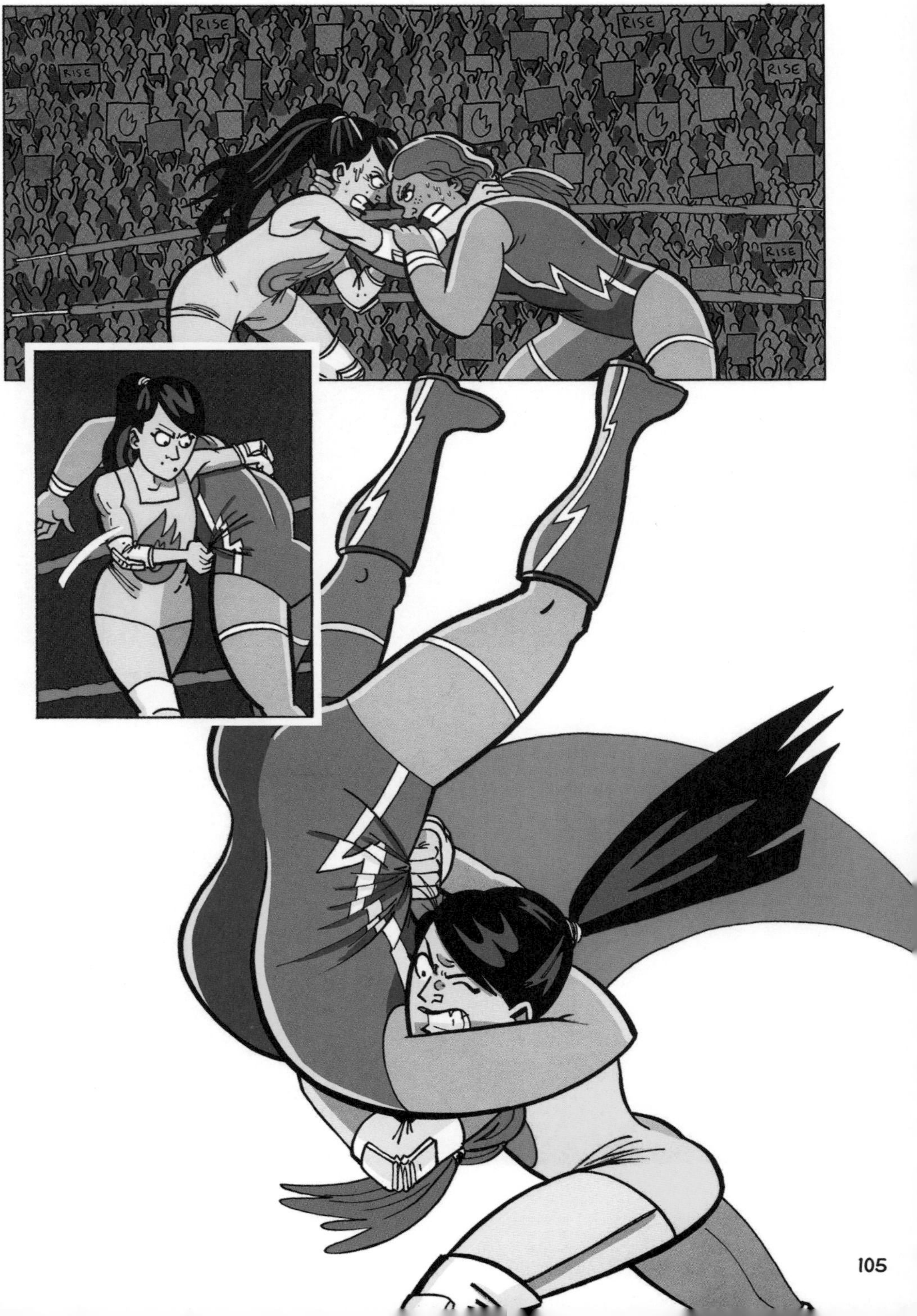
RISE
RISE
RISE
RISE
RISE

BOOM
WINNER
RISING
PHOENIX
Sports
VS
ANDREA THE GIANT
WRESTLING MONTHLY
I'M NOT SURPRISED AT WHAT I'VE DONE.

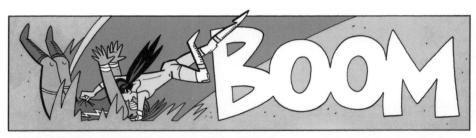

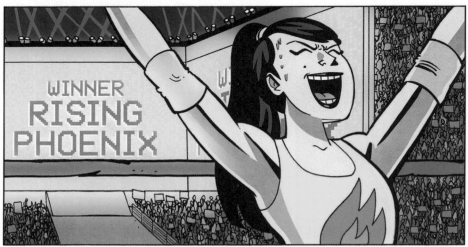

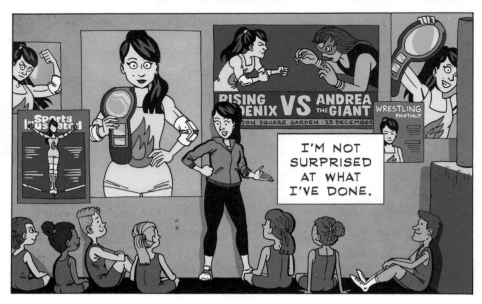

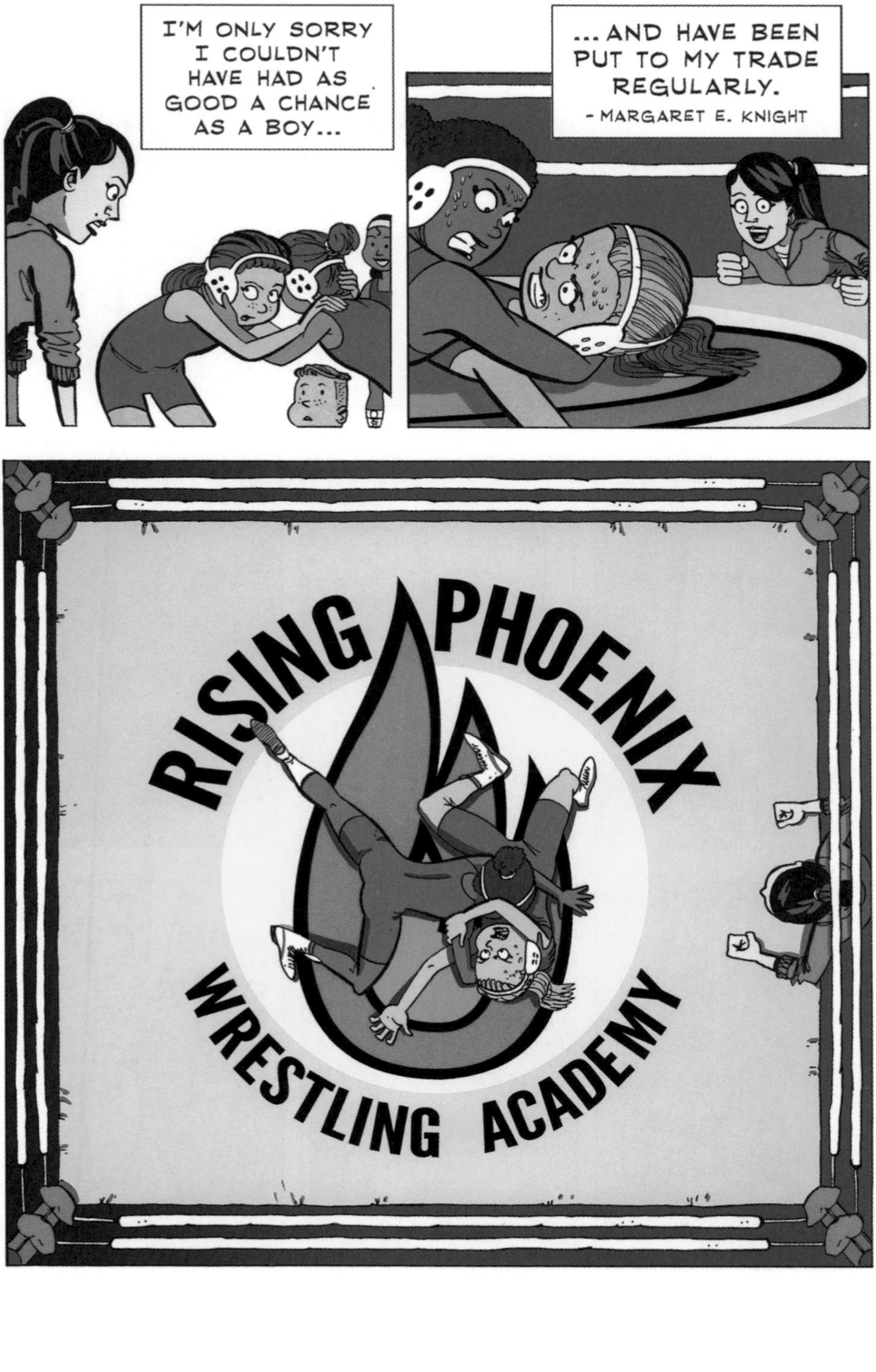
I'M ONLY SORRY I COULDN'T HAVE HAD AS GOOD A CHANCE AS A BOY...
...AND HAVE BEEN PUT TO MY TRADE REGULARLY.
- MARGARET E. KNIGHT
RISING PHOENIX
WRESTLING ACADEMY

A WORTHY CRISIS Epictetus

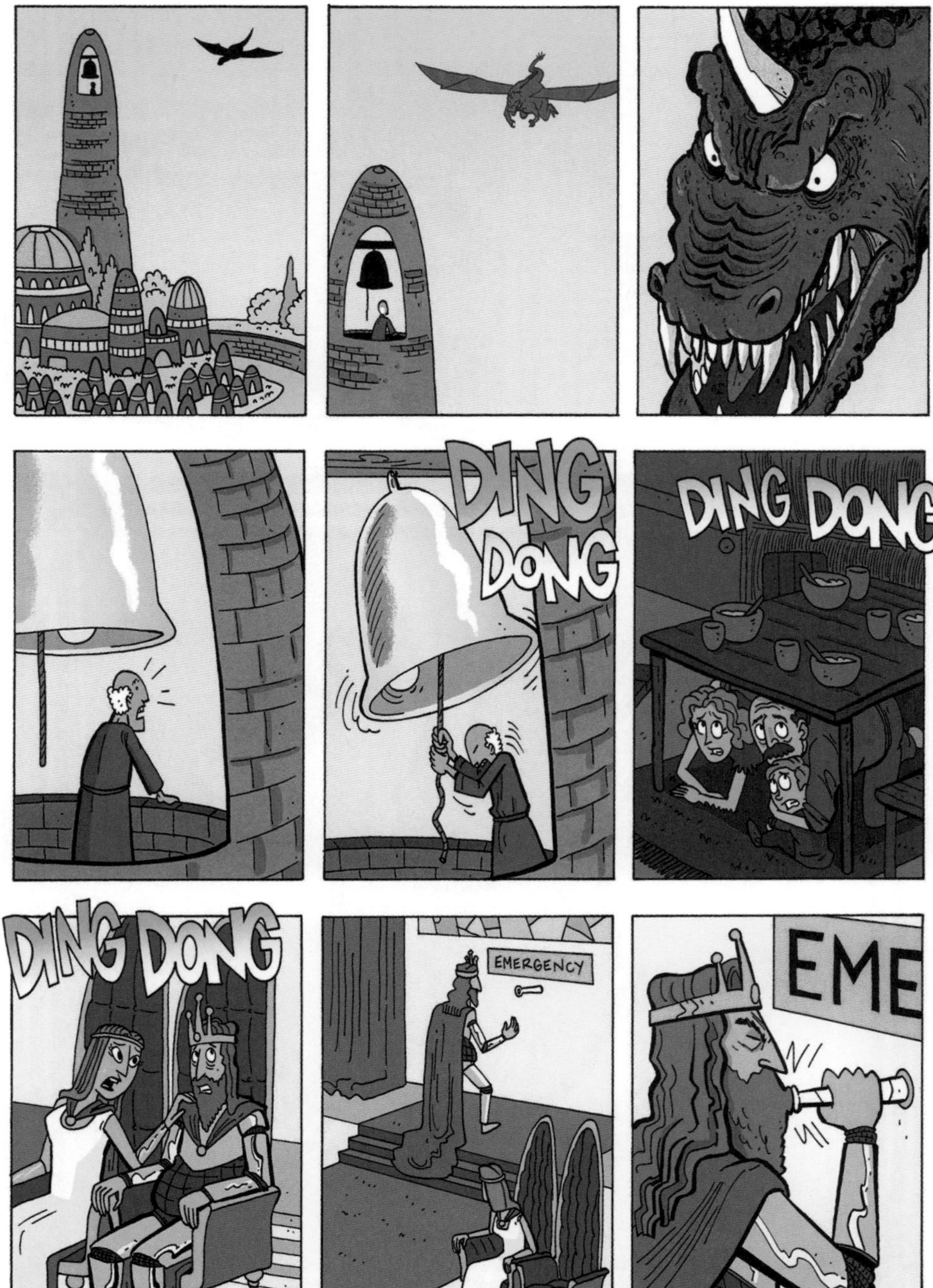
DING
DONG
DING DONG
DING DONG
EMERGENCY
EME

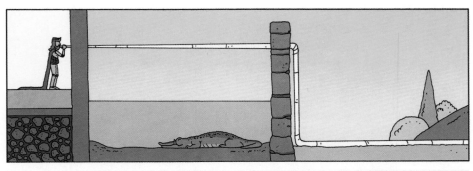

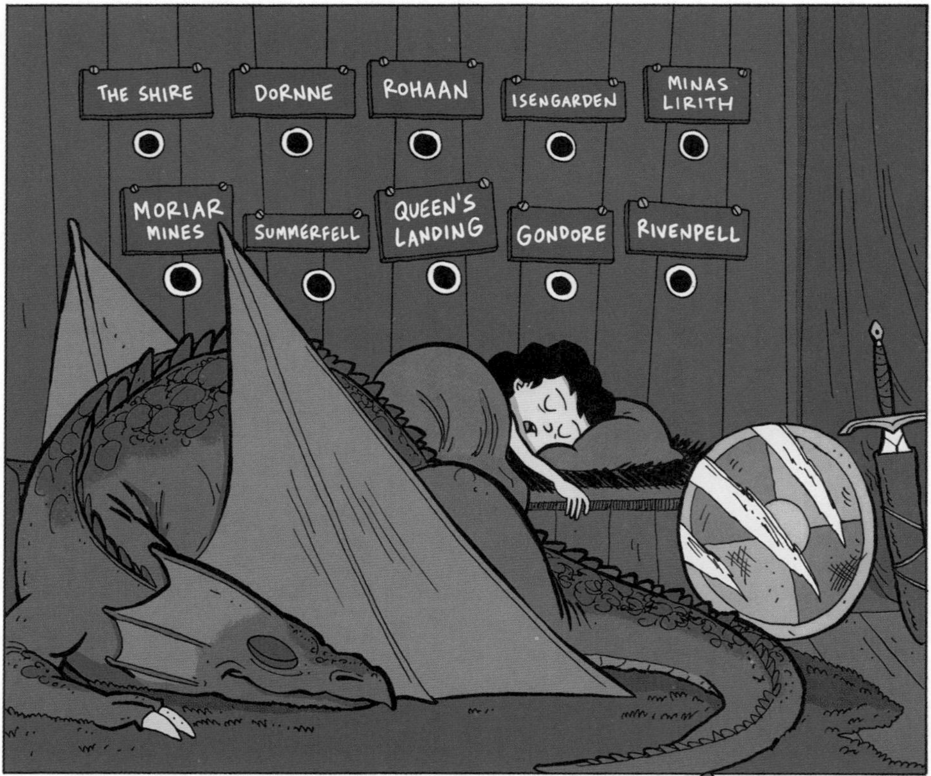
THE SHIRE
DORNNE
ROHAAN
ISENGARDEN
MINAS LIRITH
MORIAR MINES
SUMMERFELL
QUEEN'S LANDING
GONDORE
RIVENPELL

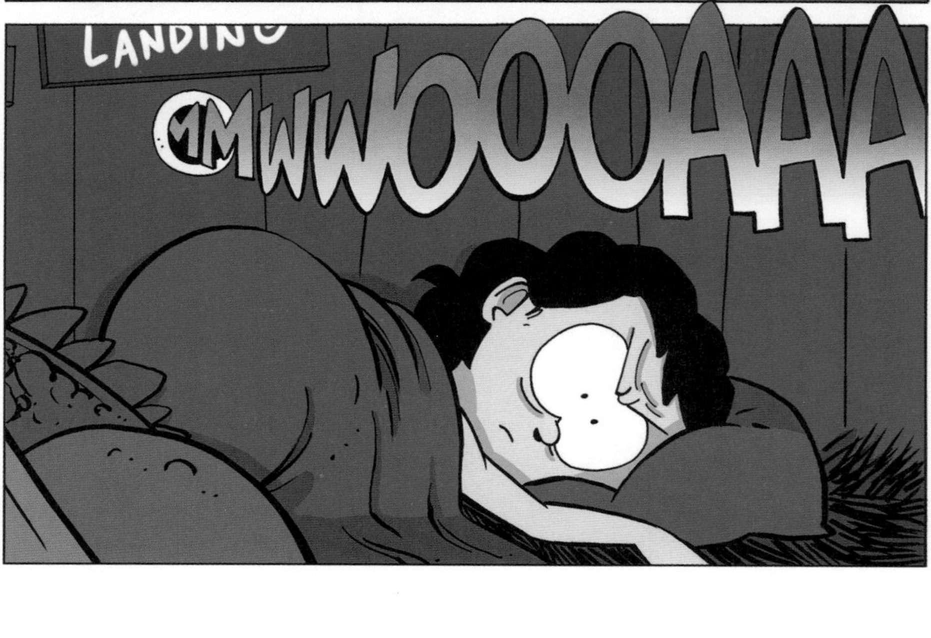
MMWWOOOAAA

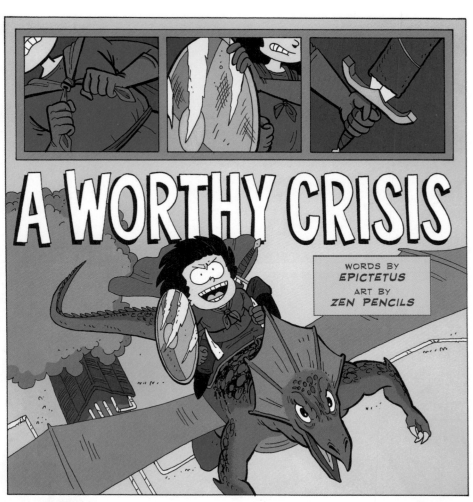

A WORTHY CRISIS

WORDS BY
EPICTETUS

ART BY
ZEN PENCILS

WHAT WOULD HAVE BECOME OF *HERCULES* DO YOU THINK ...

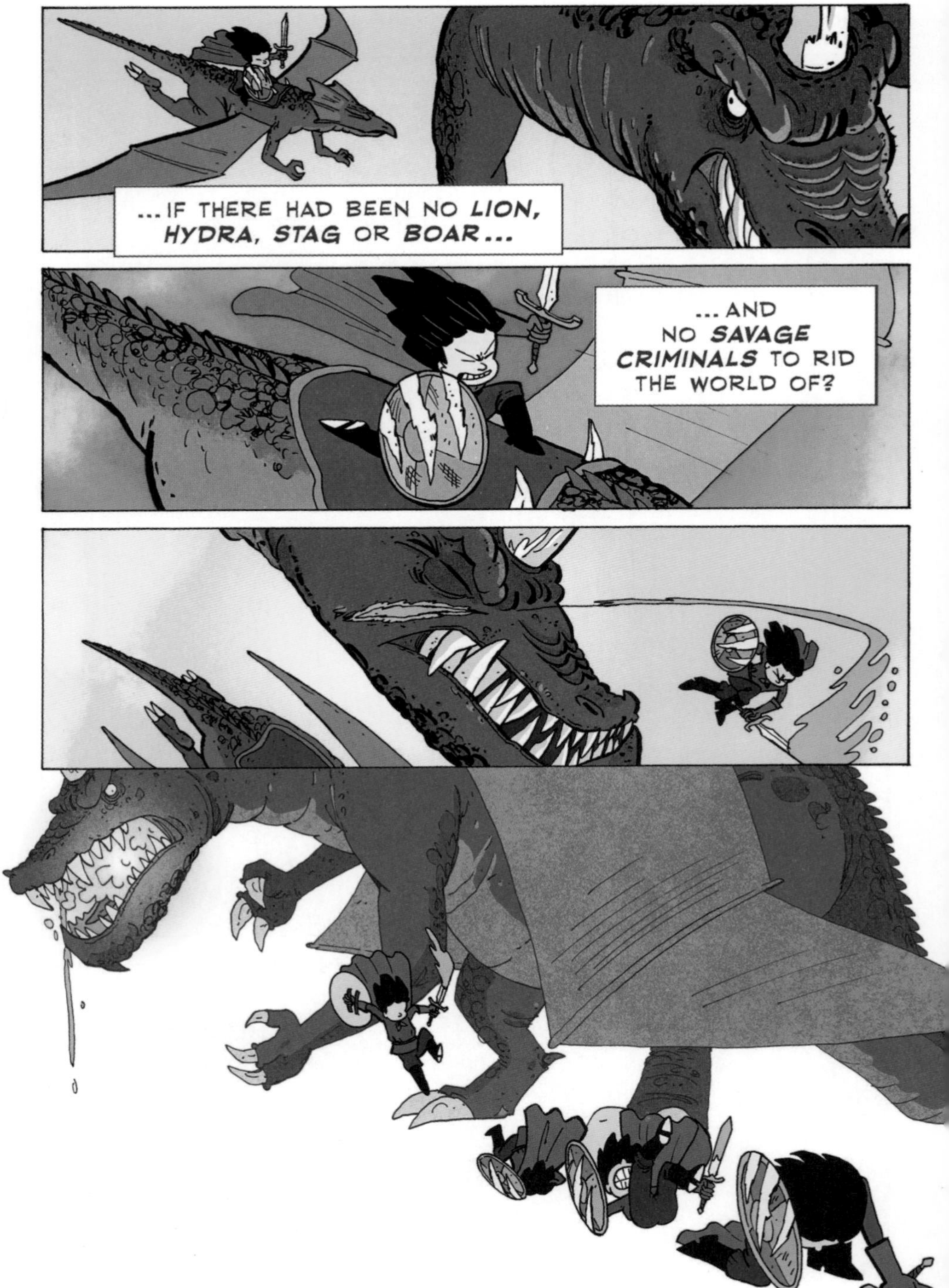
...IF THERE HAD BEEN NO *LION*, *HYDRA*, *STAG* OR *BOAR*...
...AND NO *SAVAGE CRIMINALS* TO RID THE WORLD OF?

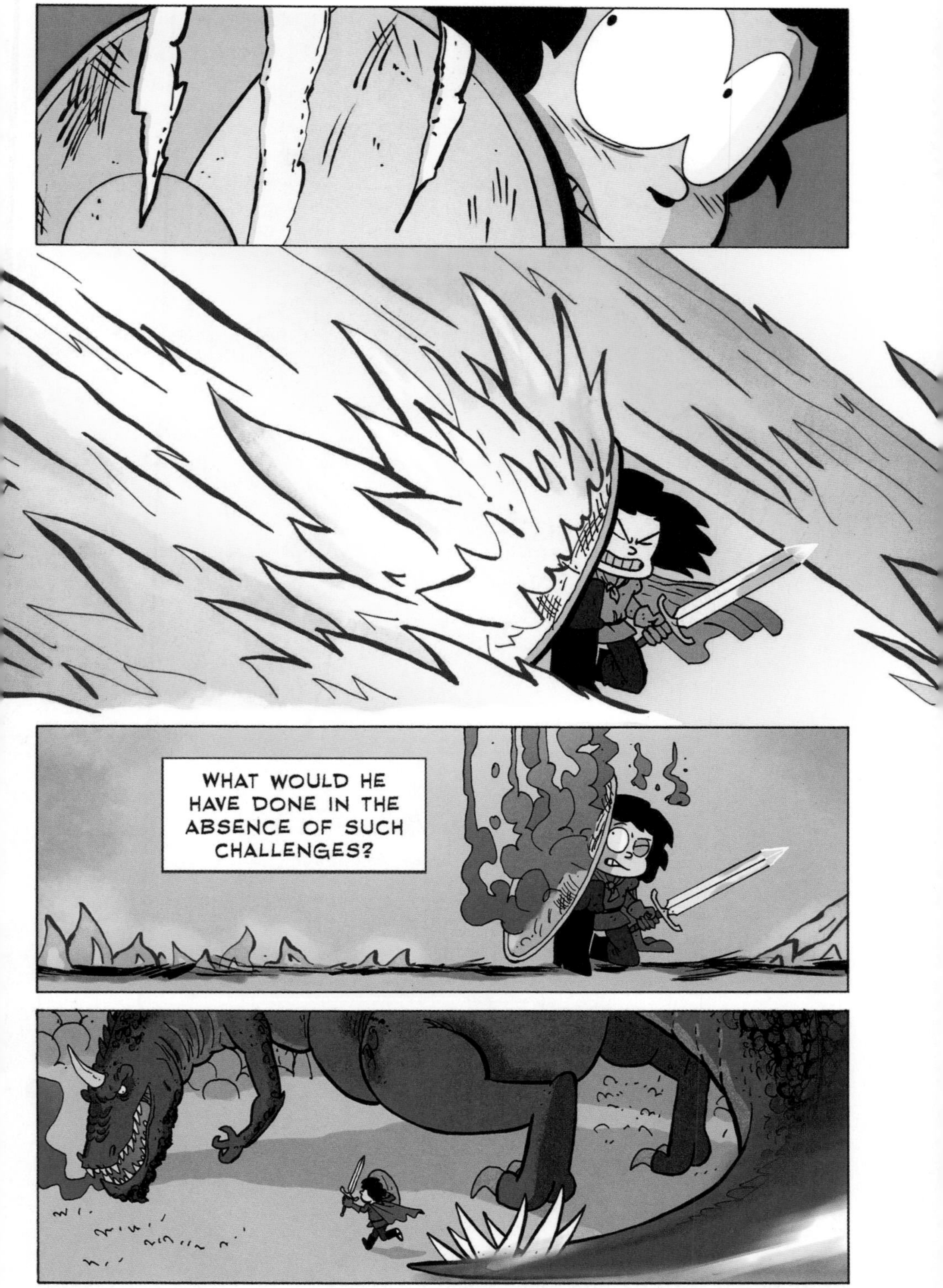
WHAT WOULD HE HAVE DONE IN THE ABSENCE OF SUCH CHALLENGES?

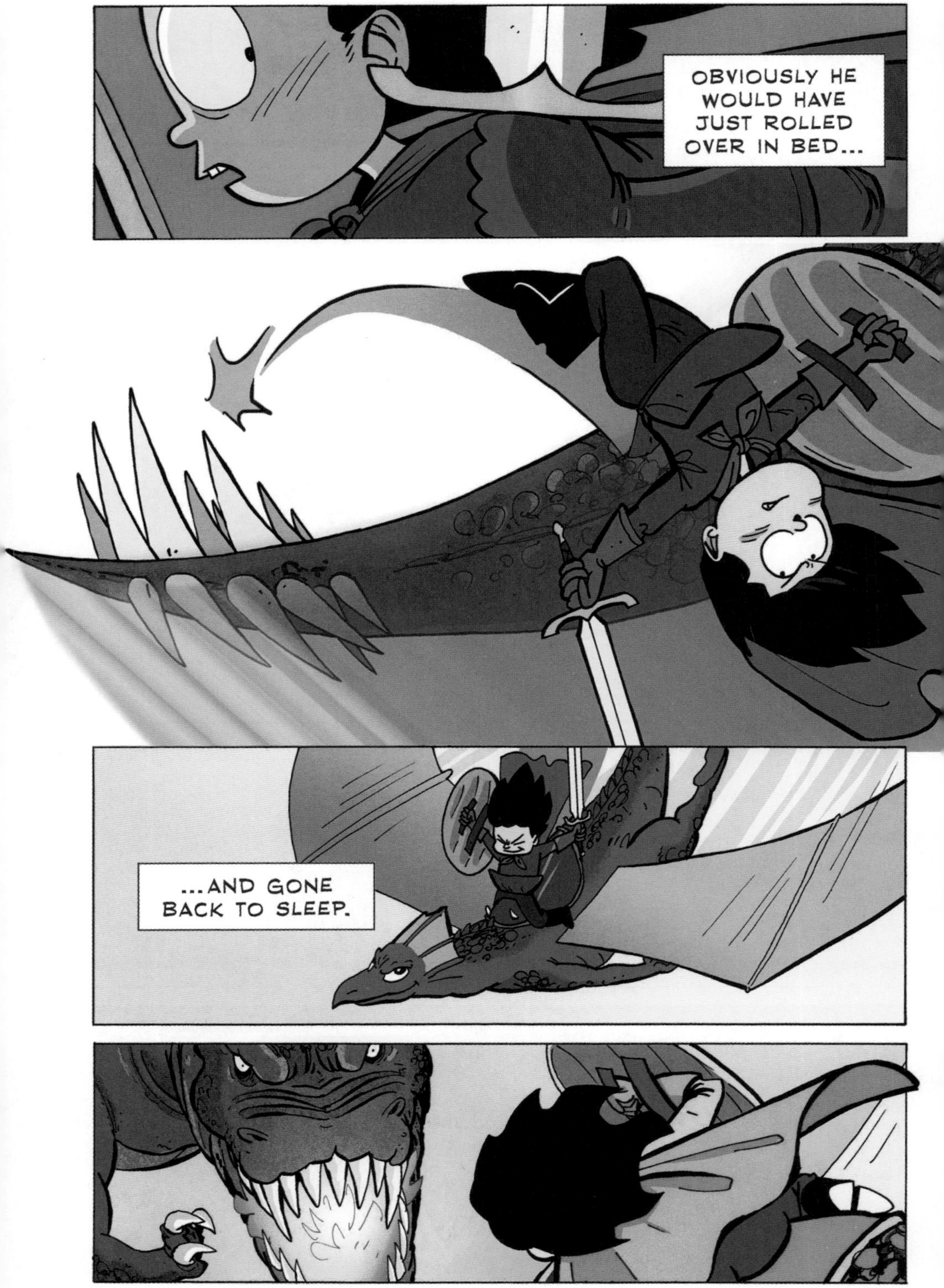

OBVIOUSLY HE WOULD HAVE JUST ROLLED OVER IN BED...
...AND GONE BACK TO SLEEP.

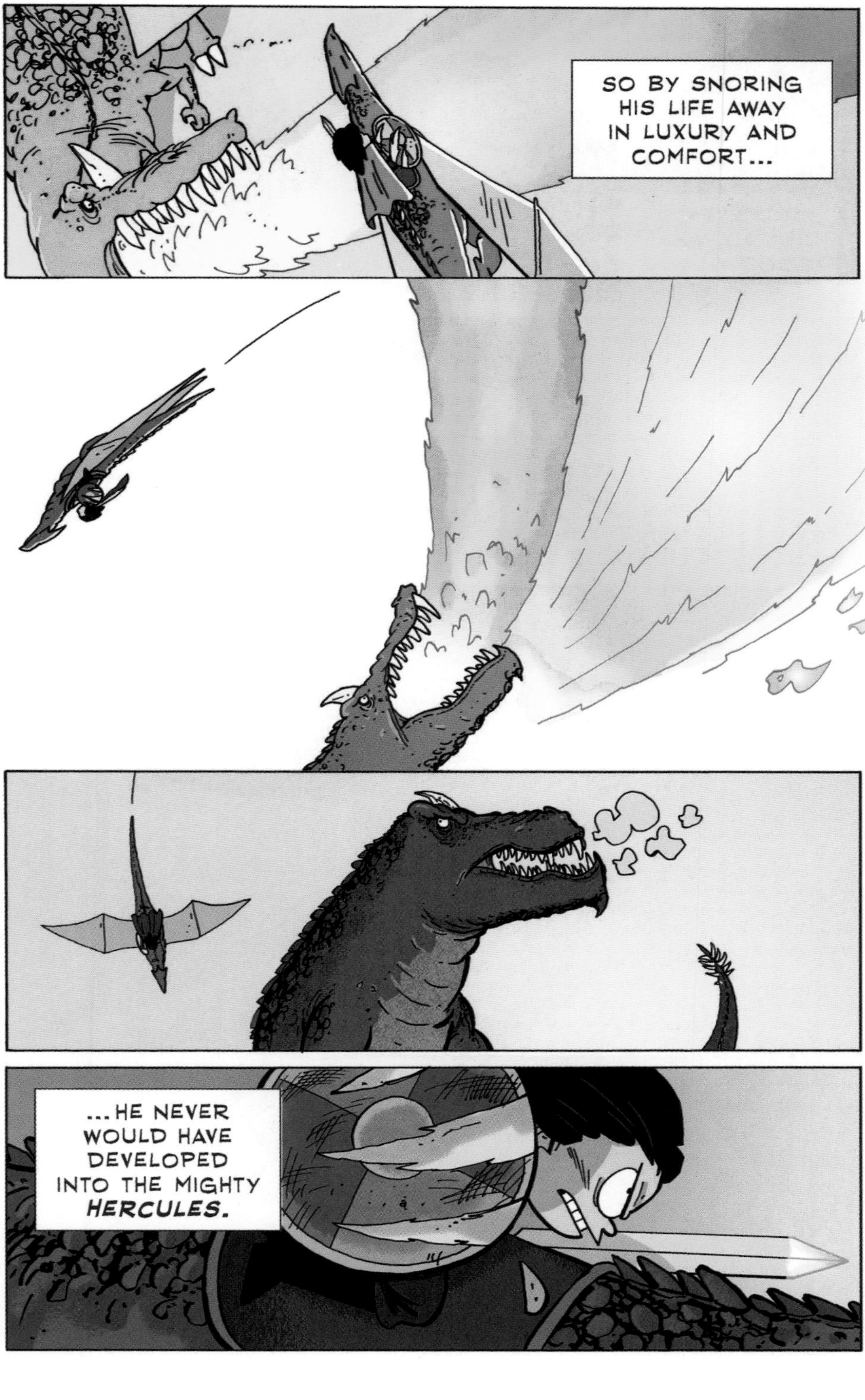
SO BY SNORING HIS LIFE AWAY IN LUXURY AND COMFORT...
...HE NEVER WOULD HAVE DEVELOPED INTO THE MIGHTY ***HERCULES.***

AND EVEN IF HE HAD, WHAT GOOD WOULD IT HAVE DONE HIM?

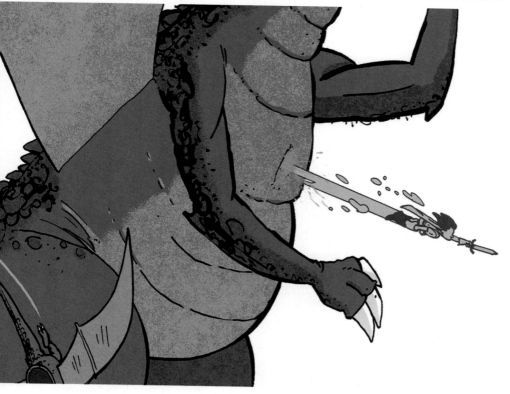

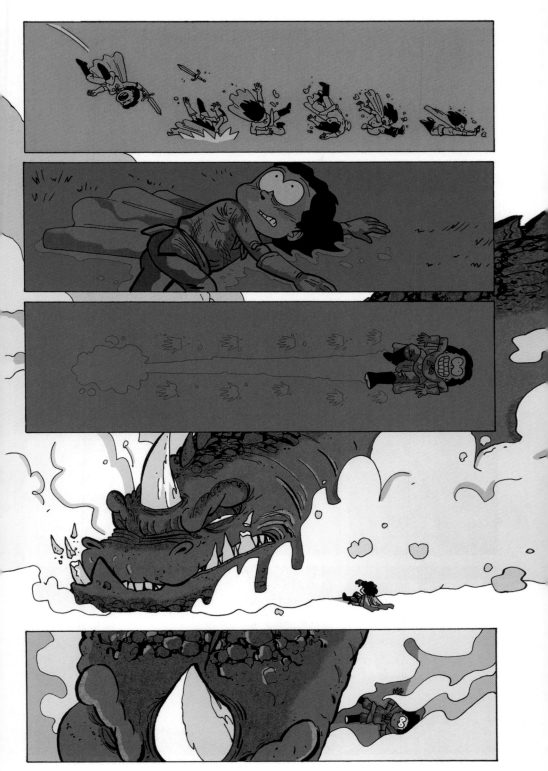

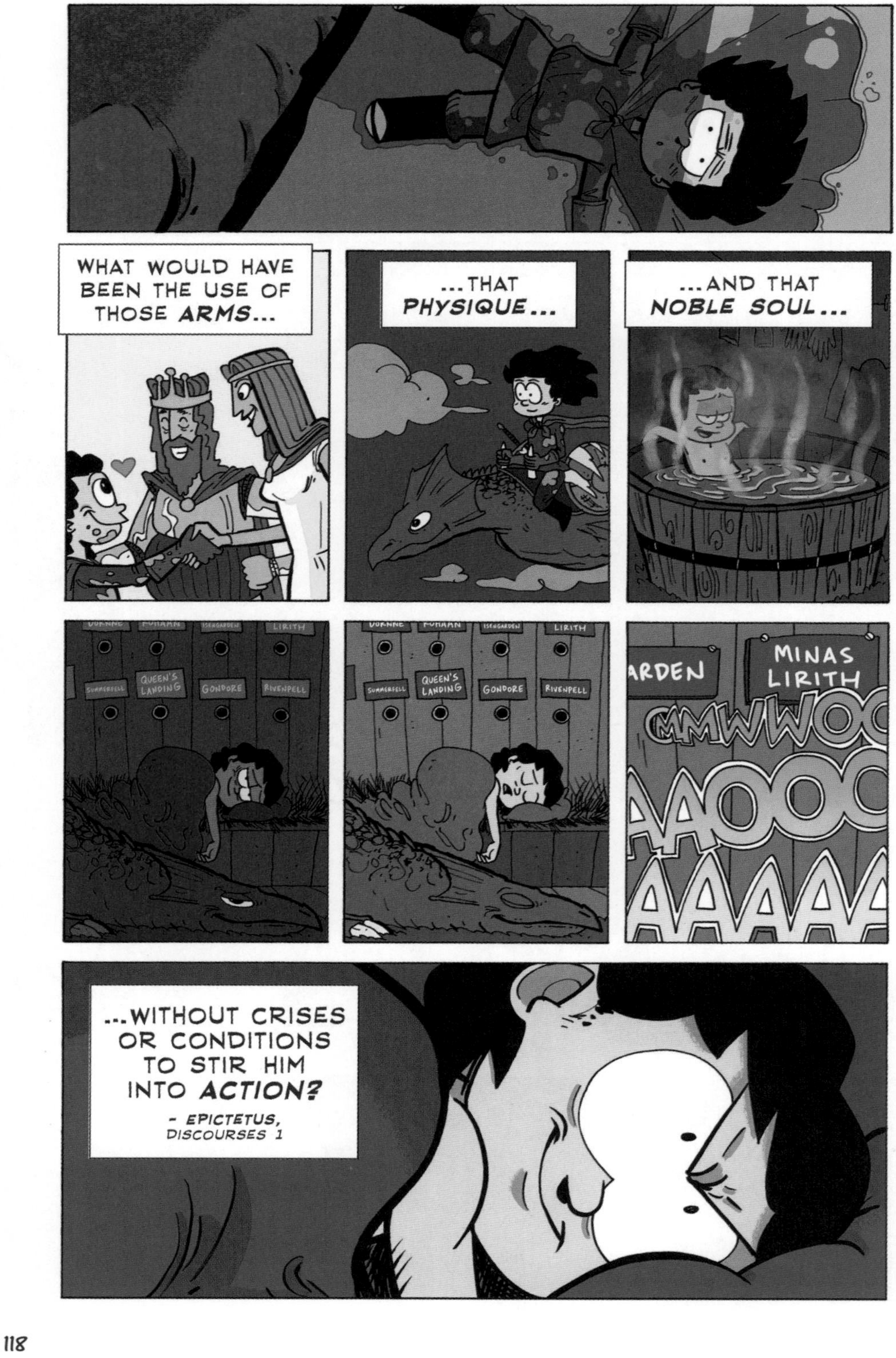
WHAT WOULD HAVE BEEN THE USE OF THOSE ARMS...
...THAT PHYSIQUE...
...AND THAT NOBLE SOUL...
LIRITH
QUEEN'S LANDING
GONDORE
RIVENPELL
LIRITH
QUEEN'S LANDING
GONDORE
RIVENPELL
ARDEN
MINAS LIRITH
CMMWWOO
AAOOO
AAAAA
...WITHOUT CRISES OR CONDITIONS TO STIR HIM INTO ACTION?
- EPICTETUS, DISCOURSES 1

ON HAPPINESS Henry David Thoreau

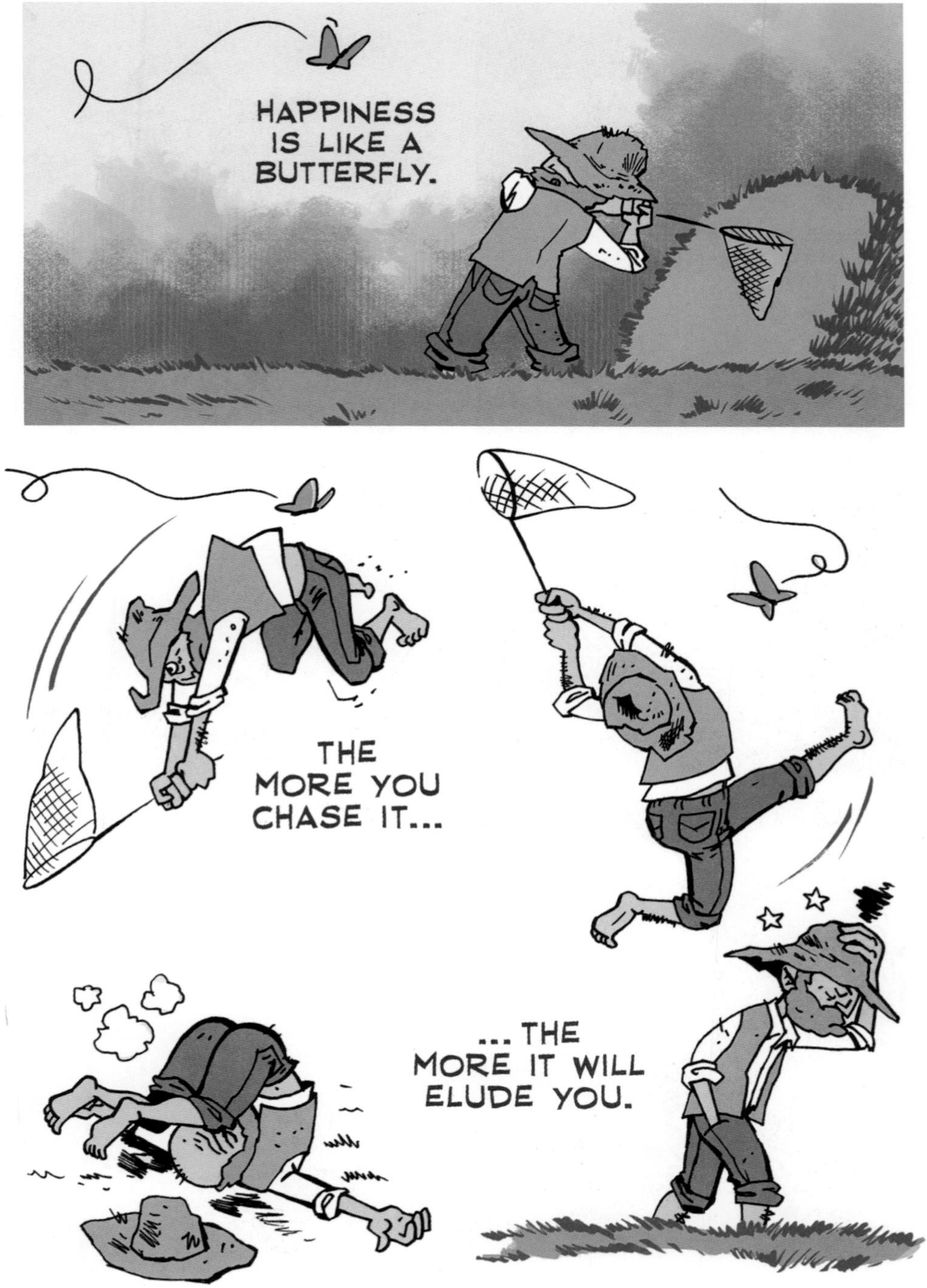
HAPPINESS IS LIKE A BUTTERFLY.
THE MORE YOU CHASE IT...
... THE MORE IT WILL ELUDE YOU.

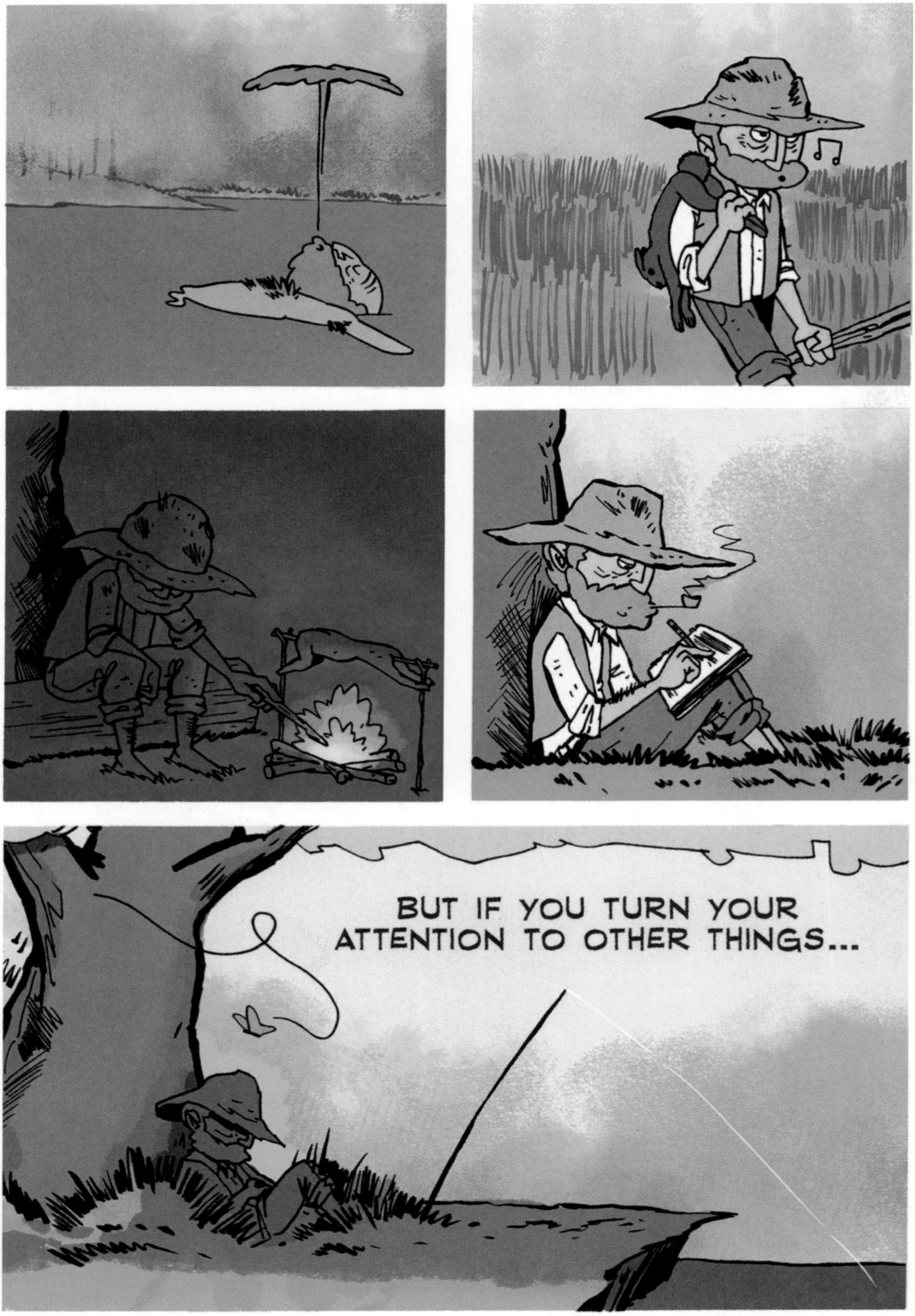
BUT IF YOU TURN YOUR
ATTENTION TO OTHER THINGS...

... IT WILL COME
AND SIT SOFTLY ON
YOUR SHOULDER.

- HENRY DAVID THOREAU

The People Behind the Quotes

Rabindranath Tagore (1861-1941) was a Bengali poet, writer, playwright, musician, and painter who helped modernize Indian culture and was the first non-European to win the Nobel Prize in Literature.

Confucius (551 BC-479 BC) was an important Chinese philosopher who taught that human beings are responsible for their happiness through their own actions toward others.

Besides being the twenty-sixth president of the United States, **Theodore Roosevelt** (1858-1919) was also a naturalist, ornithologist, cowboy, conservationist, ranchman, war hero, writer, and hunter. He lived what he called "the strenuous life" where physical activity, adventure, and action were the keys to success and happiness.

Rebecca Martin is a writer from Toronto, Canada. She wrote the "Strange Like Me" quote as a tribute to one of her heroes, the Mexican painter **Frida Kahlo** (1907-1954). Kahlo was proud of her thick eyebrows and featured them for all to see in the many self-portraits she painted.

Howard Thurman (1899-1981) was an African-American leader and prominent figure during the American Civil Rights movement. His books on philosophy and theology were a major influence on Martin Luther King, Jr.

Jack London (1876-1916) was an American writer. The quote "Ashes or Dust" was London's life motto.

Calvin Coolidge (1872-1933) was the thirtieth president of the United States. A serious and no-nonsense man, Coolidge was unassuming but had a quiet determination that saw him prosper in the White House.

Amelia Earhart (1897-1937) was a pioneering aviator. She was the first woman to fly solo across the Atlantic Ocean, first to fly across the Pacific from Honolulu to Oakland, and also set numerous altitude and speed records. www.ameliaearhart.com

Robert F. Kennedy (1925-1968) was an American politician and brother of former president, John F. Kennedy. He gave his speech "On the Mindless Menace of Violence" the day after Civil Rights leader Martin Luther King, Jr. was assassinated.

Chris Hadfield is a retired Canadian astronaut who became well-known for using social media to share what daily life was like aboard the International Space Station. The quote is taken from a Reddit "Ask Me Anything" session Hadfield took part in while aboard the ISS. www.chrishadfield.ca

John Green is the bestselling author of *Looking For Alaska*, *Paper Towns,* and *The Fault in Our Stars*. He is also one half of the Vlogbrothers and host of the Crash Course History educational series. www.johngreenbooks.com

Seneca the Younger (4 BC-AD 65) was a Roman Stoic philosopher, politician, and writer.

Winston Churchill (1874-1965) was the British Prime Minister during World War II, where he led the country against the Axis Powers. He was voted the greatest Englishman of all time. www.winstonchurchill.org

Sir Ken Robinson is a leading authority on education and the bestselling author of *The Element* and its sequel, *Finding Your Element.* The words featured are taken from Robinson's famous TED talk "How Schools Kill Creativity," which you can watch online. www.sirkenrobinson.com

Marie Curie (1867-1934) was a Polish scientist who did pioneering research on radioactivity, discovered two elements, won two Nobel Prizes, and is now a hero of the scientific world.

Tenzin Gyatso, The 14th Dalai Lama, is a Buddhist monk and the spiritual leader of Tibet. The featured quote is taken from the Dalai Lama's Nobel Peace Prize acceptance speech in 1989. www.dalailama.com

Jacob A. Riis (1849-1914) was a Danish-American social reformer, journalist, and photographer. His pioneering photojournalism work culminated in the book *How The Other Half Lives*, which for the first time documented the plight of the working class in New York.

Terence McKenna (1946-2000) was a writer, lecturer, and expert on ecology, botany, shamanism, and spiritual transformation.

George Bernard Shaw (1856-1950) was an Irish playwright. He wrote over sixty plays and is the only person to have received both a Nobel Prize (in Literature) and an Academy Award (for Adapted Screenplay).

Margaret E. Knight (1838-1914) was an American inventor. From a young age, Knight had a gift for engineering and mechanics, and loved to build gadgets. She created her first invention when she was twelve years old and became the most famous female inventor of the nineteenth century.

Epictetus (AD 55-135) was one of the key Stoic philosophers, along with Seneca and Marcus Aurelius.

Henry David Thoreau (1817-1862) was a writer, poet, and philosopher. He's most well-known for his book *Walden*, in which he tells the story of the two years he lived in a small cabin in the woods near Walden Pond in Concord, Massachusetts.

About the cartoonist

While working a corporate design job, **Gavin Aung Than** always dreamed of one day being able to draw comics for a living. He had the idea to combine his love for history and quotes with his love for cartooning and launched the *Zen Pencils* website in 2012. Now Gavin finally gets to scribble for a living. He lives in Melbourne, Australia with his wife, daughter, and two miniature schnauzers. For more cartoon quotes from inspirational folks visit www.zenpencils.com

Acknowledgments

THEODORE ROOSEVELT "The Man in the Arena" excerpt from the speech "Citizenship in a Republic" delivered at the Sorbonne, in Paris, France on April 23, 1910.

STRANGE LIKE ME quote used with permission from Rebecca Martin.

JACK LONDON words as retold by journalist Ernest J. Hopkins in the *San Francisco Bulletin*, December 2, 1916.

AMELIA EARHART quote taken from her official website: http://www.ameliaearhart.com/about/quotes.html

ROBERT F. KENNEDY "On the Mindless Menace of Violence" excerpt taken from a speech given at the Cleveland City Club, 1968.

CHRIS HADFIELD "An Astronaut's Advice" excerpt taken from his 2013 Reddit Ask Me Anything "I Am Astronaut Chris Hadfield, Currently Orbiting Planet Earth."

JOHN GREEN "Make Gifts for People" excerpt taken from his 2009 Vlogbrothers video "The Gift of Gary Busey." www.youtube.com/watch?v=j22qA39eHvw

WINSTON CHURCHILL "Never Yield to Force" excerpt from speech given at Harrow School, 1941.

SIR KEN ROBINSON "Full Body Education" excerpt taken from his 2006 TED talk "How Schools Kill Creativity." www.ted.com/talks/ken_robinson_says_schools_kill_creativity

DALAI LAMA "We Are All Human Beings" taken from his 1989 Nobel Peace Prize acceptance speech.

JACOB A. RIIS "The Stonecutter" quote taken from *The Making of an American* by Jacob A. Riis, 1901.

GEORGE BERNARD SHAW quote taken from his lecture "Art and Public Money."

Andrews McMeel Publishing
a division of Andrews McMeel Universal
1130 Walnut Street, Kansas City, Missouri 64106

www.andrewsmcmeel.com

17 18 19 20 21 SDB 10 9 8 7 6 5 4 3 2 1

ISBN: 978-1-4494-8721-8

Library of Congress Control Number: 2017930963

Editor: Dorothy O'Brien
Creative Director: Tim Lynch
Production Editor: Amy Strassner
Production Manager: Chuck Harper

Made by:
Shenzhen Donnelley Printing Company Ltd.
Address and location of manufacturer:
No. 47, Wuhe Nan Road, Bantian Ind. Zone,
Shenzhen China, 518129
1st Printing – 7/24/17

ATTENTION: SCHOOLS AND BUSINESSES

Andrews McMeel books are available at quantity discounts with bulk purchase for educational, business, or sales promotional use. For information, please e-mail the Andrews McMeel Publishing Special Sales Department:
specialsales@amuniversal.com.

Check out these and other books at ampkids.com

amp! COMICS for kids

DIARY OF AN 8-BIT WARRIOR
PATH OF THE DIAMOND
Runt's training is coming to an end!
CUBE KID
AN UNOFFICIAL MINECRAFT ADVENTURE

SNOOPY
WHAT'S WRONG WITH DOG LIPS?
PULL-OUT POSTER INSIDE
A PEANUTS Collection

Unicorn Crossing
Another Phoebe and Her Unicorn Adventure
Dana Simpson

the knights of Boo'Gar
Story & Art By
Art Roche

big NATE
A GOOD OLD-FASHIONED WEDGIE
PULL-OUT POSTER INSIDE
by LINCOLN PEIRCE
New York Times Best-Selling Author

Anne of Green Gables
a graphic novel

The Adventures of
KUNG FU ROBOT
HOW TO MAKE A
PEANUT BUTTER, JELLY & KUNG FU SANDWICH
JASON BAYS

LASER MOOSE AND RABBIT BOY
DOUG SAVAGE

SUIT YOUR SELFIE
New York Times Bestselling Author
Stephan T. Pastis
A Pearls Before Swine Collection

Also available:
Teaching and activity guides for each title.
AMP! Comics for Kids books make reading FUN!

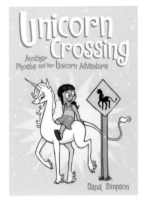

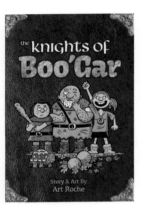

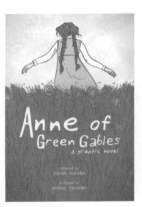

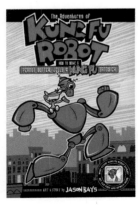